Dartmouth College Hockey
Northern Ice

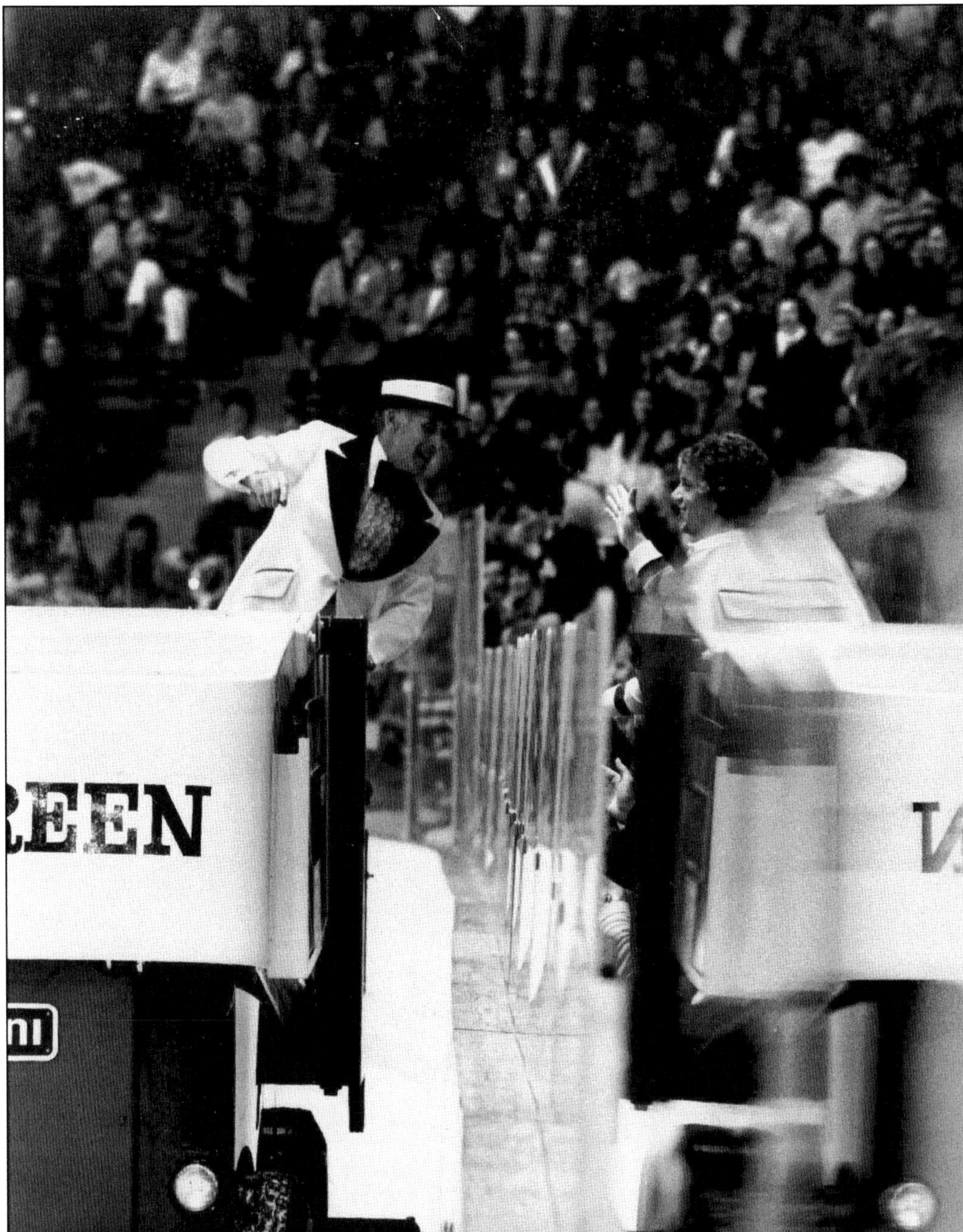

HUTCH, THE ICE MAN. For many years, in Thompson Arena and before that in Davis Rink, making ice between periods of the annual Winter Carnival game was as memorable as the game itself. No one played to the crowd better than Richard Hutchins. Dressed to the nines in a top hat and tails (rented by Dartmouth hockey players), Hutch drove the Zamboni in style, resurfacing the ice to rave reviews from the packed house. The Hanover native returned to town after a 20-year career in the navy and was superintendent of the athletic grounds crew for a decade until he retired in 1979.

DARTMOUTH COLLEGE HOCKEY
NORTHERN ICE

David Shribman and
Jack DeGange

ARCADIA

ISBN 0-7385-3885-X

Published by Arcadia Publishing
Charleston SC, Chicago IL, Portsmouth NH, San Francisco CA

Printed in Great Britain

Library of Congress Catalog Card Number: 2005927744

For all general information contact Arcadia Publishing at:
Telephone 843-853-2070
Fax 843-853-0044
E-mail sales@arcadiapublishing.com
For customer service and orders:
Toll-Free 1-888-313-2665

Visit us on the internet at http://www.arcadiapublishing.com

Front cover, left: Bill Riley '46, the all-time scoring leader of Dartmouth men's hockey.
Front cover, right: Gretchen Ulion '94, the all-time scoring leader of Dartmouth women's hockey.
Back cover: A crowd of more than 4,000 in Rupert Thompson Arena, the home of men's and women's hockey at Dartmouth College.

Contents

ACKNOWLEDGMENTS

This story has been accomplished with the benefit of unlimited access to the photographic images and reference material retained by the Dartmouth College Athletic Department (DCAD), the Rauner Special Collections Library, and the Alumni Records Office at Dartmouth College. With few exceptions, the images and information in this book come from these resources. Where appropriate, specific photograph credit is noted.

First, we wish to thank the DCAD. The authors are indebted to Josie Harper (director of athletics), Kathy Slattery (director of sports information), and Kathy's staff, especially Cindi Mansell. The thorough research of Dartmouth's athletic records by Dan Connolly has been as invaluable as the proofreading by Jane DeGange.

The Special Collections Library and the Alumni Records Office were equally helpful, including Jay Satterfield (the special collections librarian) and members of his staff: Barbara Krieger, Sarah Hartwell, Eric Esau, Phyllis Gilbert, and Joshua Shaw. Also, Michelle Brown of the Alumni Records Office provided much support.

Special thanks are also extended to Edward Connery Lathem '51, dean of libraries and librarian emeritus; to the Friends of Dartmouth Hockey, particularly Barbara Crowe, Michael Choukas '51, and Seaver Peters '54; to Chuck Gibson, graphic designer; and to the coaches of men's and women's hockey at Dartmouth.

About the Authors

David Shribman '76 became executive editor of the *Pittsburgh Post-Gazette* in 2003 after more than 25 years as a writer and editor for the *Buffalo Evening News*, the *Washington Star*, the *New York Times*, the *Wall Street Journal*, and the *Boston Globe*. He was awarded a Pulitzer Prize in 1995 for his national political coverage. Shribman was a trustee of Dartmouth College from 1993 to 2003.

Jack DeGange, a graduate of Bates College, was sports information director at Dartmouth from 1968 to 1977 and has been a newspaper, corporate and academic communicator for more than 40 years. He lives in Lebanon and continues to write about Dartmouth and Ivy League athletics.

Previously, Shribman and DeGange published *Dartmouth College Football: Green Fields of Autumn* (Arcadia Publishing, 2004).

INTRODUCTION

The Dartmouth of legend and lore is a frost-encrusted outpost, a frigid, forbidding institution perched on the frontier, a lonely academic redoubt planted in the frozen North Country by a visionary preacher. All that is true, at least for part of the year. Northern New England is famous for its seasons: the renewal that comes with springtime, the easy early evenings of summer, the brilliant color of autumn. But it is winter that gives the region its character, and it is winter that gives northern New England's most storied college its game.

Hockey is the winter game, and Dartmouth is the winter college. The sounds and shouts of the game—the screech of skates coming to an abrupt halt on new ice, the chant of the crowd in the last moments of a close game against Harvard or Cornell, the "ooohhh" that accompanies a furious slap shot from the point—are part of the sound track of the place. This is an outdoor game, even when it is played indoors. It had its origins on frozen ponds in Dartmouth's frigid corner of New Hampshire. This game sprung from the earth at Dartmouth, and it has flourished there for 100 years.

This college of legends has legends galore in hockey. Its coaches, including Eddie Jeremiah '30 and George Crowe, are part of the history of the game. The contemporary coaches, Bobby Gaudet '81, Judy Parish Oberting '91, and now Mark Hudak, are making history, game by game, along with the men and women who play at Hanover and who are coaching across North America. Its players—Lee Stempniak '05, a Lou Gehrig of the ice whose stamina is matched only by his flexibility; Lea Bolling '78, so much a trailblazer in women's hockey that you might think of her as one of the founding mothers of the sport; Bill Riley '46, one of three brothers (with Jack '44 and Joe '49) in the U.S. Hockey Hall of Fame; Gretchen Ulion '94, the all-time leading women's scorer and one of several women Olympians—all are part of the heritage of hockey and of Dartmouth. Its venues—the venerable Davis Rink, the palace beloved even by people who never stepped into it and loathed by opponents who still resent the fans hanging belligerently over the ragged chicken wire, and Thompson Arena, still among the most magisterial sites in eastern collegiate hockey—hold the echoes of the ages.

Dartmouth players have left big skates to fill and have filled big roles in many arenas. Seaver Peters '54, captain of the 1953–54 team, was for many years Dartmouth's athletic director and a formidable figure in collegiate sports in America. Mike McGean '49 came to Hanover from Cleveland and toyed with hockey but perfected figure skating, becoming a major figure in that world. (He lost his two front teeth, and some of his innocence, in hockey practice in Hanover.) Walter Bush '51, Bob Naegele '61, and Gordie Russell '55 are on the roster of National Hockey League owners. Buddy Teevens '79 cut a figure on the ice as much as on the gridiron, where he is once again Dartmouth's head football coach. (Two of his predecessors in those dual sporting roles were Myles Lane '28, the rare inductee in both the hockey and football halls of fame, and

Bill Morton '32, an All-American in both sports and, later, the head of American Express.) Jackie Brennan '76, also a lacrosse student, left hockey in his senior year but left an impact outside the rink; he went on to be the leader of the multibillion-dollar Vanguard financial empire. And, of course, there are Stempniak and Hugh Jessiman '06, tooling around the Hanover ice before heading to hockey's big show.

Mostly, though, there are the memories. The days when Nick Pelton created new ice by pushing a 55-gallon drum of hot water on wheels across Davis Rink. The Saturday Winter Carnival games, when out-of-town dates crowded the stands and showered the Yale six with opprobrium (and cuss words they learned only the night before). The drumbeat of "Go Green Go" reaching the rafters and raining back into the stands and onto the ice. The tip of the hat from Richard "Hutch" Hutchins, sitting on the Zamboni as if it were a surrey with a fringe on top. The dedication of Ted Wingate '78, volunteer coach with the early women's teams on fundamentals on the Davis Rink ice to prepare them for scrimmage games with Hanover High. The coming of age of the women's game in Hanover, a reign of success that has placed 17 Dartmouth women on national teams—and a concentration of talent so rich that, on the 2004–05 team, several players had been named to Canadian or American national teams.

In the end, the thing about hockey is the thing about Dartmouth. There is no room for pretense, no room for the poseur. It rewards grit, guts, ingenuity, and above all, great spirit. It puts a premium on individual skills even as it prizes teamwork. It is grounded in equal opportunity, which is why the men's team turns out for women's games, and vice versa, and why the tradition of this sport, and the pages of this book, are shared with pride by men and women alike. It is at once old-fashioned and modern, rough and smart, and fast and fun. It does not see ice as an obstacle; it sees it as a playing surface.

ONE

The Early Years for Men 1905–1937

Befitting the college of Robert Frost, hockey's first Green at Dartmouth were gold. Today's skaters are creating their own glorious history, but they measure themselves against players who were not only revolutionary in their style but also enduring in their impact. They shaped the game far beyond the confines of their early playing surfaces—playing surfaces (including marked-off corners of the frozen Connecticut River) that survive only in memory and photographs.

So much of that past is unrecognizable to us now: the rivals they played, the outfits they wore, the positions they occupied (rovers today are confined to lunar vehicles and gridiron secondaries), the teams they sent to the ice (seven players rather than today's six), particularly the game they played (slower, less sophisticated). To hockey fans today, they look like daguerreotypes from another age. Their hockey was not mannered, but it was manly.

Their success is a reminder of how, even in team sports, individuals have the power to mold a game. Gerry Geran '18 envisioned a players' association long before labor disputes resulted in the cancellation of an entire professional hockey season. Myles Lane '28 played a brand of hockey that matched the man: brainy, contemplative, innovative, judicious. Eddie Jeremiah '30 played in the pros, but his legacy was here, at the college level and at Dartmouth. He may not have been one of the game's founding fathers, but for an important time in the game's history he was its favorite son.

These early years tell so little about the game, and yet it is everything we need to know about this game. They tell us that it is, at base, a game of pure, refined skill. They tell us that it has its origins in the cold outdoors and thus is closer to nature than its cousins, baseball, basketball, and football. They tell us that it is a game of imagination, rewarding the imaginative even as it produces matches of unimaginable excitement. They tell us that even with the greatest advances in technology (for hockey has been marked more by technology than any other team sport), it is pure mental sharpness that makes the difference on the ice.

And so we begin our look at the winter game where it started, in the wintry confines of Hanover, in the place where the ice was thick, where the skaters were strong, where the frigid air was made for hockey, though really it might have been the other way around.

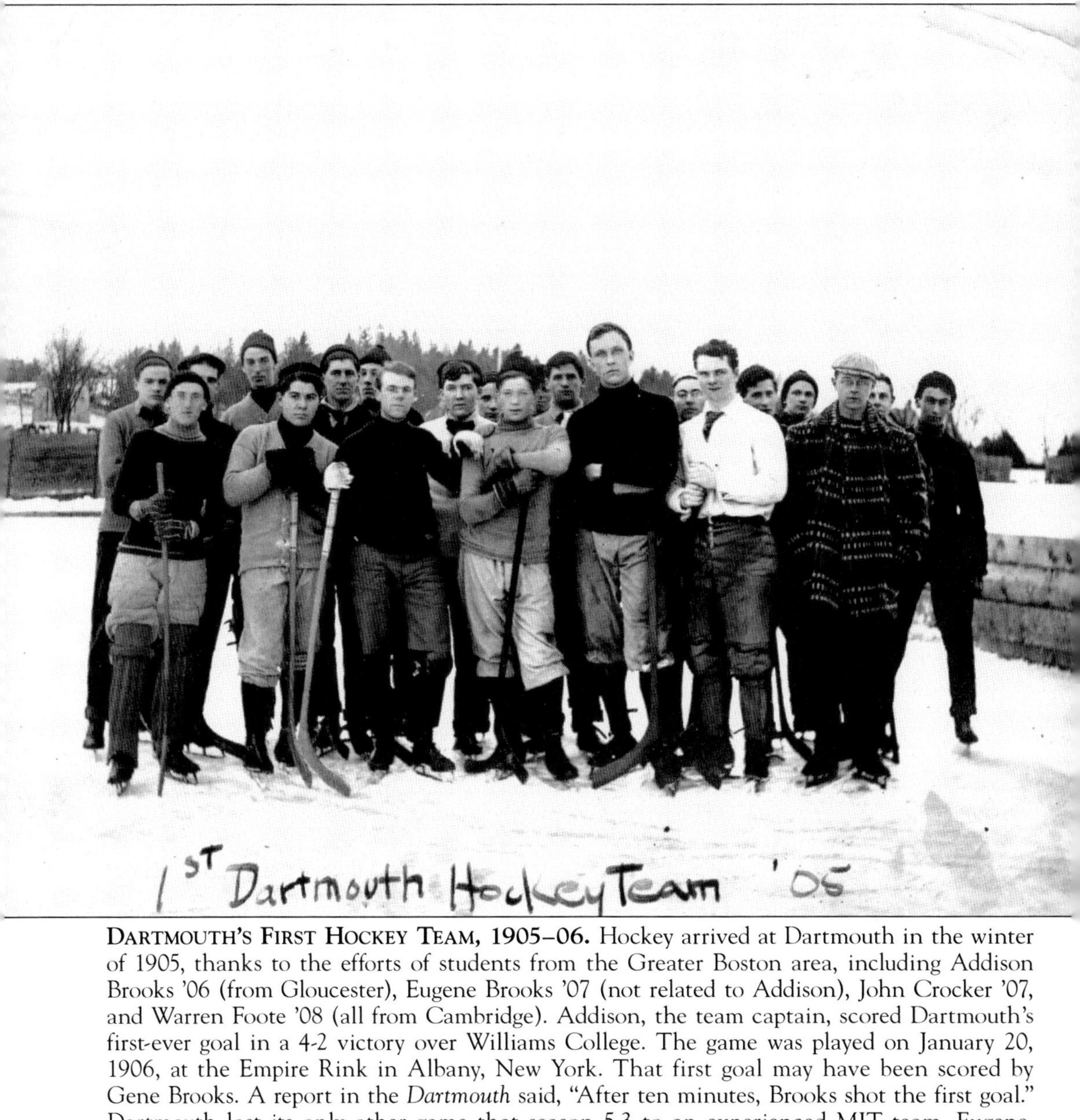

DARTMOUTH'S FIRST HOCKEY TEAM, 1905–06. Hockey arrived at Dartmouth in the winter of 1905, thanks to the efforts of students from the Greater Boston area, including Addison Brooks '06 (from Gloucester), Eugene Brooks '07 (not related to Addison), John Crocker '07, and Warren Foote '08 (all from Cambridge). Addison, the team captain, scored Dartmouth's first-ever goal in a 4-2 victory over Williams College. The game was played on January 20, 1906, at the Empire Rink in Albany, New York. That first goal may have been scored by Gene Brooks. A report in the *Dartmouth* said, "After ten minutes, Brooks shot the first goal." Dartmouth lost its only other game that season 5-3 to an experienced MIT team. Eugene, also a quarterback on the football team, was elected captain of Dartmouth's second team. A knee injury forced him into a coaching role with Foote in 1906, as Dartmouth compiled a 5-2 record. In this photograph, Gene Brooks is second from left in the front row. (Courtesy of Virginia Hutton, daughter of Gene Brooks.)

WARREN FOOTE '08. During Dartmouth's first three seasons, Foote was the Green's dominant player. The rangy forward-rover led Dartmouth in scoring each year. In 1906–07, Dartmouth joined the Intercollegiate Hockey League with Princeton, Harvard, Yale, and Columbia. Foote scored every Dartmouth goal in a 4-2 win at Yale that season. In 1907–08, he had Dartmouth's three goals against Harvard (the Crimson won 10-3).

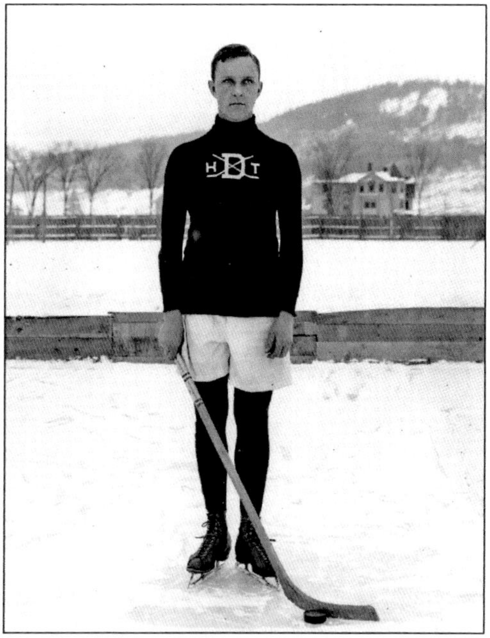

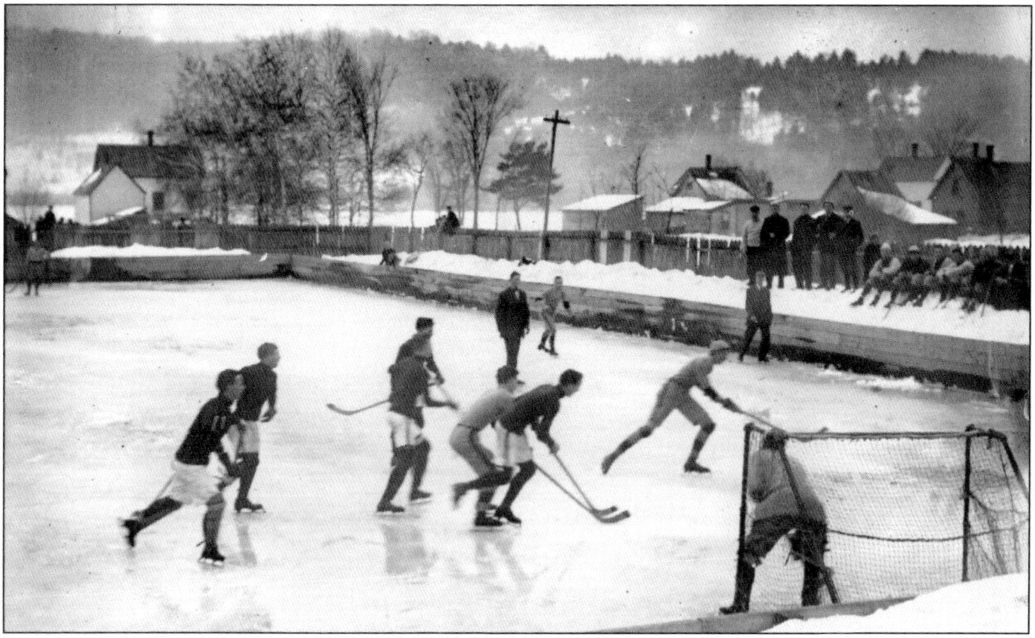

DARTMOUTH'S FIRST RINK. During the first 25 years of hockey at Dartmouth, the Green played outdoors in Hanover. The vast majority of games were played in locales where indoor ice was available. Dartmouth's first rink was built on the current site of Leverone Field House, adjacent to South Park Street. Hanover's Velvet Rocks can be seen in the background. Over the years, Dartmouth's home games were played on three seasonal rinks in proximity to Alumni Gymnasium (completed in 1910). Games were also played on Occom Pond north of the campus. Dartmouth's first home game was played on January 11, 1907, against the Coaticook Club from Quebec (Dartmouth won 9-5). The first intercollegiate hockey game in Hanover was on January 24, 1908, a 3-0 loss to Bishop's University, located near Sherbrooke, Quebec.

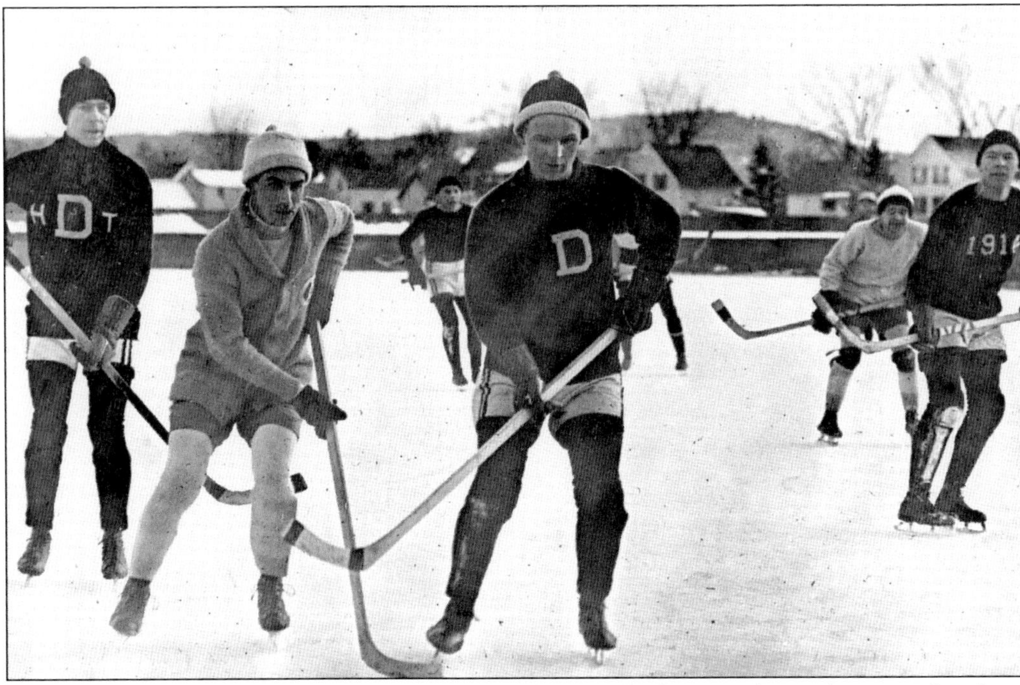

THE EARLY YEARS. As collegiate hockey evolved, teams had seven players (compared with six today). Positions included a rover and a coverpoint. These games at Dartmouth, played prior to World War I on the original rink, reveal that uniforms emphasized warmth rather than protection, though shin pads were not unknown.

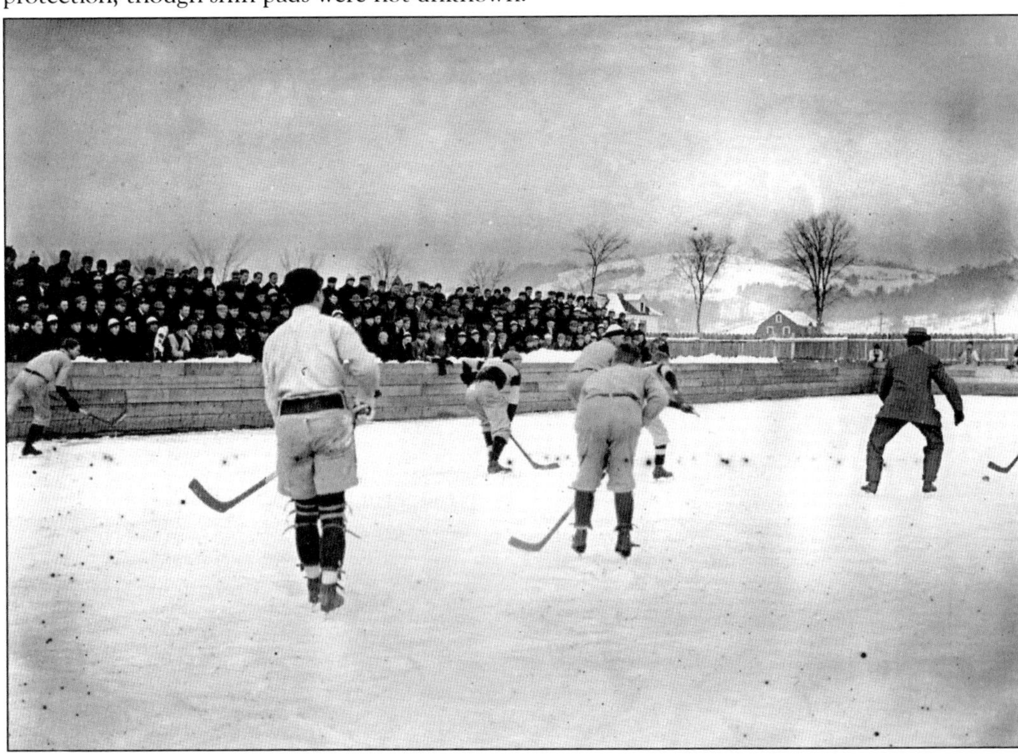

CLARENCE "BAGS" WANAMAKER '15. From 1912 to 1915, Wanamaker, the rover, led Dartmouth in scoring while classmate Arthur "Jiggs" Donahue protected the goal. Wanamaker scored 32 goals as Dartmouth won 18 of 28 games. From 1915 to 1920, Wanamaker coached Dartmouth to a 21-16 record. He then coached Yale from 1921 to 1928, compiling a 76-41-4 record. A catcher in baseball, Wanamaker got into a uniform but not a game for the New York Giants.

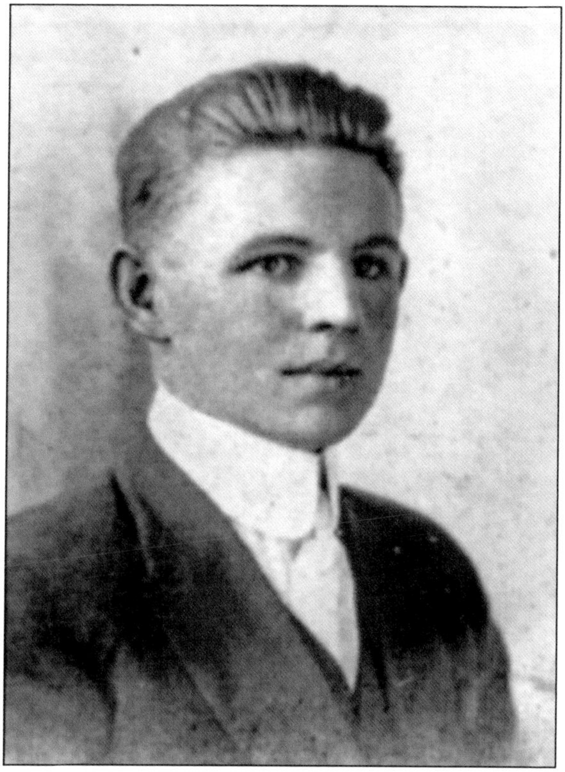

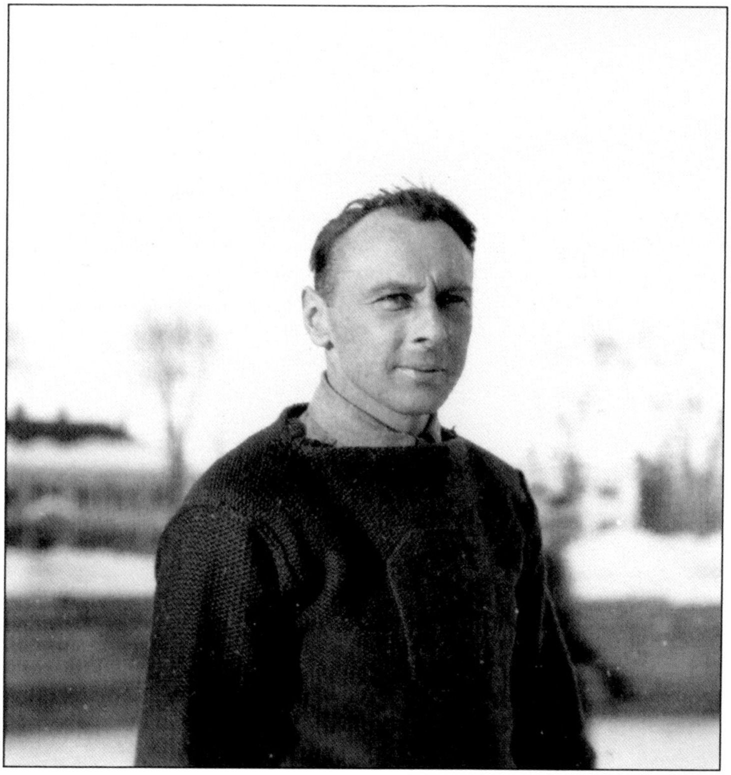

LEON TUCK '15. Another member of the team from 1912 to 1915, Tuck was a center who scored 23 goals for the Green and earned a place on the first U.S. Olympic hockey team at Antwerp, Belgium, in 1920. Tuck succeeded Bags Wanamaker as Dartmouth's coach. Over three seasons from 1920 through 1924, Tuck's teams built a 26-11-3 record. He did not coach in 1921–22 but returned to direct a 13-2 season in 1922–23.

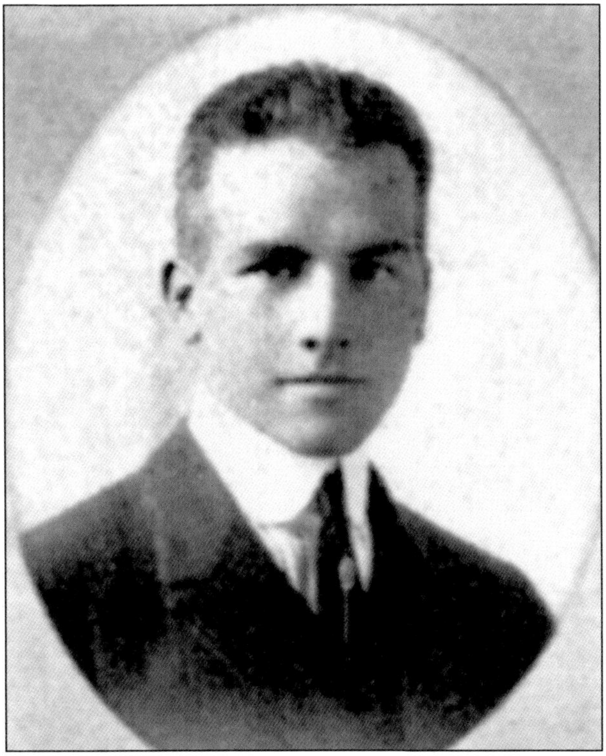

RALPH "TUG" TYLER '16. Tug Tyler played from 1914 to 1917. He was Dartmouth's scoring leader in 1916, then the captain and an All-American rover in 1917. Though Dartmouth had an informal golf team until 1920, Tyler became a golf pro and golf architect. His subsequent business, Ralph Tyler & Company in Muncie, Indiana, specialized in handmade clubs for several decades.

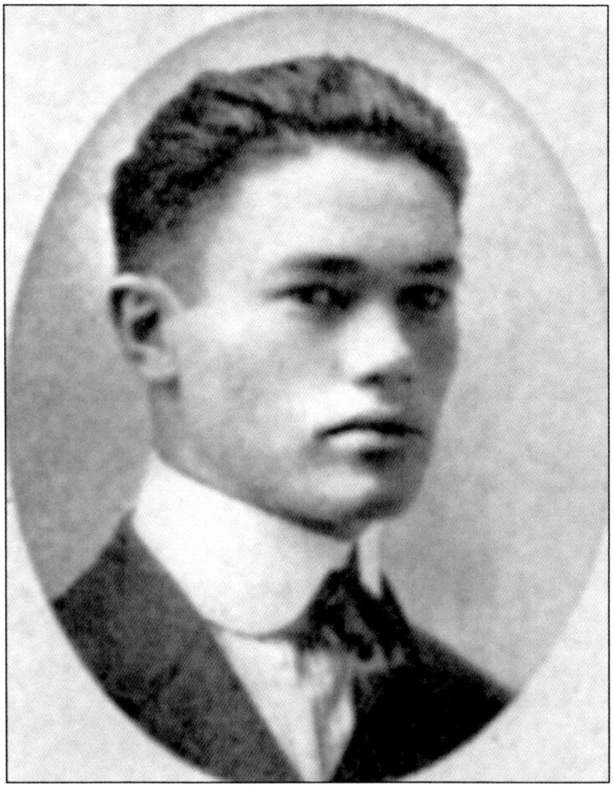

GEORGE "GERRY" GERAN '18. Geran played briefly at Dartmouth before joining the navy during World War I. He was a member of the 1920 U.S. Olympic hockey team and one of the first American players in the National Hockey League. Twenty years later, he promoted creation of an NHL players association. As an outspoken player, he raised the ire of owners with long memories. His idea failed.

JOHN MURPHY '19. Recognized as an All-American wing as a sophomore in 1917, Murphy was captain and leading scorer for the 1917–18 team. Due to World War I, Dartmouth had no hockey team in 1918–19 (the only break in play for more than a century). Murphy was a shortstop and second baseman for Dartmouth's baseball team, serving as captain in 1918.

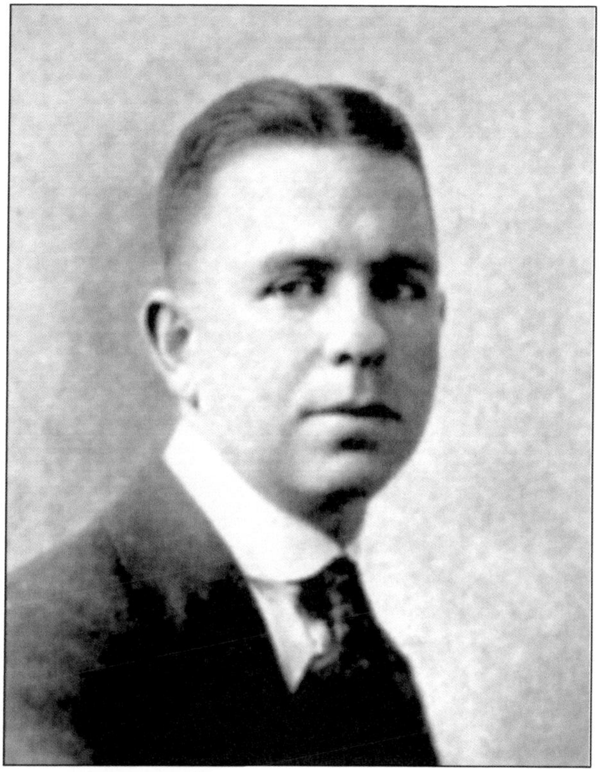

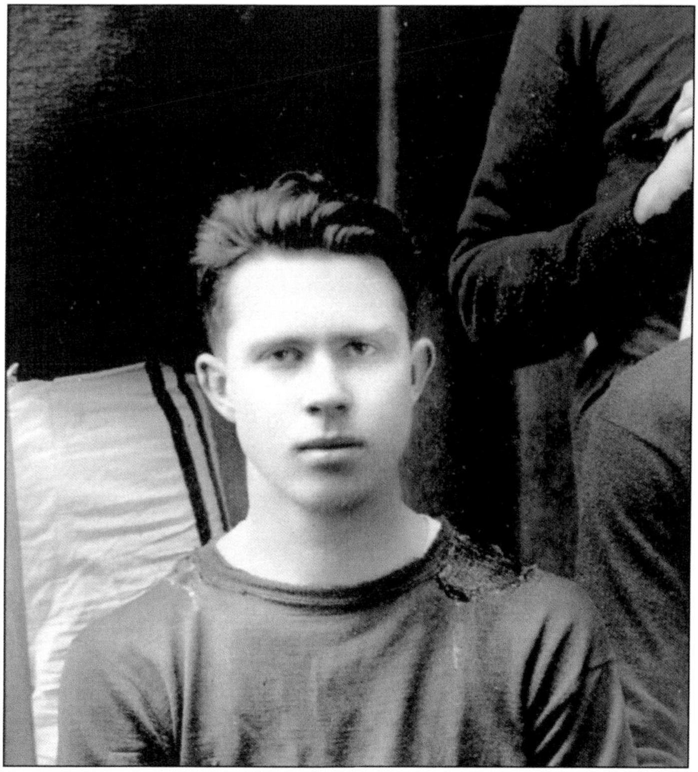

ROBERT PAISLEY '19. Bob Paisley returned to Dartmouth after serving during World War I as a member of the first Marine Aviation Force, flying DeHaviland bombers out of Dunkirk, Belgium. Paisley was captain and an All-American center for the 1919–20 team. He was also considered for the U.S. Olympic hockey team in 1920, when the sport was contested as part of the Summer Games at Antwerp.

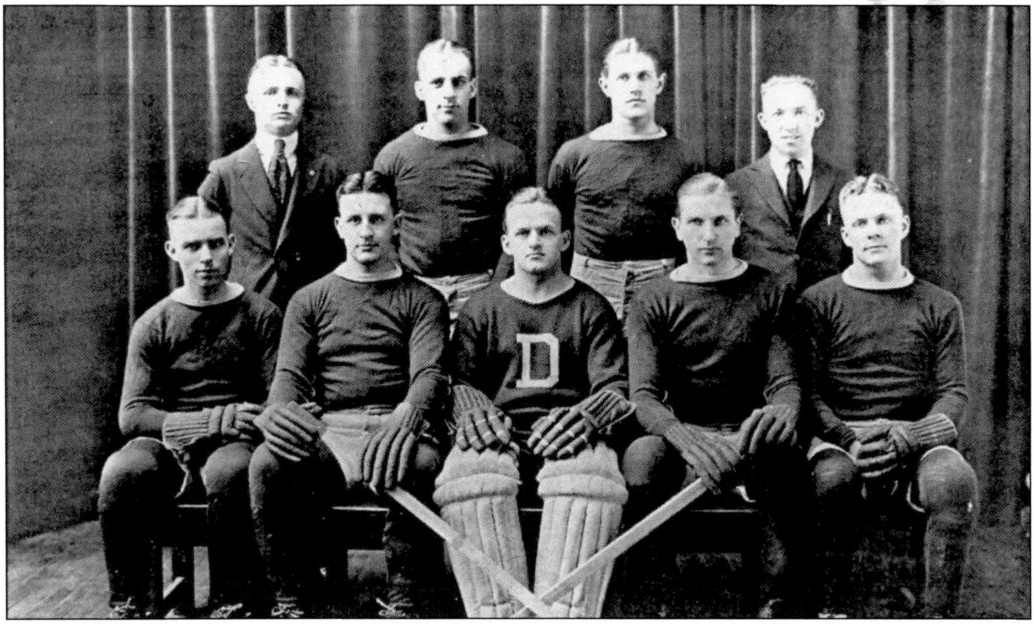

Chester Gale '19. During a career that spanned World War I, Gale (front row, center) was Dartmouth's premier goaltender. In 1919–20, he set a record that still stands—five shutouts in a season. Gale had a 1.60 goals-against average as Dartmouth compiled a 6-4 record. Gale also lettered in baseball and tennis and won the Archibald Prize as Dartmouth's outstanding scholar-athlete in 1920.

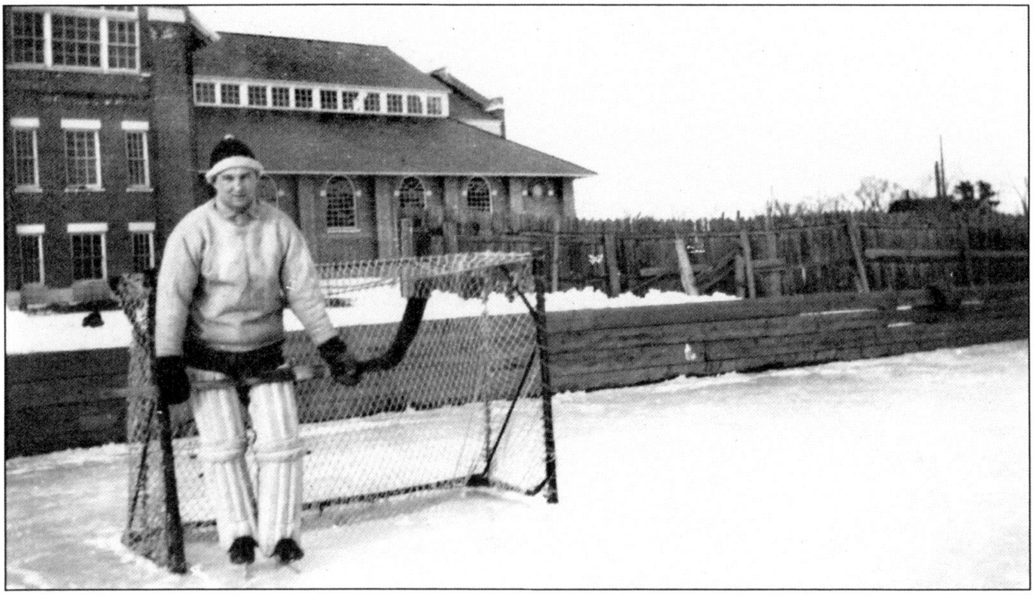

Rink Relocation. In the early 1920s, Dartmouth set up a rink on Alumni Oval, now Memorial Field and home of Dartmouth football. Games, however, were frequently played on Occom Pond. The goalie in this photograph could be Lloyd "Pudge" Neidlinger '23. Neidlinger was the goalie in nine games as Dartmouth built a 13-2 record in 1922–23. In 1922, he was chosen by Walter Camp as a second team All-American tackle in football. And, for two decades (into the early 1950s), Neidlinger was the dean of Dartmouth College.

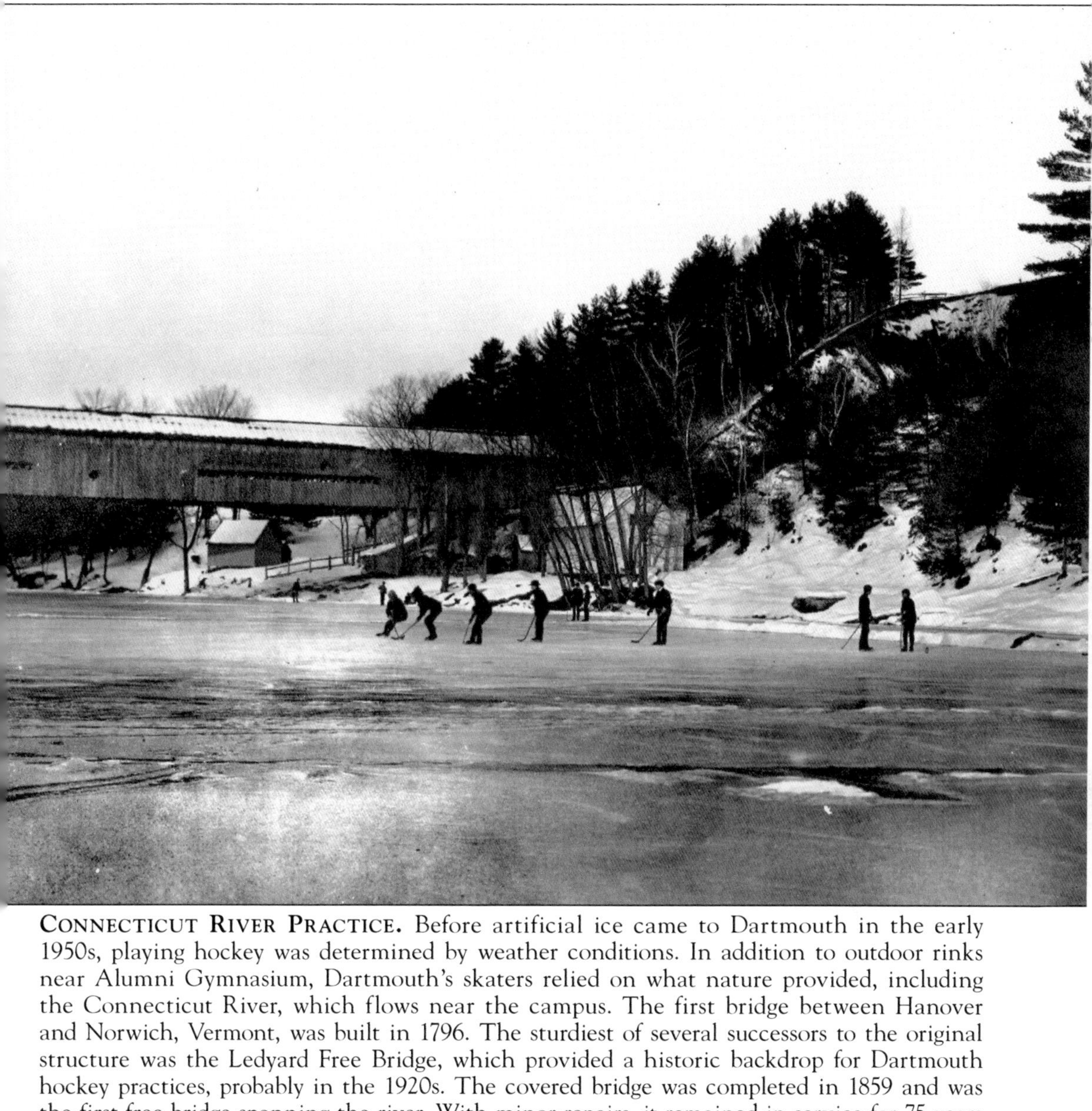

Connecticut River Practice. Before artificial ice came to Dartmouth in the early 1950s, playing hockey was determined by weather conditions. In addition to outdoor rinks near Alumni Gymnasium, Dartmouth's skaters relied on what nature provided, including the Connecticut River, which flows near the campus. The first bridge between Hanover and Norwich, Vermont, was built in 1796. The sturdiest of several successors to the original structure was the Ledyard Free Bridge, which provided a historic backdrop for Dartmouth hockey practices, probably in the 1920s. The covered bridge was completed in 1859 and was the first free bridge spanning the river. With minor repairs, it remained in service for 75 years until it was replaced in 1935 by the steel-and-concrete Ledyard Bridge, which (with recent replacement) has served automotive traffic ever since.

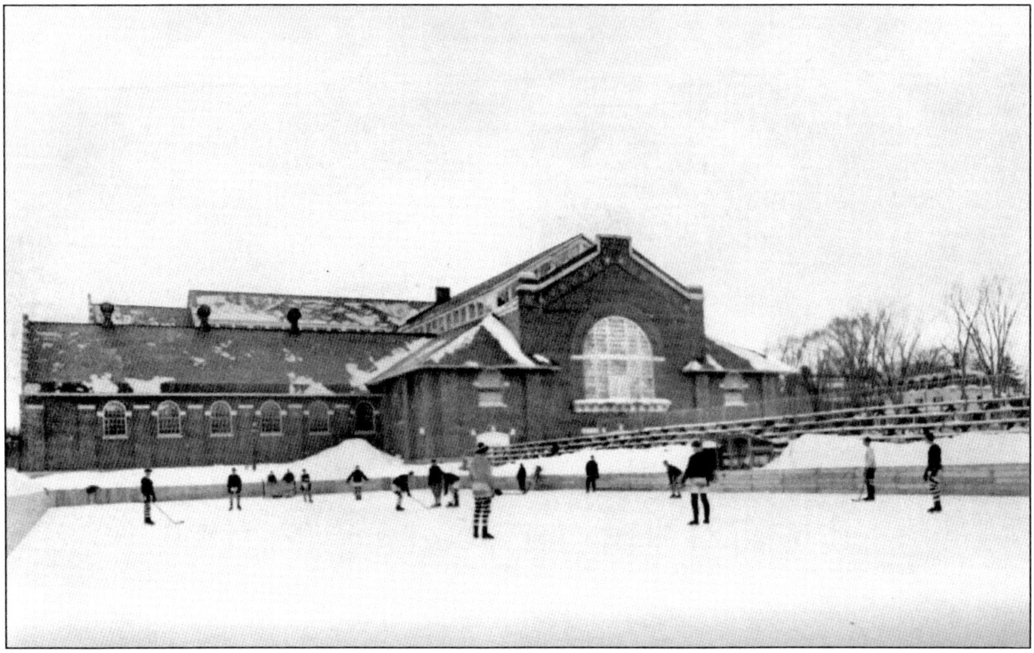

LAST OF THE OUTDOOR RINKS. With the completion of Memorial Field in 1923 as the home for football at Dartmouth, a new site for hockey was created adjacent to the east wing of Alumni Gymnasium, completed in 1921. Along with Occom Pond, the rink served as the home for hockey until Davis Rink was completed in 1930.

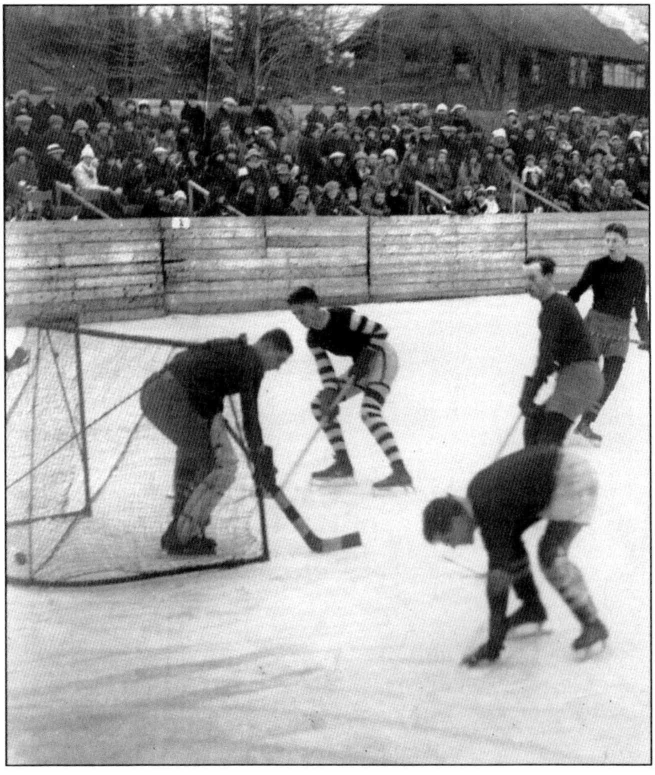

OCCOM POND. Another of Dartmouth's outdoor rinks during the 1920s was located on Occom Pond, north of the campus near the Hanover Country Club. It was frequently used for games, including Winter Carnival games. One especially memorable Winter Carnival game was the 1922 match with Columbia. Scoreless in the second period, play was called due to a heavy snowfall.

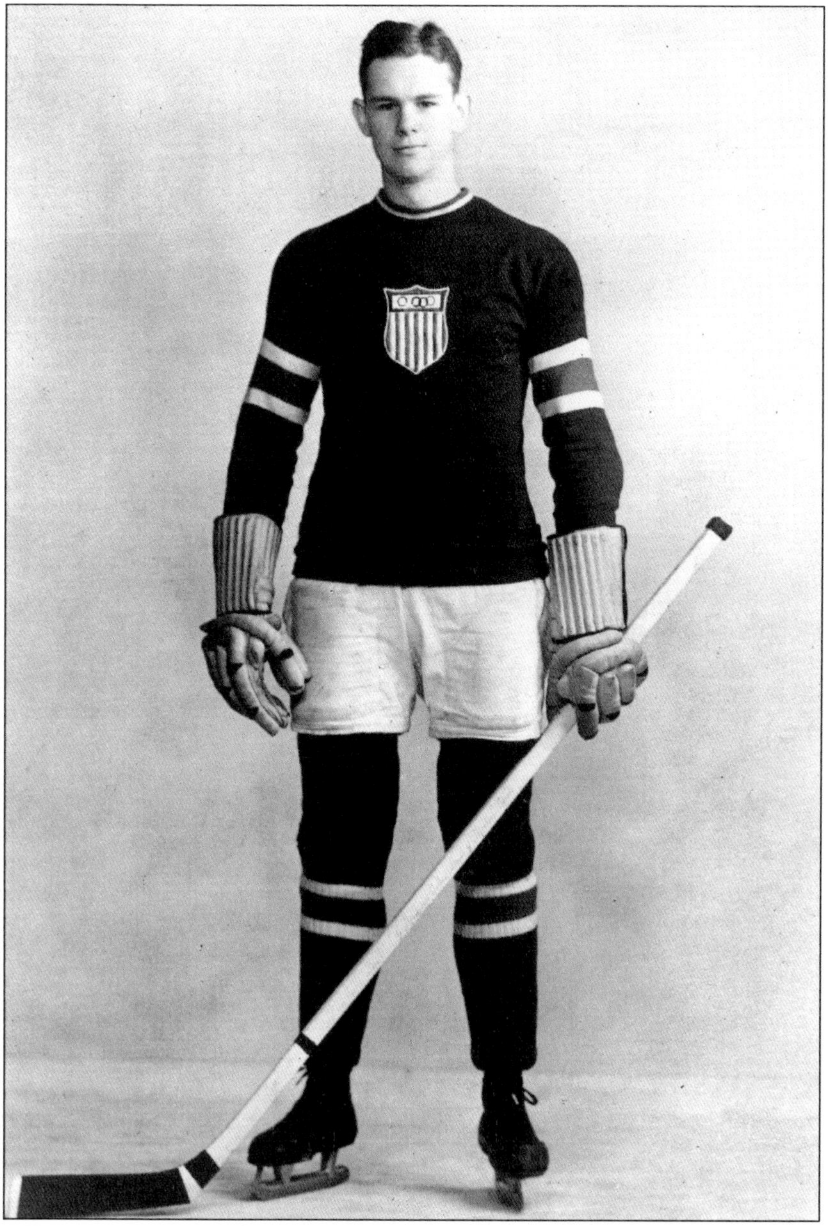

DOUGLAS EVERETT '26. In the mid-1920s, there was no finer skater at Dartmouth than Everett. The rangy wing from Concord, New Hampshire, lived on the ice from age five. While he never led the Green in scoring (30 goals from 1923 to 1926), his talent was obvious. During Everett's collegiate career, the Green built a cumulative record of 26-11-3, including a 12-3-0 mark in 1925–26, when Everett earned All-American selection. He was pursued by three NHL teams: the Boston Bruins, New York Rangers, and Toronto Maple Leafs. Everett refused all offers and joined an insurance firm in Concord, where he remained for 40 years. He continued to play amateur hockey and crowned his playing career with the U.S. Olympic team that won the silver medal at Lake Placid in 1932. He was elected to the U.S. Hockey Hall of Fame in 1974. Concord's municipal arena, a mecca of scholastic and amateur hockey, is named in his honor.

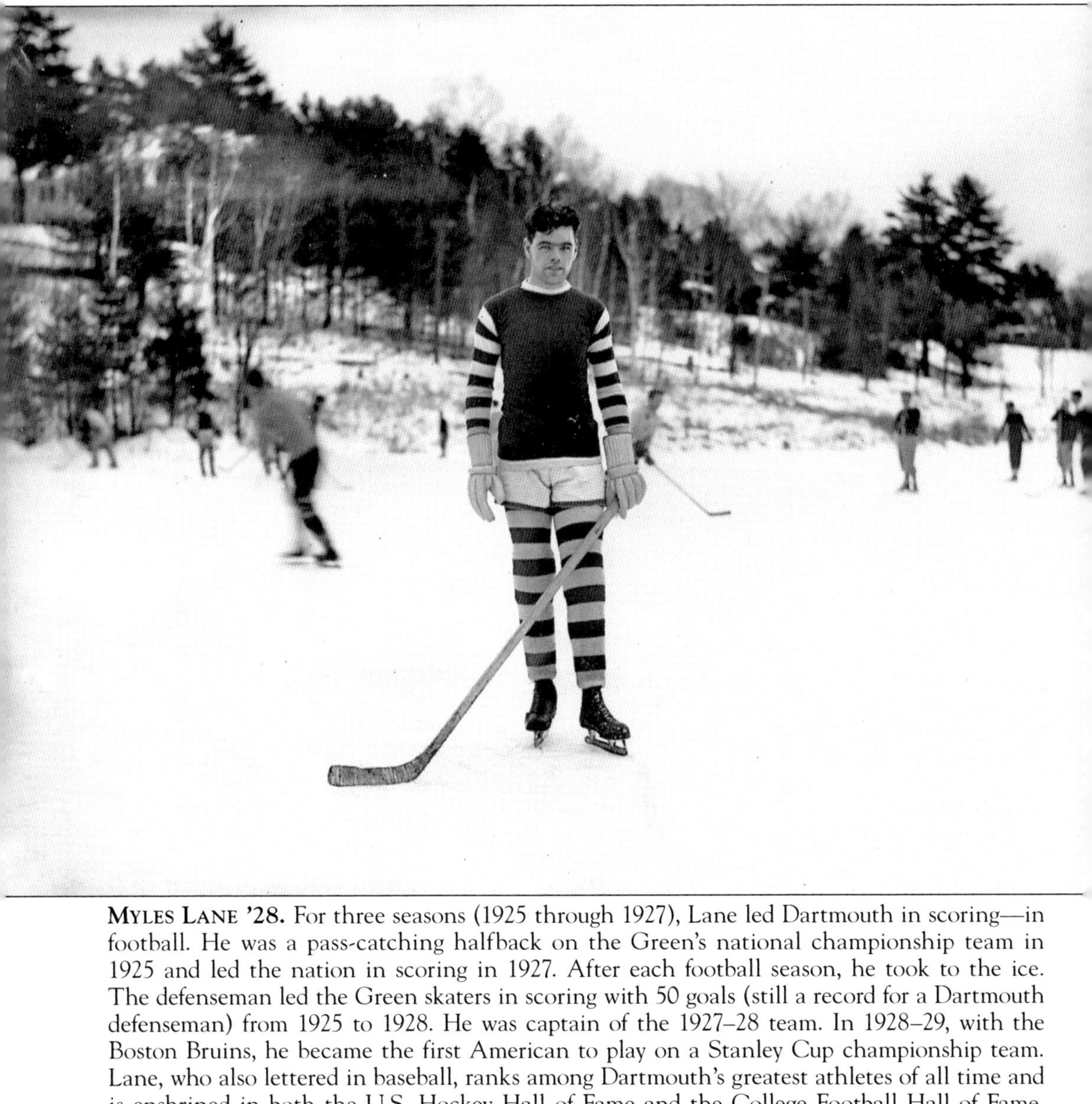

Myles Lane '28. For three seasons (1925 through 1927), Lane led Dartmouth in scoring—in football. He was a pass-catching halfback on the Green's national championship team in 1925 and led the nation in scoring in 1927. After each football season, he took to the ice. The defenseman led the Green skaters in scoring with 50 goals (still a record for a Dartmouth defenseman) from 1925 to 1928. He was captain of the 1927–28 team. In 1928–29, with the Boston Bruins, he became the first American to play on a Stanley Cup championship team. Lane, who also lettered in baseball, ranks among Dartmouth's greatest athletes of all time and is enshrined in both the U.S. Hockey Hall of Fame and the College Football Hall of Fame. Playing professional hockey and serving as head football coach at Boston University financed his law school studies at Boston College. Lane became one of the nation's most successful trial lawyers and was a justice of the New York State Supreme Court. His former teammate on the Bruins, Eddie Shore, said, "You're the only person I know who ever played professional hockey and eventually wound up on the bench—the judicial bench, I mean."

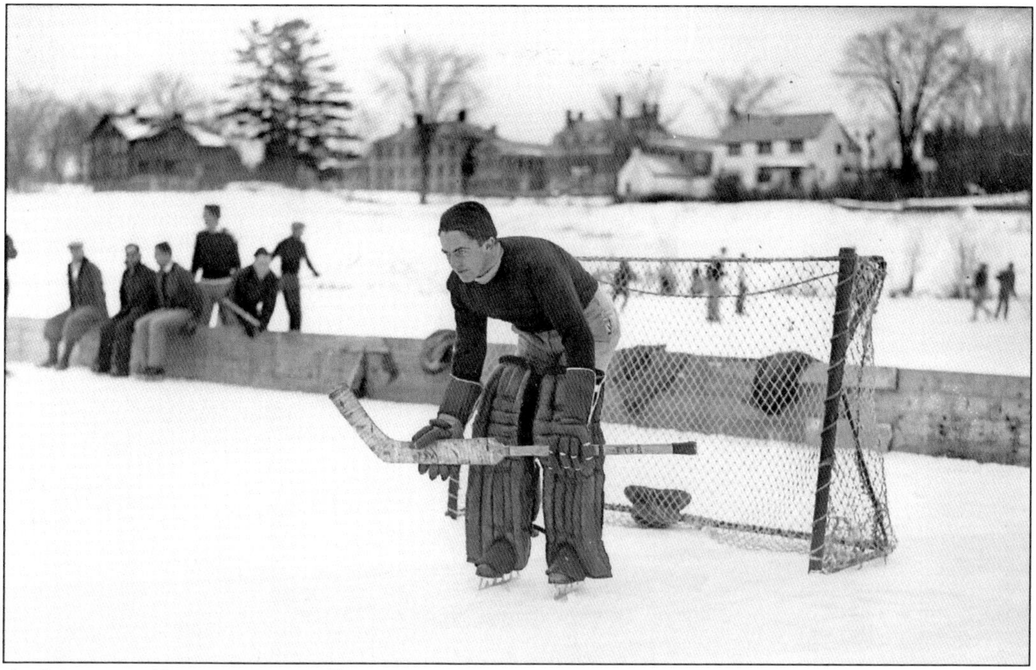

G. MORRILL BOTT '29. "Molly" Bott came to Dartmouth via Phillips Exeter Academy and capped a three-year career in the nets by earning All-American honors in 1929. Bott had a career goals-against average of 1.60 (48 goals in 30 games). During his senior season, Bott shut out four of 16 opponents. His total of seven career shutouts remains a record at Dartmouth.

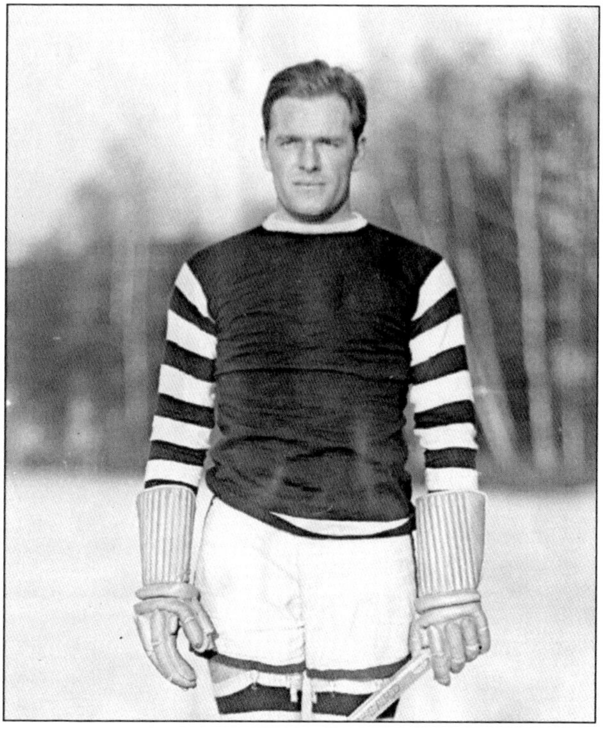

RICHARD ROGERS '29. While Bott backstopped the defense, Dick Rogers paced Dartmouth's attack. In 1926–27, the sophomore teamed with senior Myles Lane as a 1-2 scoring punch on a team that had an 11-2-2 record. For the next two years, Rogers was Dartmouth's leading scorer. As a senior, he joined Bott on the All-American team.

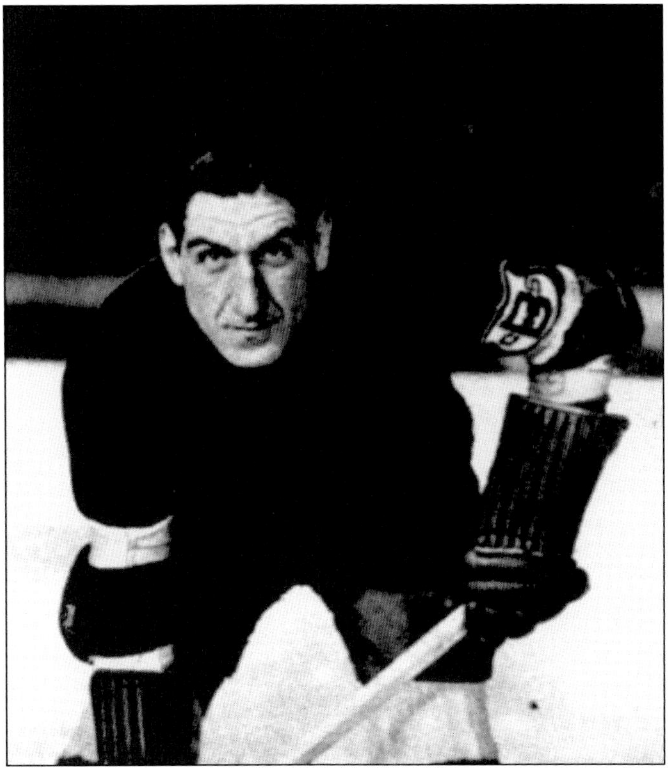

EDDIE JEREMIAH '30, THE PLAYER. Hailing from Massachusetts, Jeremiah won nine letters in three sports at Somerville High and received a scholarship to Hebron Academy. He arrived at Dartmouth in 1926 as a freshman but survived to letter in football, hockey, and baseball. He was an All-American on the first team to play in Davis Rink in 1930. His legendary coaching career is the subject of chapter 3.

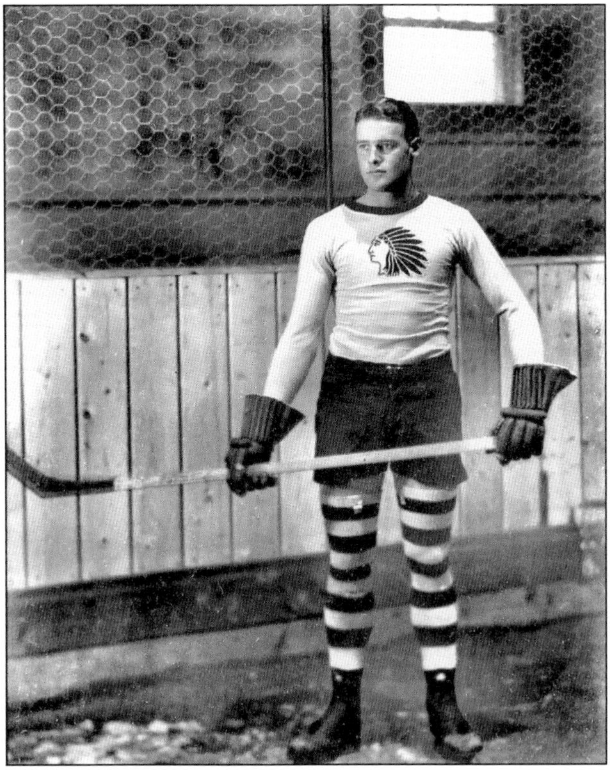

WILLIAM MORTON '32. He was known widely as "Air Mail" Bill Morton for his football exploits as an All-American and Hall of Fame quarterback who kicked a historic field goal to tie Yale 33-33 in 1931. Morton was also an All-American defenseman in hockey. His last-minute goal—in his last game—decided a 3-2 win over Princeton in 1932. Morton's brother, Roald "Rollie" '34, led Dartmouth in scoring twice.

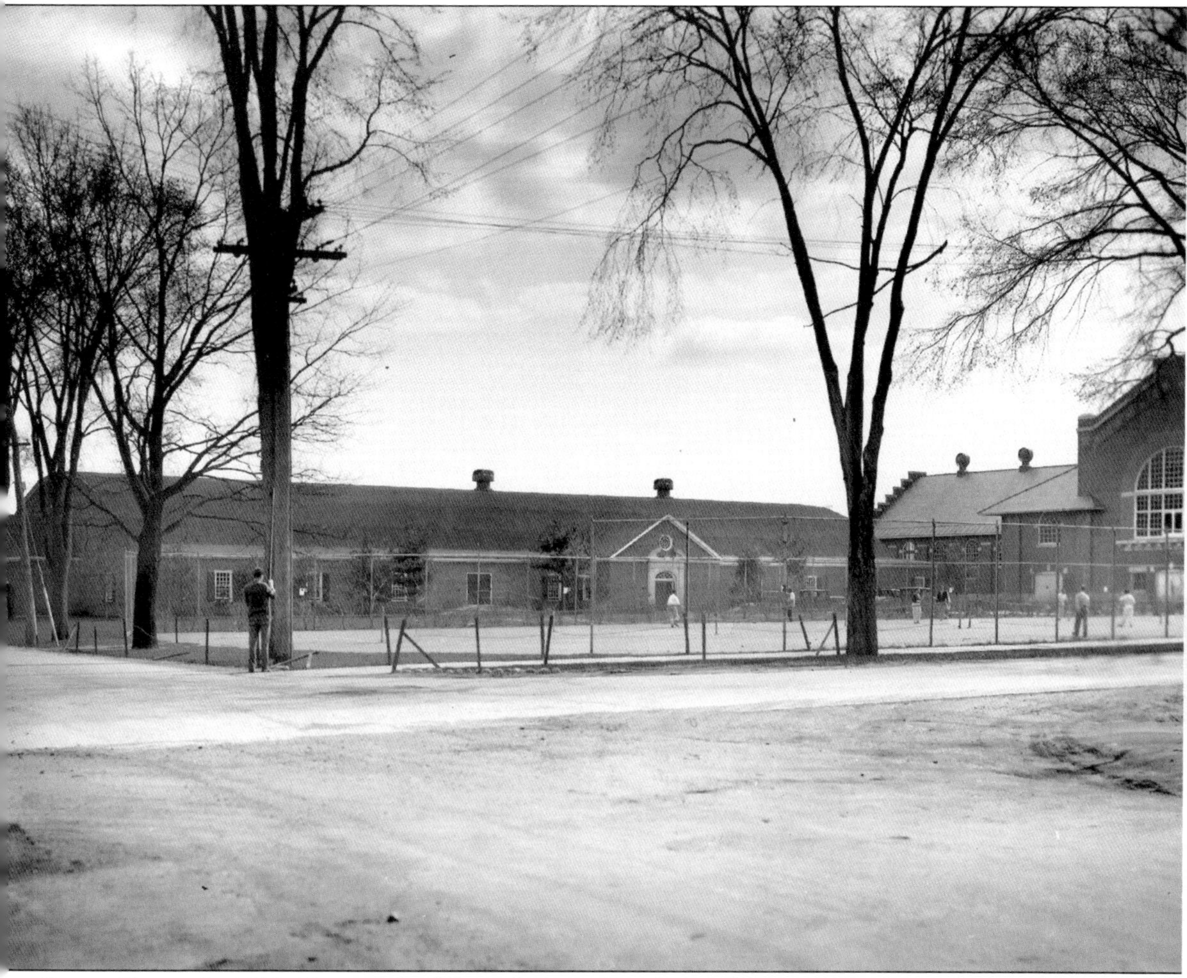

DAVIS RINK. In 1929, Howard C. "Shorty" Davis '06 donated $60,000 for Dartmouth's new covered hockey rink. Davis also made gifts to satisfy the mortgage on Alumni Gymnasium and for construction of Davis Varsity House. In the foreground of this picture, from the early 1930s, today's busy intersection of East Wheelock and Park Streets is still unpaved. Though Davis Rink answered Dartmouth's need for an indoor rink, the ice was still natural and subject to the weather. As the 1929–30 season began, the team still practiced on Occom Pond and experimented with the new surface. The first game in Davis Rink was between Dartmouth's freshman team and the Hebron Academy team that included Charles "Hafey" Arthur '34, later Dartmouth's coach during World War II. The first varsity game was played on February 1, 1930, a 7-2 loss to Bishop's University. The Green also lost to Harvard 2-1 in the first Winter Carnival game in Davis. Four days later, on February 12, 1920, Dartmouth's first victory in the new facility came in an 11-1 decision over Amherst. The rink served skaters at Dartmouth for more than a half-century.

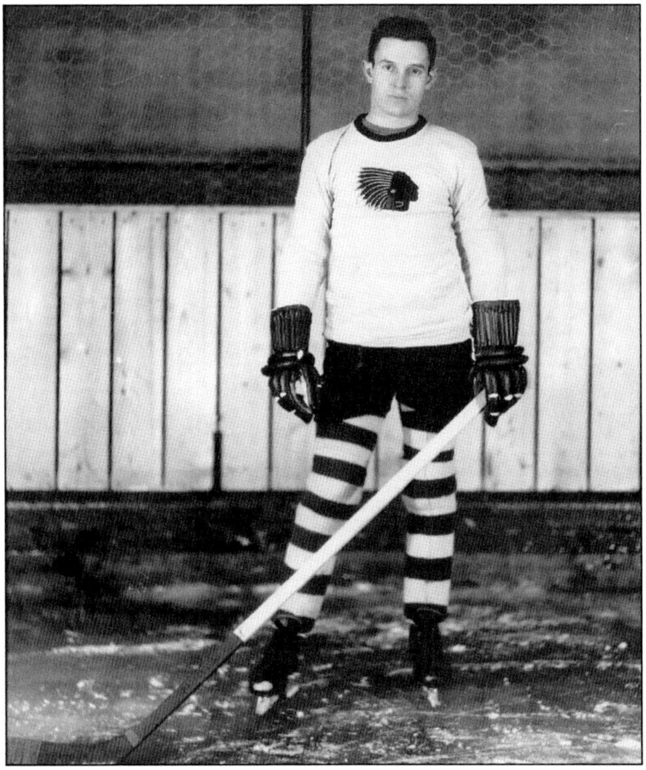

FRANK SPAIN '34. Spain came to Dartmouth from Phillips Exeter Academy in 1930 and earned All-American honors as he scored 41 points (14 goals, 27 assists) as the center on the 1933–34 team that had a 12-5 record. Spain did not play in 1932–33, and he did not return for his last season of eligibility in 1934–35, though he had been elected captain. Spain played exhibition games to prepare for the 1936 Olympics, where he helped the United States win the bronze medal.

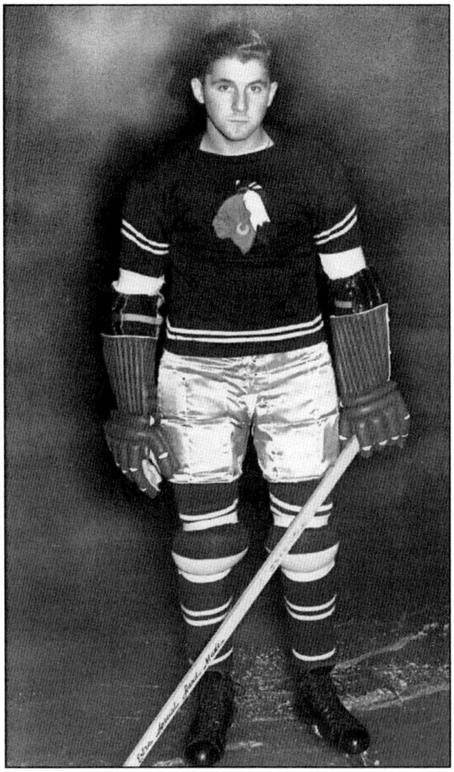

PAUL GUIBORD '36. When Spain departed, Guibord was elected Dartmouth's captain in 1934–35. He was also captain of the 1935–36 team. Guibord was a three-time All-American who became the first collegiate player to score more than 100 career points (66 goals, 37 assists, 103 points). An outstanding tennis player throughout his life, Guibord declined an invitation to play on the U.S. Olympic team in 1936. He also turned down professional hockey offers.

TWO

The Early Years for Women 1974–1986

What seems completely unremarkable today seemed beyond comprehension then: women playing hockey for Dartmouth. The advent of women's hockey at Hanover was a team effort: men and women working together for the pure love of the game. The assists may have come from the men, such as Ted Wingate '77, Mark Panella '78, and Bob Ceplikas '78, but the goal was set by women, including Aggie Kurtz, the assistant athletic director. By the time a dozen years had passed, women's hockey was part of the normal order of things.

The story of the early days is, in some ways, more remarkable than the tale of how the women in Green tore up the ice once the team, and the sport, reached full maturity. It was, in the early years, a notion—a grand notion, to be sure, but a tentative one. Hand-me-down uniforms. Players who didn't know how to stop on the ice. No formal record keeping. No formal practices, either. Then, as if by spontaneous combustion, a fire was lit on the ice. This was something good. This was something big. This was something as Dartmouth as Davis Varsity House.

This was also something hard. In the beginning, the college gave the women—not a varsity team, not even a club—about $3,000 and free ice time, two one-hour slices a week (plus all they could steal at Occom Pond). Peggy Epstein '79 was lucky; her sister's roommate was on a term abroad and so she borrowed a pair of skates. The players rustled up sticks and borrowed helmets. They raised money on their own, even paying dues. But the spirit was theirs, and it was infectious. A sport that barely had any participants soon became not merely a participatory sport, but also a spectator sport.

These early women played Hanover High and, according to Lea Bolling '78, "got mooshed, 9 to 4" by the University of New Hampshire. Things changed. Women's hockey became a club, and then a team, and the women in green eventually did not get mooshed very often, and hardly ever by five goals.

Before long, they were turning away players and attracting a turnout of viewers. They won games and attention. They won, too, a following. What followed was quite something, for in truth the glory of these women is more than what they did with so little. It is the trail they blazed for a sport that is now a fixture on the Hanover scene—and the national stage.

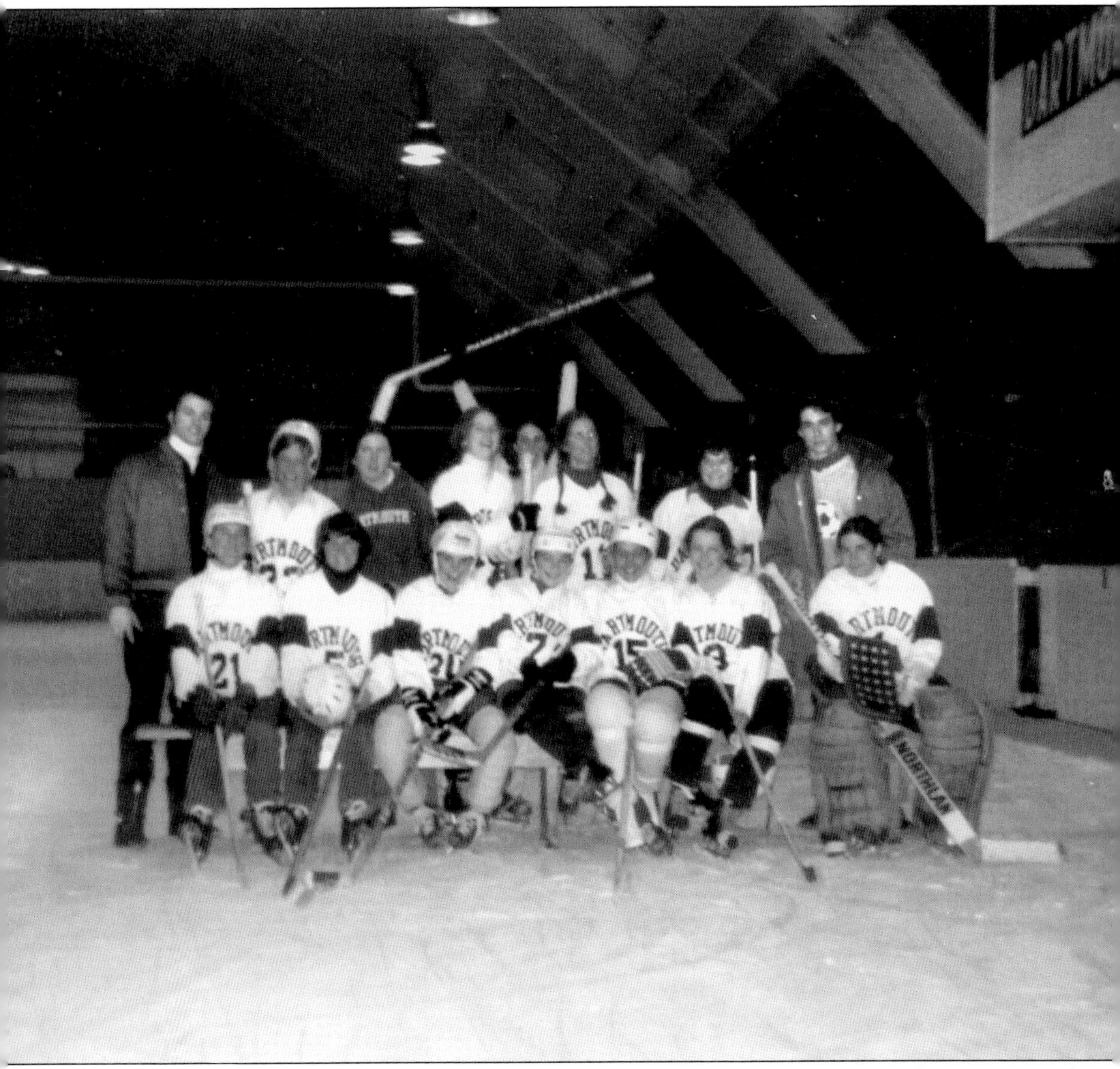

DARTMOUTH'S FIRST WOMEN'S TEAM, 1974–75. In 1974, two years after coeducation arrived at Dartmouth, the first women's hockey team was comprised of freshman and sophomores interested in learning how to play the game. They were allocated an occasional hour of ice time in Davis Rink, attired in intramural league helmets and goalie pads (many wore figure skates) and loosely classified as an intramural team. These women mark the genesis of a hockey program that is now among the nation's best: Bolling, Boyer, Cammann, Duffy, Heller, Kurkjian, Leggat, Miller, Singer, Smallwood, Steele, Stone, and Teel. Many had to learn how to skate backwards and stop on hockey skates (not the same as with figure skates). Their volunteer coaches, Ted Wingate '77 and Dave Richardson '77, were former players from the men's team. They had two scrimmage victories against the Hanover High School girls team and, as Wingate recalled, "a disastrous encounter with the University of New Hampshire," a dominating team in the early years of women's intercollegiate hockey. For them, and their sport at Dartmouth, it was a defining experience.

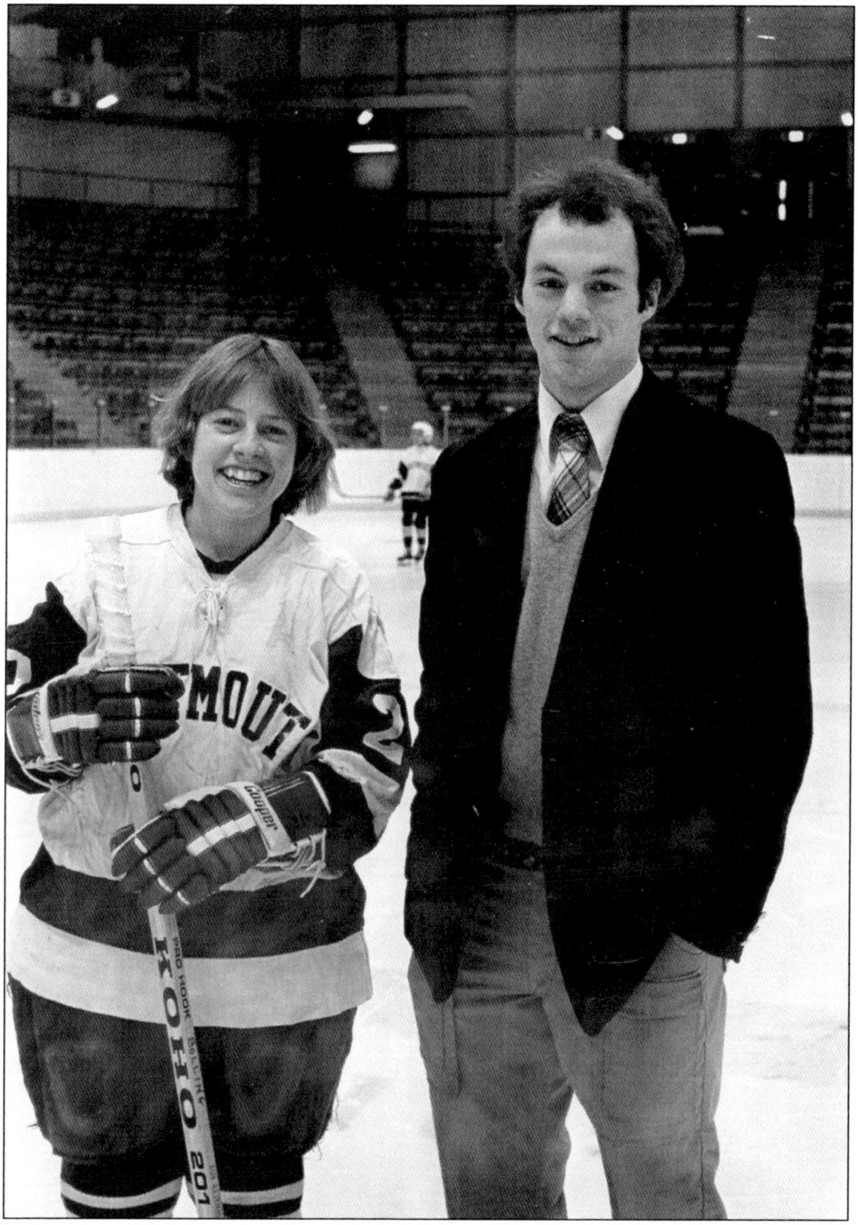

LEA BOLLING '78 AND TED WINGATE '77. In 1975, Dartmouth women's hockey was given club sport standing and more ice time; it did not become an intercollegiate sport until 1979. The prime movers as the team developed were Bolling (left) and Wingate. Bolling was an avid fan of the Philadelphia Flyers and played pond hockey (as a goalie in galoshes) with her older brothers. Wingate played freshman hockey at Dartmouth and then was the unpaid women's coach for three seasons. After graduating, Wingate was paid a modest stipend to coach in 1977–78 and used the money to purchase the team's first shoulder-breast pads. "[Hockey] was the best thing I ever did at Dartmouth," said Bolling, who played right wing. "Ted was the reason it all was successful. We didn't know anything." The team grew to 17 players but was winless (0-6) in 1975–76. The program's first victory came in the first game of the 1976–77 season 2-0 against Middlebury.

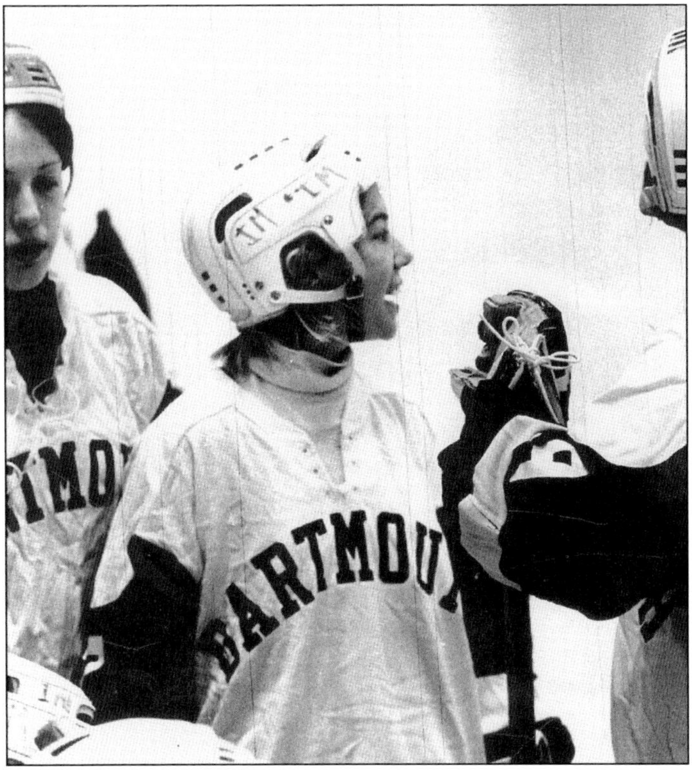

AMY CAMMANN '77. "We were a dilapidated crew of former figure skaters who loved athletics, wanted to play a team sport, and were excited about starting a women's team at Dartmouth," said Amy Cammann. When Dartmouth played at Yale in 1977, Cammann tried to emulate the guys by heaving herself over the boards. She recalled, "At four-foot, 11 inches and 95 pounds, with all those pads, I got stuck half-way and was helpless, until someone pulled me onto the ice."

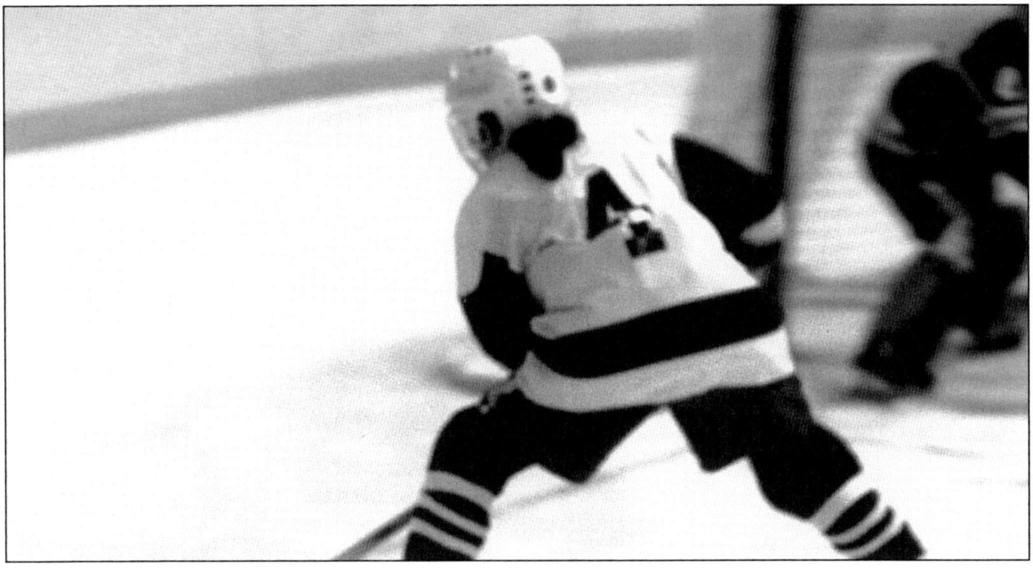

MARY LOU TEEL '78. In the Dartmouth Invitational Tournament in 1978, Teel lines up a shot against Connecticut. With Nancy Wilder '79, she played at Phillips Exeter Academy. Their mentor was George Crowe, who came to Dartmouth from Exeter in 1975. After graduating, she attached this photograph to her resume "to illustrate what a toughie I could be" when she applied for a job with CBS News. "I couldn't type but I got an interview," she said. It worked. She's still there—as an Emmy Award–winning producer at CBS News Sunday Morning. (Photograph by Barry Braverman '76.)

KAREN KURKJIAN '78. When this photograph of Karen Kurkjian appeared in a story about the evolving women's hockey team in the *Dartmouth Alumni Magazine* in 1977, the caption read, "The mask is standard equipment, the pigtails optional for the goalie." Kurkjian and Barbara "Chip" Stone '77 minded the nets for Dartmouth's first four teams.

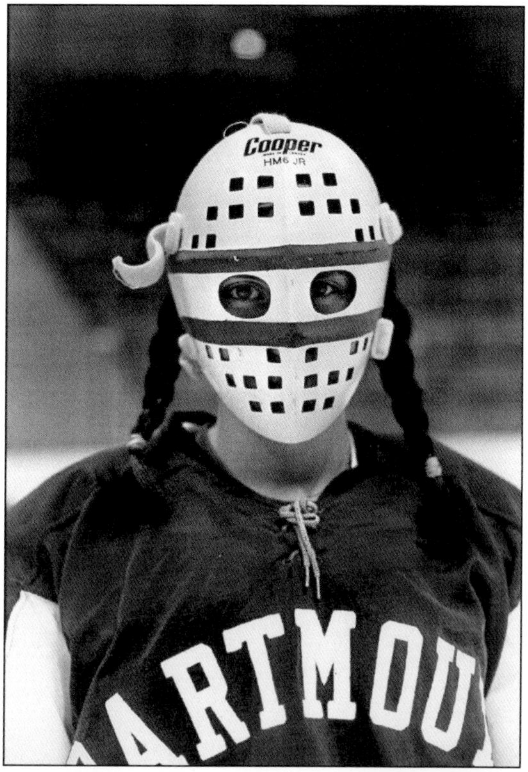

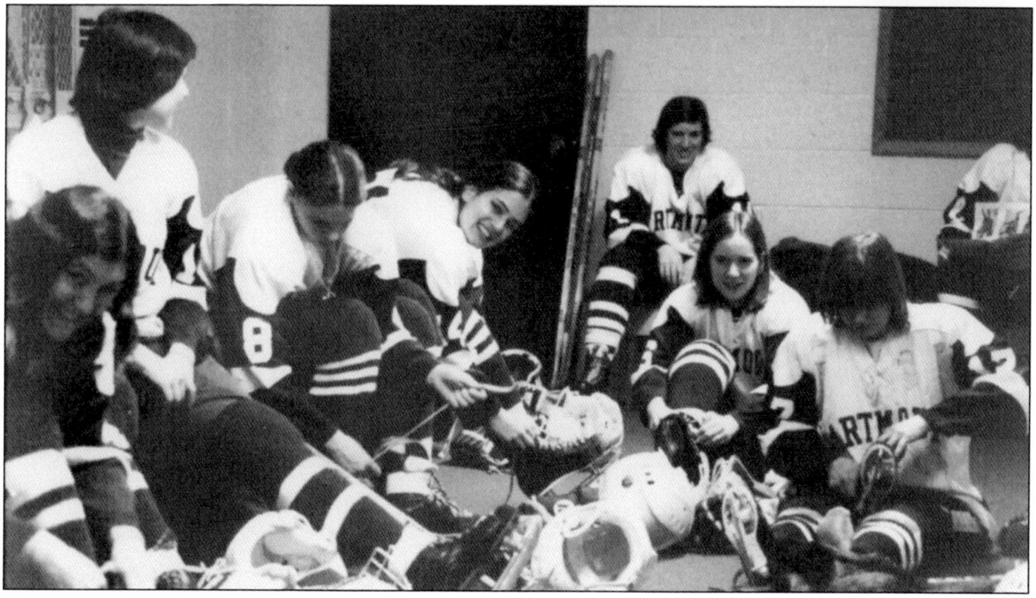

THE LOCKER ROOM. Though they still practiced occasionally in Davis Rink and were still a club sport, the women's team was assigned a locker room in Thompson Arena, which opened in 1975. The evolution to varsity status was being discussed but was a slow process. The hurdles included cost, since it would be the most expensive of all women's team sports, and whether the growing number of women at Dartmouth would be sufficient to sustain the sport. Those questions were answered in the affirmative.

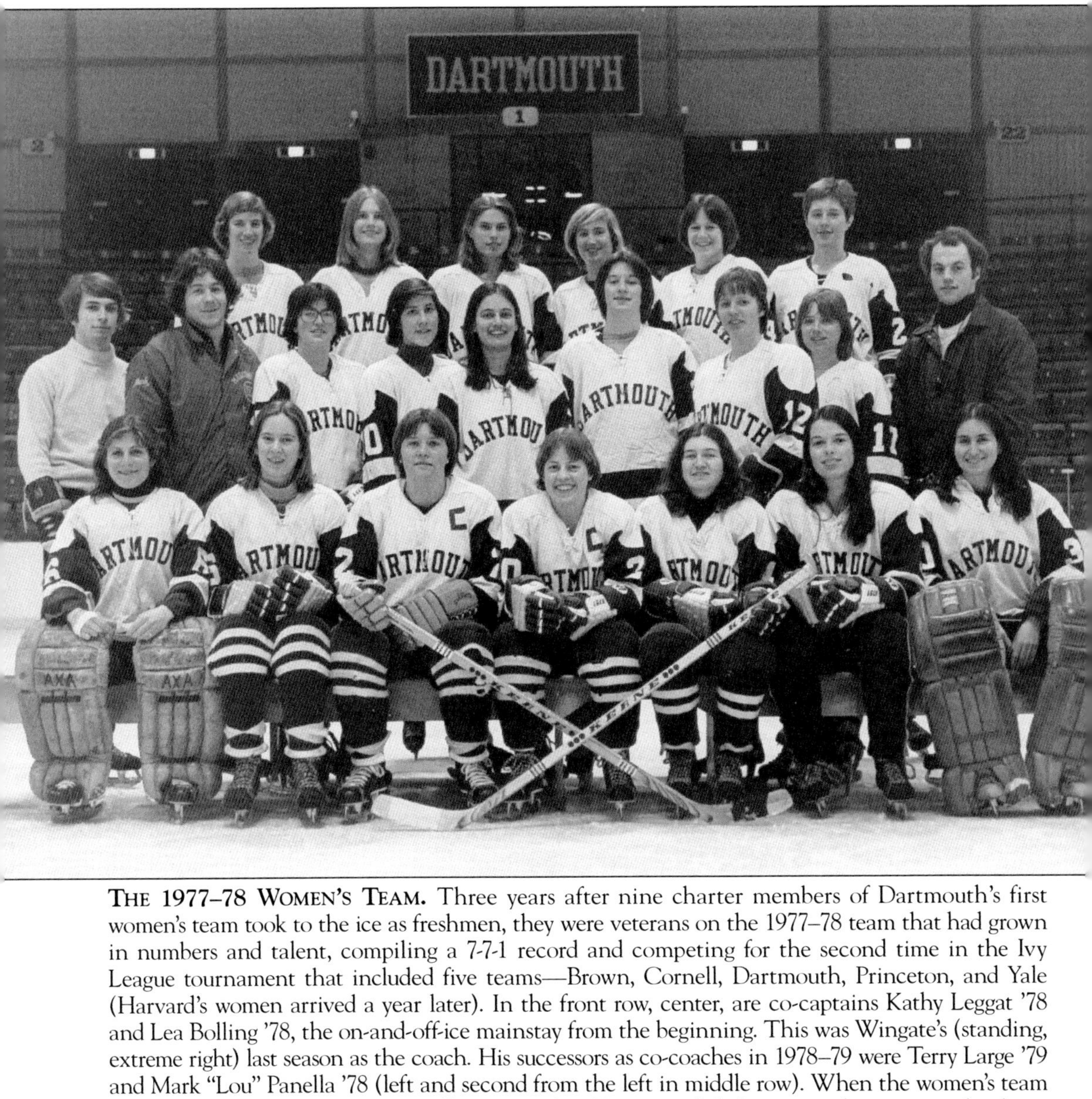

The 1977–78 Women's Team. Three years after nine charter members of Dartmouth's first women's team took to the ice as freshmen, they were veterans on the 1977–78 team that had grown in numbers and talent, compiling a 7-7-1 record and competing for the second time in the Ivy League tournament that included five teams—Brown, Cornell, Dartmouth, Princeton, and Yale (Harvard's women arrived a year later). In the front row, center, are co-captains Kathy Leggat '78 and Lea Bolling '78, the on-and-off-ice mainstay from the beginning. This was Wingate's (standing, extreme right) last season as the coach. His successors as co-coaches in 1978–79 were Terry Large '79 and Mark "Lou" Panella '78 (left and second from the left in middle row). When the women's team reached varsity status in 1979, Panella remained in Hanover while beginning his career in banking. He coached the Dartmouth women's first five varsity campaigns to a record of 60-46-1.

PEGGY EPSTEIN '79. Epstein arrived at Dartmouth with a pair of figure skates that she used to play pond hockey. She borrowed hockey skates from Jana Singer '77, a roommate of Peggy's sister and a member of the first team in 1974–75. She recalled, "The biggest problem: It took me two weeks to learn how to stop on ice."

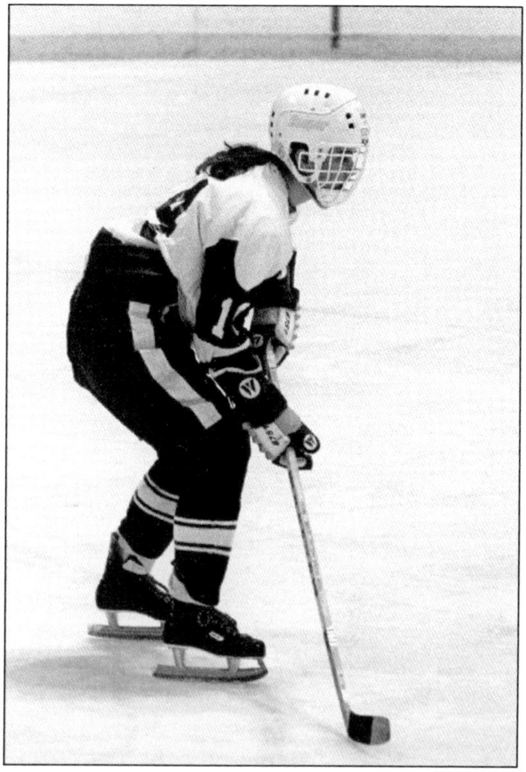

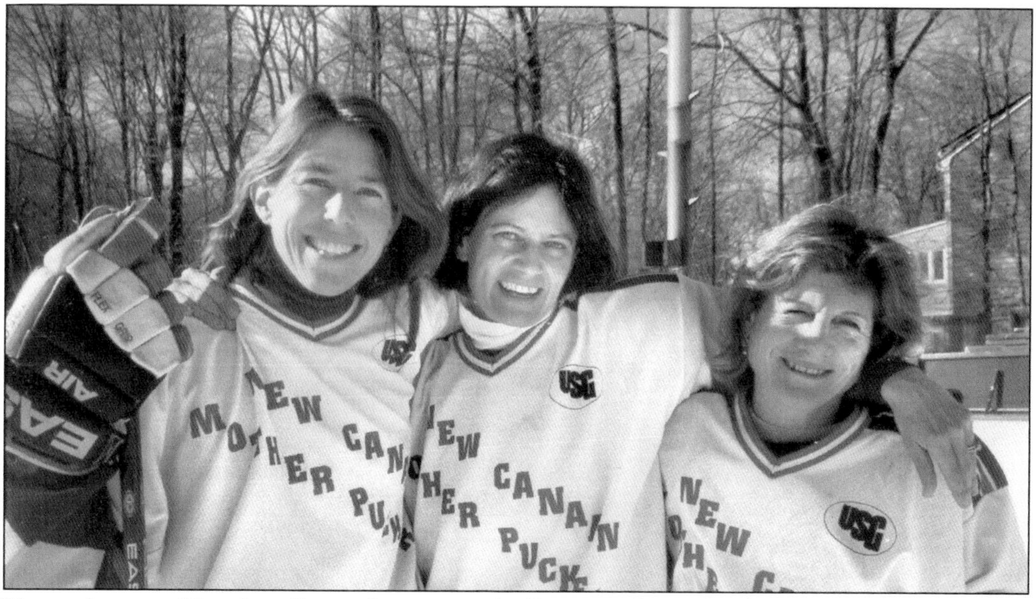

YEARS LATER, THEY'RE STILL SKATING. At Dartmouth in the late 1970s, Peggy Epstein Tanner '79 (center) and Ellen Gomprecht Oppenheim '79 were teammates. Tanner was a center. Oppenheim a goalie. In recent years, with Kit O'Brien Rohn '86 (left), who played in the early 1980s and whose brother, Don '80, was a member of two Dartmouth men's teams that reached the NCAA tournament, they are hockey parents and still playing with the New Canaan Mother Puckers in Connecticut, a team co-founded by Oppenheim.

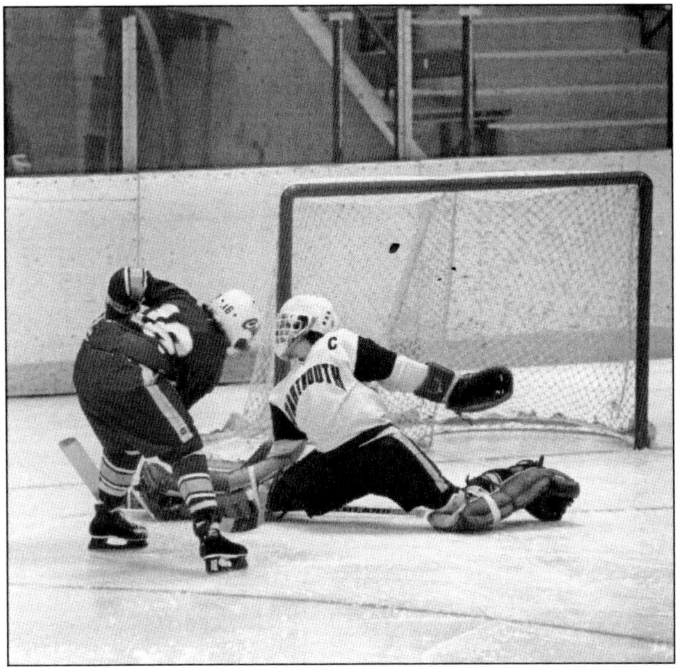

JANICE ELLIS '81. Ellis honed her hockey skills at the Pomfret School in Connecticut. Over three seasons, including 1979–81, when she was joined by defenseman Nancy Wilder '79 on the first All-Ivy League women's hockey team, Ellis was honored as the All-Ivy goaltender. Formal record keeping for women's hockey at Dartmouth began in 1979–80. As a junior and senior, Ellis had a 3.16 goals-against average, playing in all of the Green's 43 games.

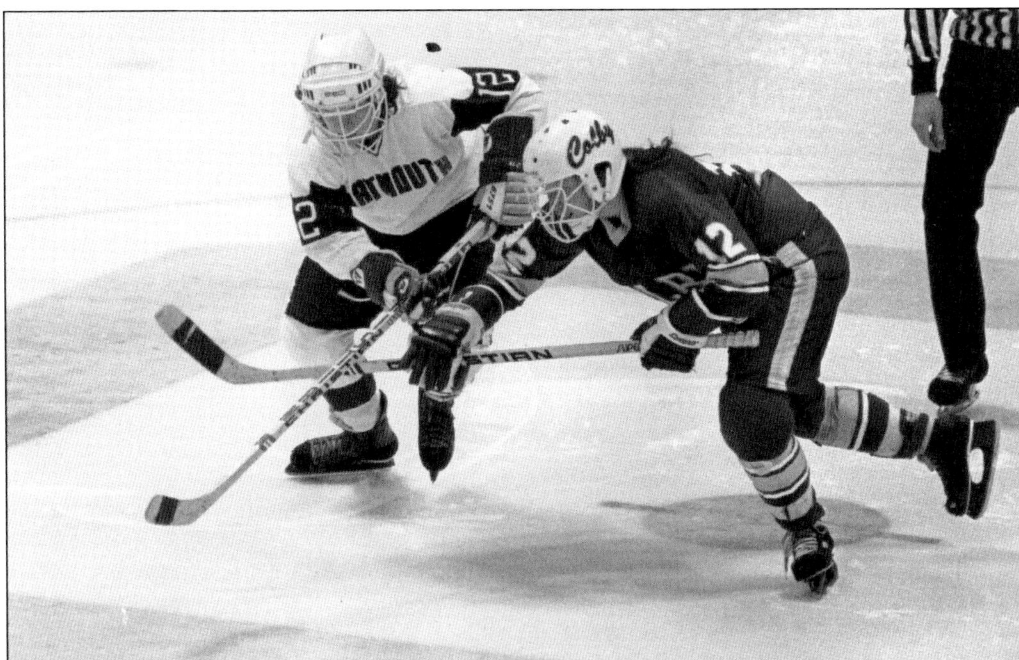

PAULA JOYCE '84. Like Ellis, defenseman Joyce was named first team All-Ivy three times from 1982 to 1984. During four seasons, Joyce scored 93 points, including 39 goals, in 85 games. As a senior, she had the distinction of being captain of both the women's hockey and field hockey teams. Joyce's last three campaigns saw Dartmouth start a string of winning records that continues to the present day.

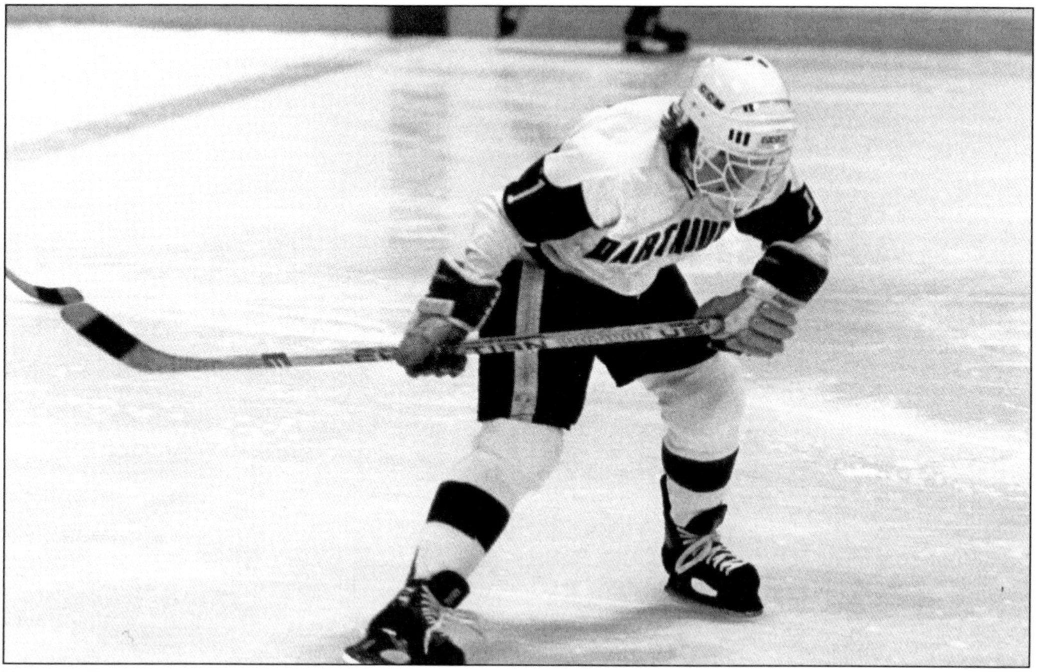

ESTEY TICKNOR '85. Named to the All-Ivy team as a junior and senior, center Ticknor became the Dartmouth women's first 100-point career scorer, matching 66 goals with 67 assists (133 points). Among five three-goal games, Ticknor had a five-goal performance against Colby as a sophomore. She was also a standout with the Green women's soccer team.

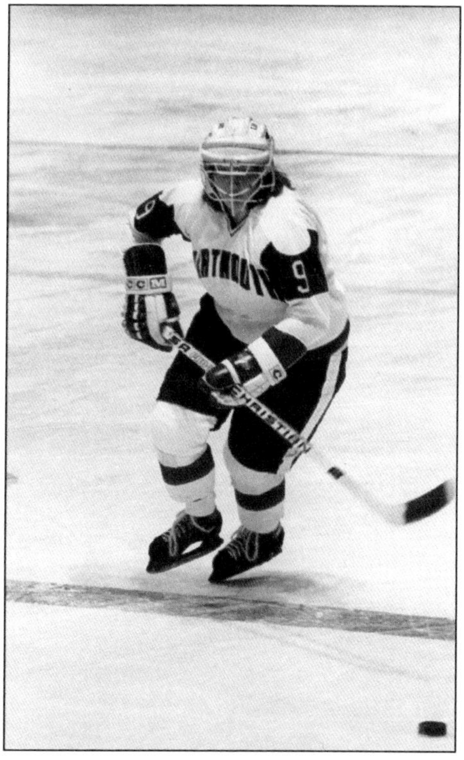

9 SANDERS '86. Her full name is Wendy 9 Sanders, but in the annals of Dartmouth hockey she's known as 9. "I don't know why my parents named me 9," she said. "I also have a brother named 7." Sanders followed her father, two uncles, and a grandfather to Dartmouth. Sanders was the Ivy League rookie of the year in 1983 and earned All-Ivy honors as a defenseman in 1985, her last season on the ice.

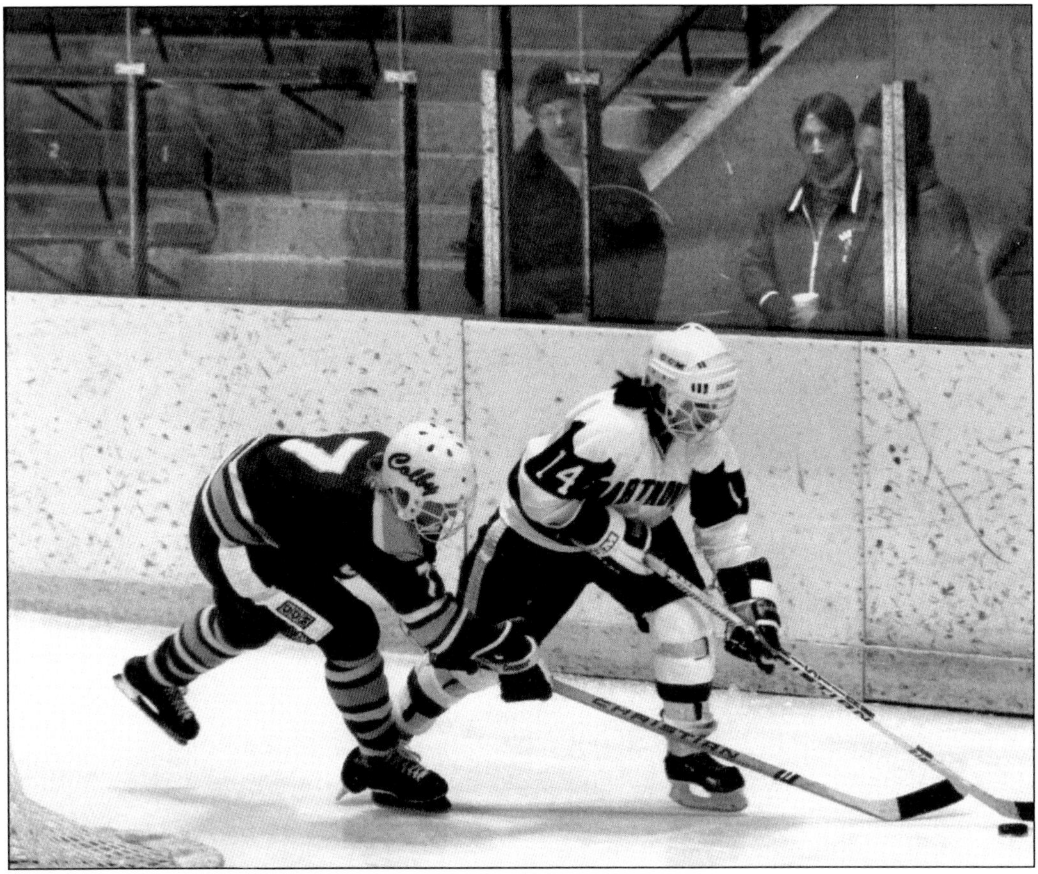

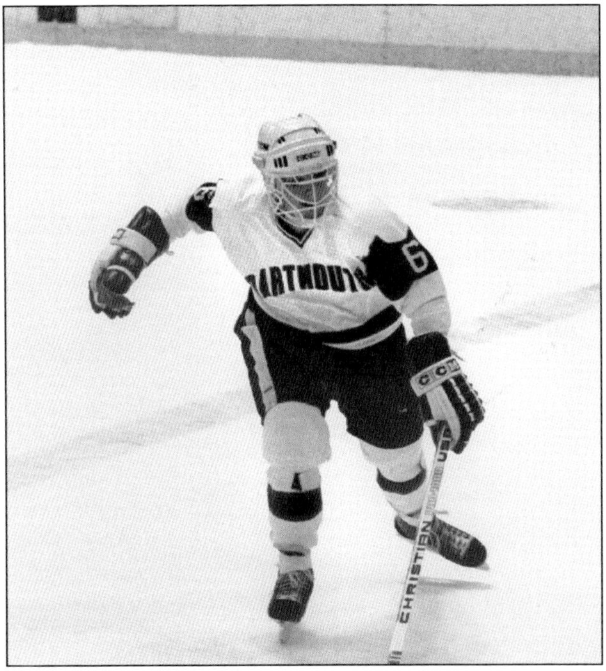

LINDA DUVA '87 AND KARIN CLOUGH '87. Duva (above), a wing, and Karin Clough (left), a center, were a one-two scoring punch behind Estey Ticknor for Dartmouth in the mid-1980s. Duva generated 105 points (56 goals) from 1983 to 1987. She was co-captain and an All-Ivy selection in 1986–87. Clough chose to sit out the 1986–87 season but returned to lead the Green in 1987–88 and finish with 104 career points (54 goals). Dartmouth had single-season coaches from 1984 to 1986 (Chuck Metz and Amy Crafts), a time of transition that preceded the 12-year tenure of George Crowe.

THREE

The Jeremiah Era 1937–1967

He was known, far and wide, on the ice and off, as Jerry. His greatest tools were his insight and his moral force. He produced teams that won a mythical national championship and that were perennial forces in American collegiate hockey. In an eight-year period that included the World War II years, his teams won seven times as many games as they lost. There is no record in Dartmouth sports that quite matches up.

Eddie Jeremiah was a Dartmouth man. He was a hockey man, too, and the genius of the man was how he married the two, taking Dartmouth men to arenas across the continent, leading them to Ivy League championships, guiding them to NCAA tournaments, contributing them to Olympic teams. One year, he placed Dartmouth men on two Olympic teams, a remarkable achievement made possible by a dispute over just who would represent the United States. No one, however, disagreed that Dartmouth men should.

His teams were prominent fixtures in Colorado Springs and Montreal. They filled the All-American ranks. His teams learned the lessons that filled his hockey books. (One of them, titled simply *Ice Hockey*, went into seven printings and still, nearly a half-century later, is the subject of brisk trade in secondhand bookstores and on the Internet.) His teams lived by the motto "Look up and keep fighting," but the enduring thing was how the first part of that credo ("look up") defined their outlook. Jeremiah's teams—and this extended to the Olympic sixes and even the amateur hockey teams he coached—were optimism on ice.

The record he established (308-246-10 in all regular and postseason play) is not the only reason he was inducted into the U.S. Hockey Hall of Fame. He grew up in Somerville, Massachusetts; Greater Boston was the hockey hotbed, in part because of his efforts. He won seven letters at Dartmouth, played professional hockey for five years and coached at Dartmouth during four decades, a period that spanned FDR's Second New Deal to LBJ's Great Society. He inspired several Dartmouth men to enter the coaching ranks, including Charlie Holt '45 and Jack Riley '44, who eventually joined him in the hall of fame (along with Riley's two brothers), Jeremiah protégés all. Over the years, he learned the harsh lessons of the world outside the white boards of the rink; two of his leading scorers, Bud Foster '39 and Bill Smoyer '67, perished in military missions. Jeremiah himself died only weeks after coaching his last game at Davis Rink.

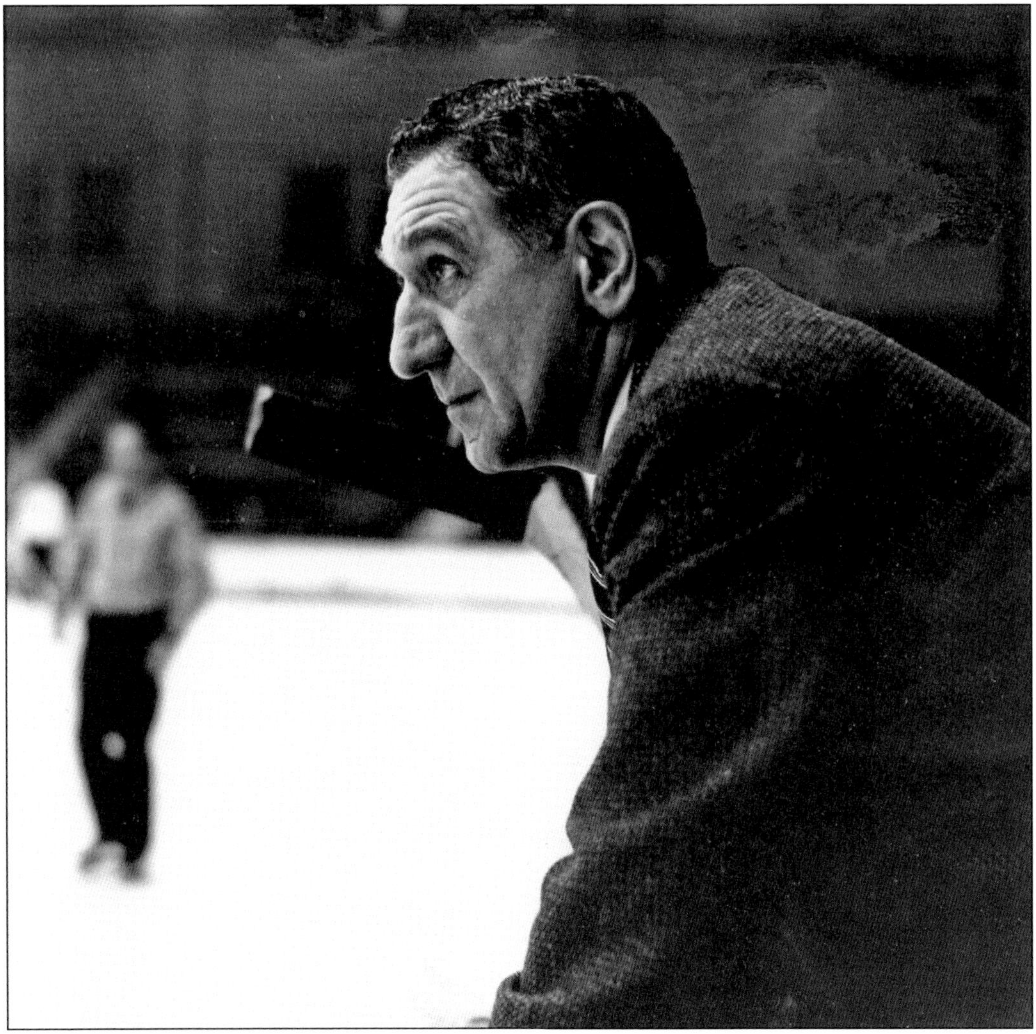

COACH EDDIE JEREMIAH '30. Under coach Herb Gill, Dartmouth had a 16-5-1 record in 1935–36, but a year later, the Green stumbled to a 12-13-0 record. The word on the streets of Hanover was "There's trouble in the hockey woodpile." Gill resigned in February 1937. Jeremiah, passed over in favor of Gill in 1934, was working at Boston Garden and coaching the Boston Olympics, the Garden's amateur team, to the 1936 National AAU championship. In 1937, he signed a one-year "trial" contract for $2,500 to coach at Dartmouth. That contract was torn up three times as Jerry led the rejuvenated Green to an 18-4 record and perfect (6-0) record in the Quadrangular League (formed by Harvard, Yale, Princeton, and Dartmouth in 1933). Defenseman Roger Conant '40, recalled, "I learned more tricks of the trade in one season under Jerry than all my other coaches put together." Jerry's coaching acumen benefited the football and baseball teams as well, but for the next three decades "Jeremiah" and "Dartmouth hockey" were synonymous.

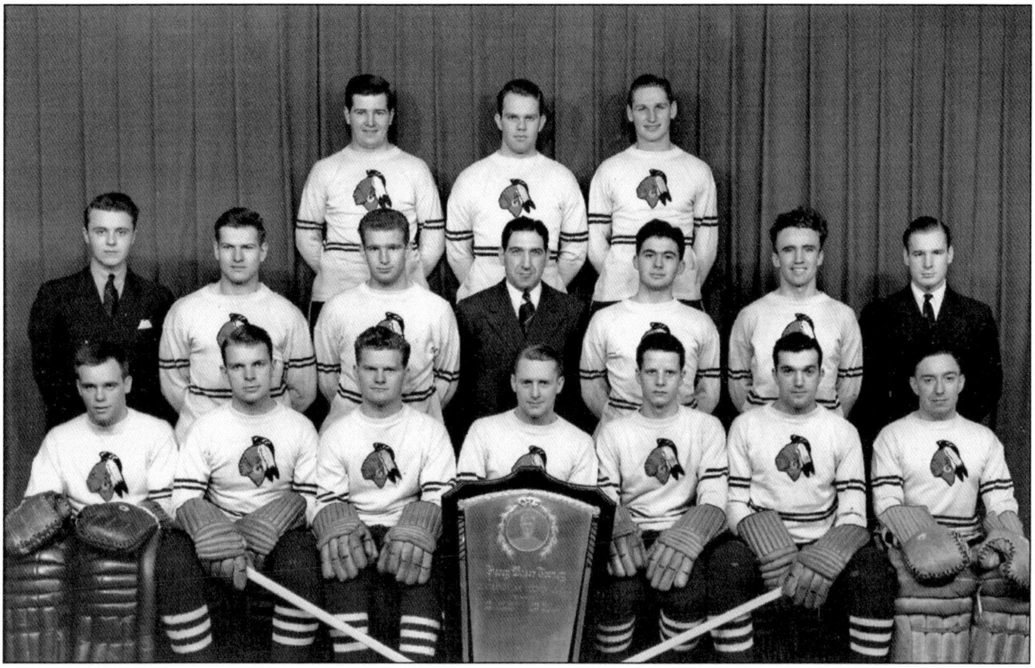

THE 1937–38 TEAM. Eddie Jeremiah's first team at Dartmouth set the stage for more than a decade of great hockey teams in Hanover. Led by captain Dick Lewis '38, balanced scoring, defense, and goaltending produced an 18-4 record that would be followed by a 17-4 record in 1938–39. In both seasons, the Green was perfect (6-0) in the Quadrangular League and launched a run of near perfection against archrival Harvard (18-0-2) that continued until 1950.

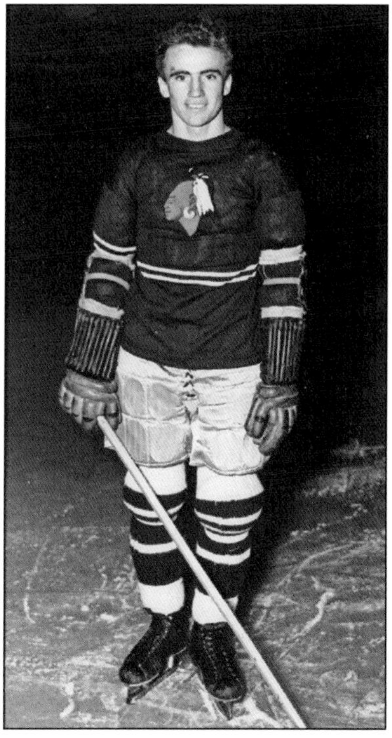

DAVID "HARPO" WALSH '39. From 1936 to 1939, left wing Harpo Walsh was one of the Green's top five scorers with Jack Costello '37, Forest Mather '38, Bud Foster '39, and Dan Sullivan '40—a group that produced 204 goals. Walsh collected 107 points (59 goals). Walsh was one of seven players in the class of 1939 who were nicknamed the "Seven Grand Old Men."

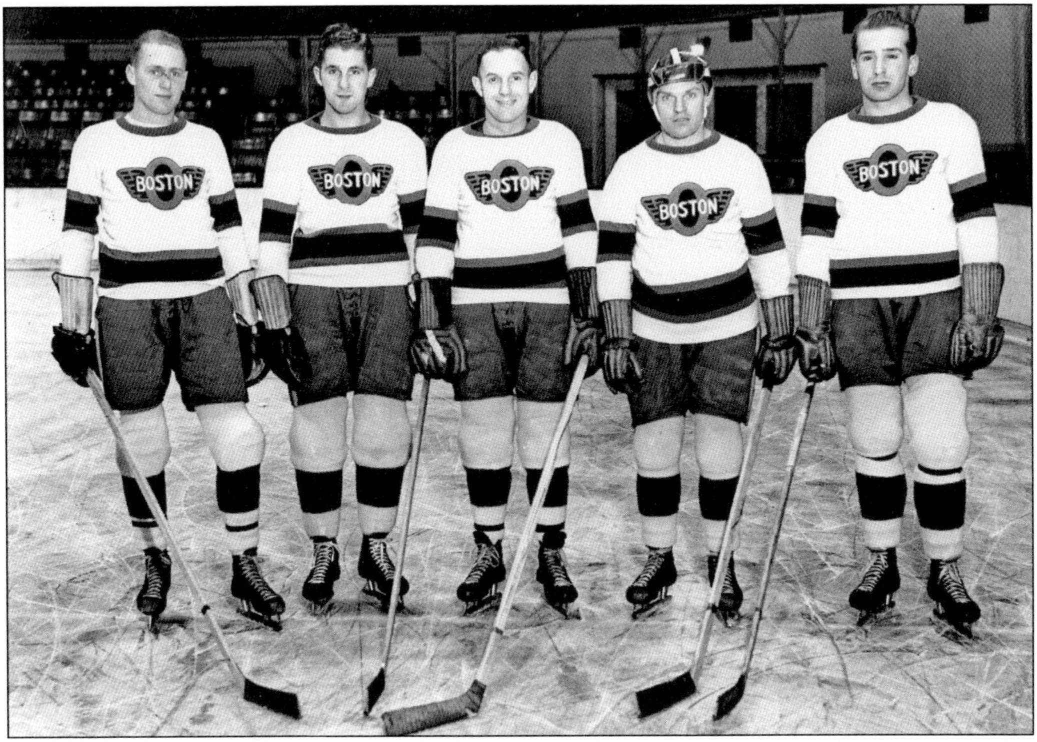

"GREENING" OF THE BOSTON OLYMPICS. The Olympics were based out of the Boston Garden and were perennial powers in national amateur hockey circles prior to World War II. In 1938–39, the team had a distinct tinge of Dartmouth green in the lineup. From left to right are Dick Lewis '38, the 1937–38 captain; Paul Guibord '36, Dartmouth's two-time captain from 1934 to 1936; Frank Spain '34, the 1933–34 captain and U.S. Olympic team member in 1936; Walter "Junie" Allen '36, the two-year center on Guibord's line at Dartmouth from 1934 to 1936; and Jack Costello '37, who scored 41 goals as a wing from 1935 to 1937.

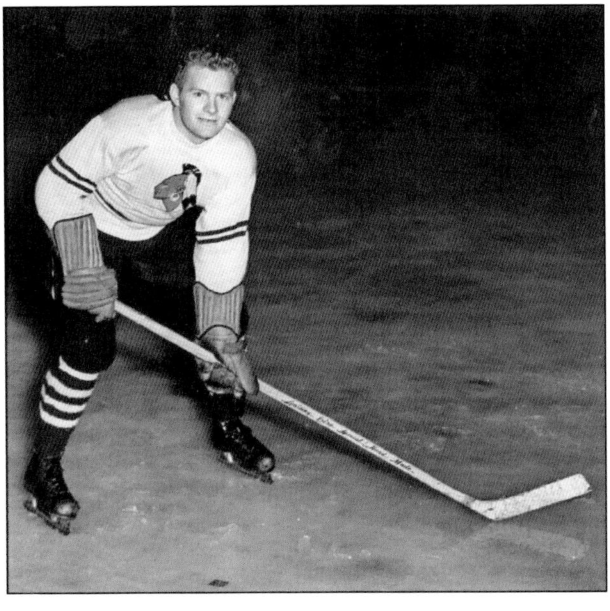

ALBERT "BUD" FOSTER '39. Center Bud Foster was Dartmouth's scoring leader as a sophomore in 1936–37 and again as a senior. Over three seasons, he netted 52 goals and 119 points overall (10th all-time at Dartmouth). Foster won the Distinguished Flying Cross as a navy fighter pilot in the Pacific during World War II. He returned to the navy in 1948 and died in 1949 when his Corsair fighter became lost in rain and fog, ran out of fuel, and crashed into the Atlantic Ocean.

"A BUNDLE OF DYNAMITE." Wes Goding '39 was the All-American goalie in 1939 and was a candidate for the U.S. Olympic hockey team in 1940 (the games were cancelled due to World War II). Goding, later a lawyer and insurance executive, was the mainstay in the Dartmouth nets for three seasons. The "little bundle of dynamite" had a 3.41 goals-against average in 58 games.

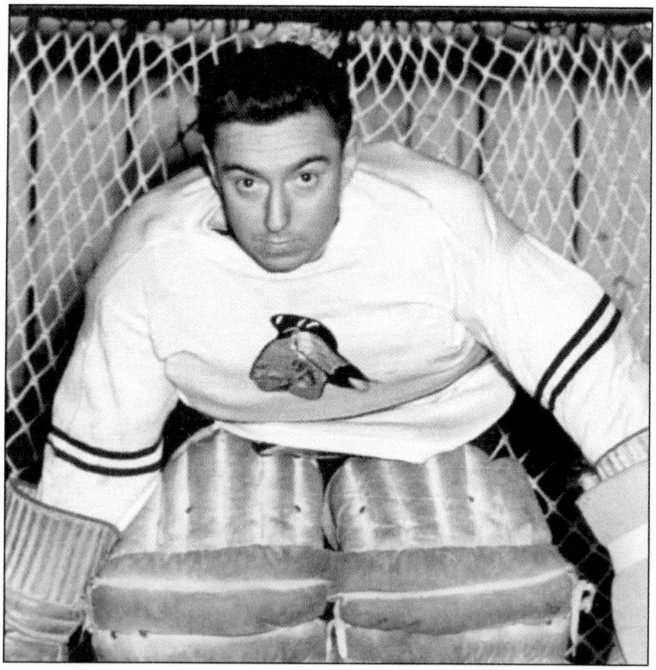

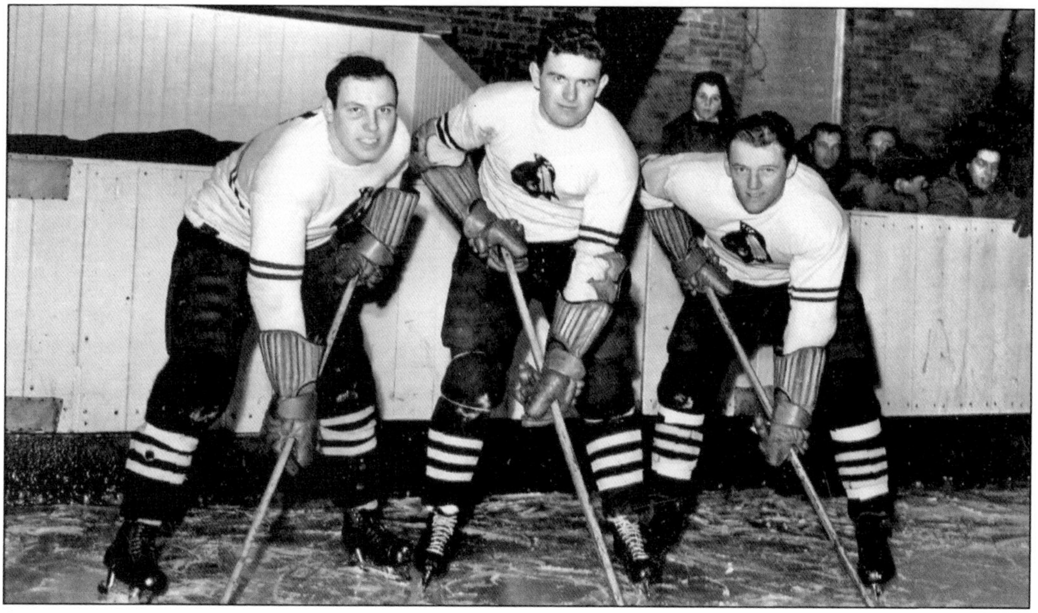

SPECTACULAR SOPHOMORES, 1941–42. They were only sophomores, but their firepower was incessant; they combined for 101 of Dartmouth's 148 goals during the great 1941–42 season (see page 40). From left to right are right wing Bill Harrison '44, center Dick Rondeau '44, and left wing Jack Riley '44. Rondeau had 45 goals, while Harrison added 38 and Riley another 18 (he missed eight games with a broken finger). This was the only season they played together. In 1942–43, Jack Riley was serving in World War II. His brother, Bill '46, took his place as a freshman and launched his career as Dartmouth's all-time scoring leader. Harrison went on to build a coaching record of 128-47-6 at Clarkson from 1948 to 1958, where he was also honored as a professor of civil engineering.

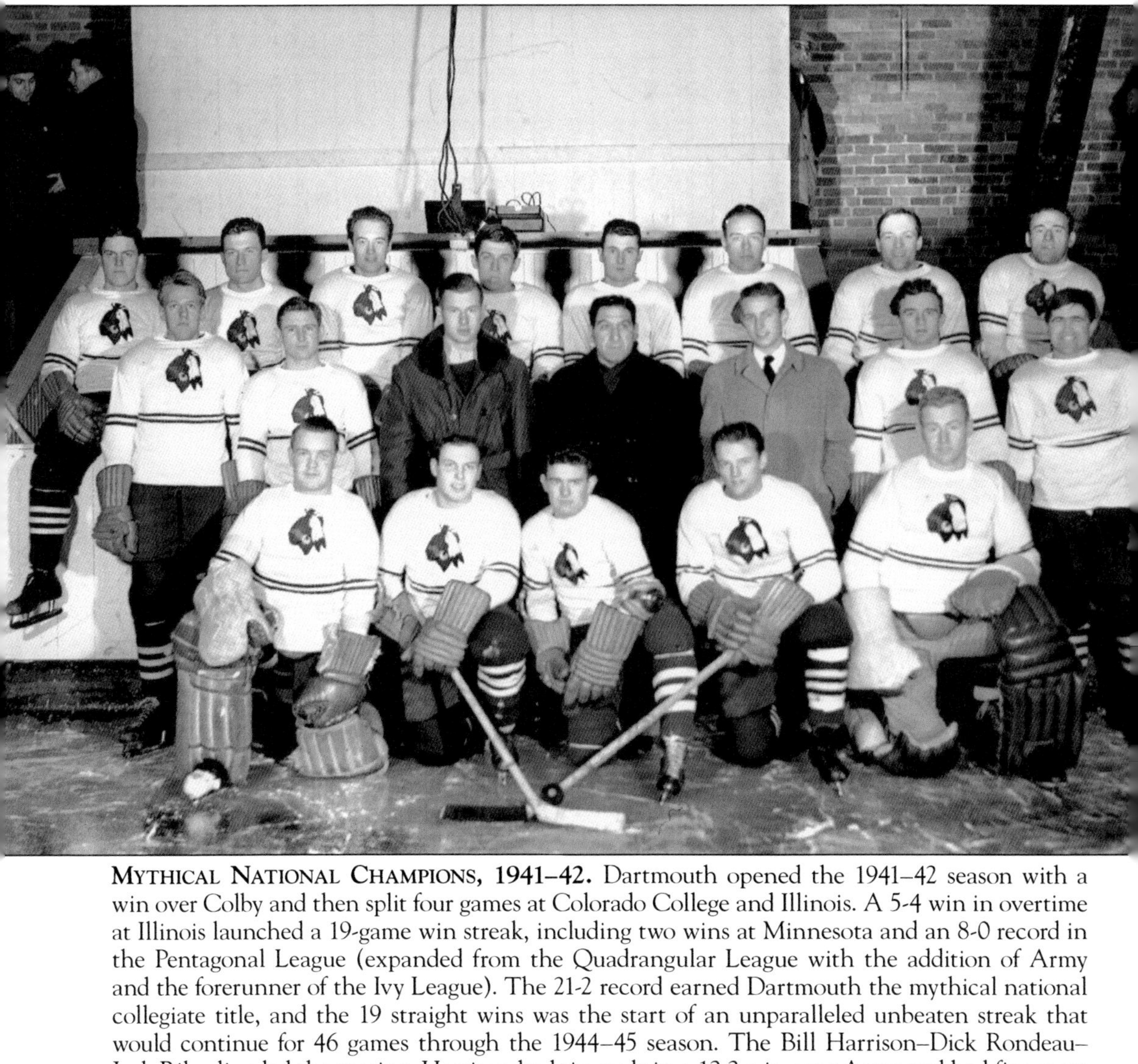

MYTHICAL NATIONAL CHAMPIONS, 1941–42. Dartmouth opened the 1941–42 season with a win over Colby and then split four games at Colorado College and Illinois. A 5-4 win in overtime at Illinois launched a 19-game win streak, including two wins at Minnesota and an 8-0 record in the Pentagonal League (expanded from the Quadrangular League with the addition of Army and the forerunner of the Ivy League). The 21-2 record earned Dartmouth the mythical national collegiate title, and the 19 straight wins was the start of an unparalleled unbeaten streak that would continue for 46 games through the 1944–45 season. The Bill Harrison–Dick Rondeau–Jack Riley line led the scoring. Harrison had six goals in a 12-2 win over Army and had five more in a 14-5 romp over Clarkson. Rondeau had a five-goal outing against Yale. Ted Lapres '42 capped three outstanding seasons in the Dartmouth nets with a 2.76 goals-against average. This team was the launch point for the most memorable decade in the history of hockey at Dartmouth.

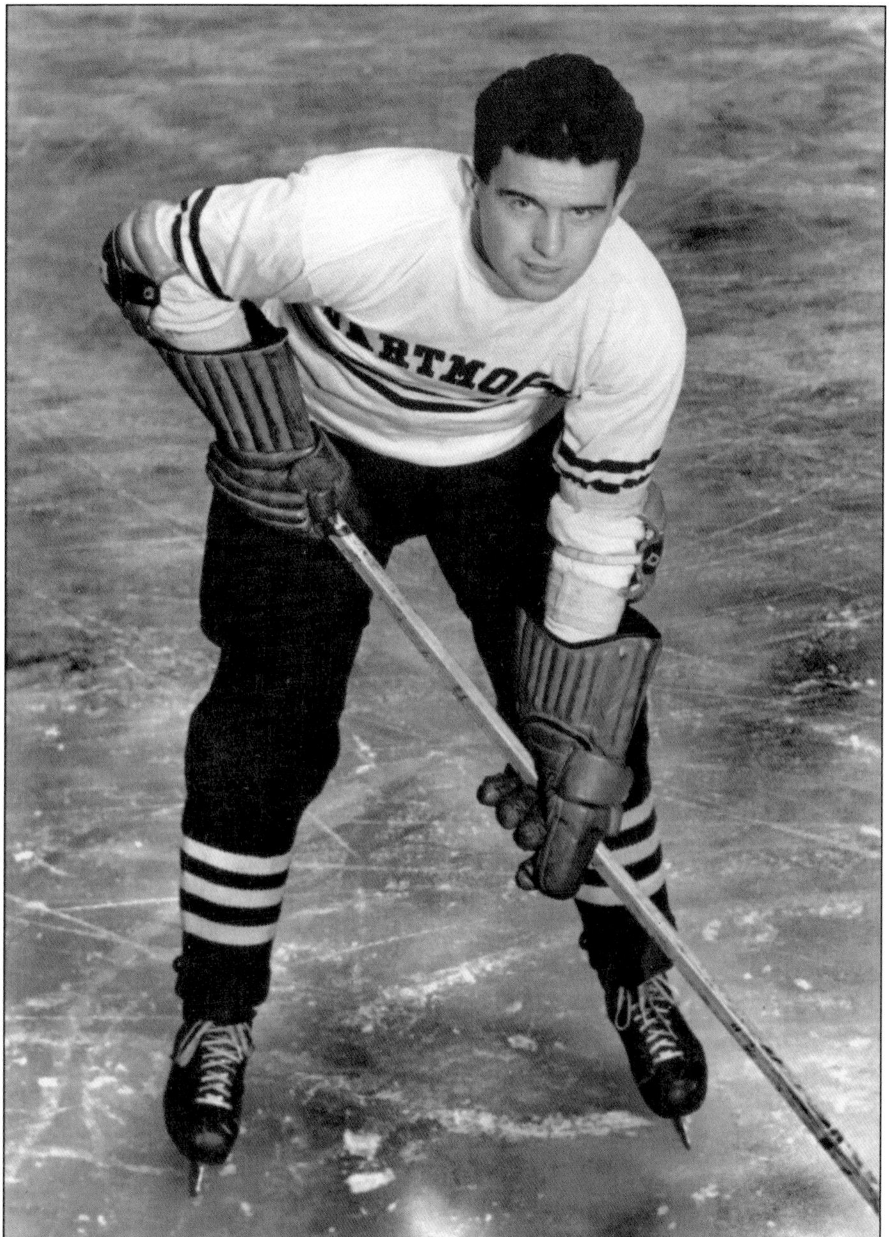

Dick Rondeau '44. It is unlikely the last game of Dick Rondeau's hockey career at Dartmouth will ever be matched. On February 8, 1944, Dartmouth bombarded Middlebury 30-0 at Davis Rink. Rondeau, a center, closed his career by scoring 12 goals and adding 11 assists (his linemates, right wing John Cunniff USMC and freshman Bruce Mather '47, had eight and four goals, respectively). Rondeau ranks second all-time in scoring at Dartmouth with 176 points (103 goals, 73 assists) in only 40 games. In 1942, Eddie Jeremiah departed for service in the navy. Rondeau was captain and co-coach with George Barclay of the 1942–43 team that was 14-0-1 (the tie was with Harvard 4-4). He was also captain of the 1943–44 team (7-0-0) as Dartmouth's unbeaten streak grew to 40 games. He later coached at Holy Cross and Providence College. In 1985, he was elected to the U.S. Hockey Hall of Fame.

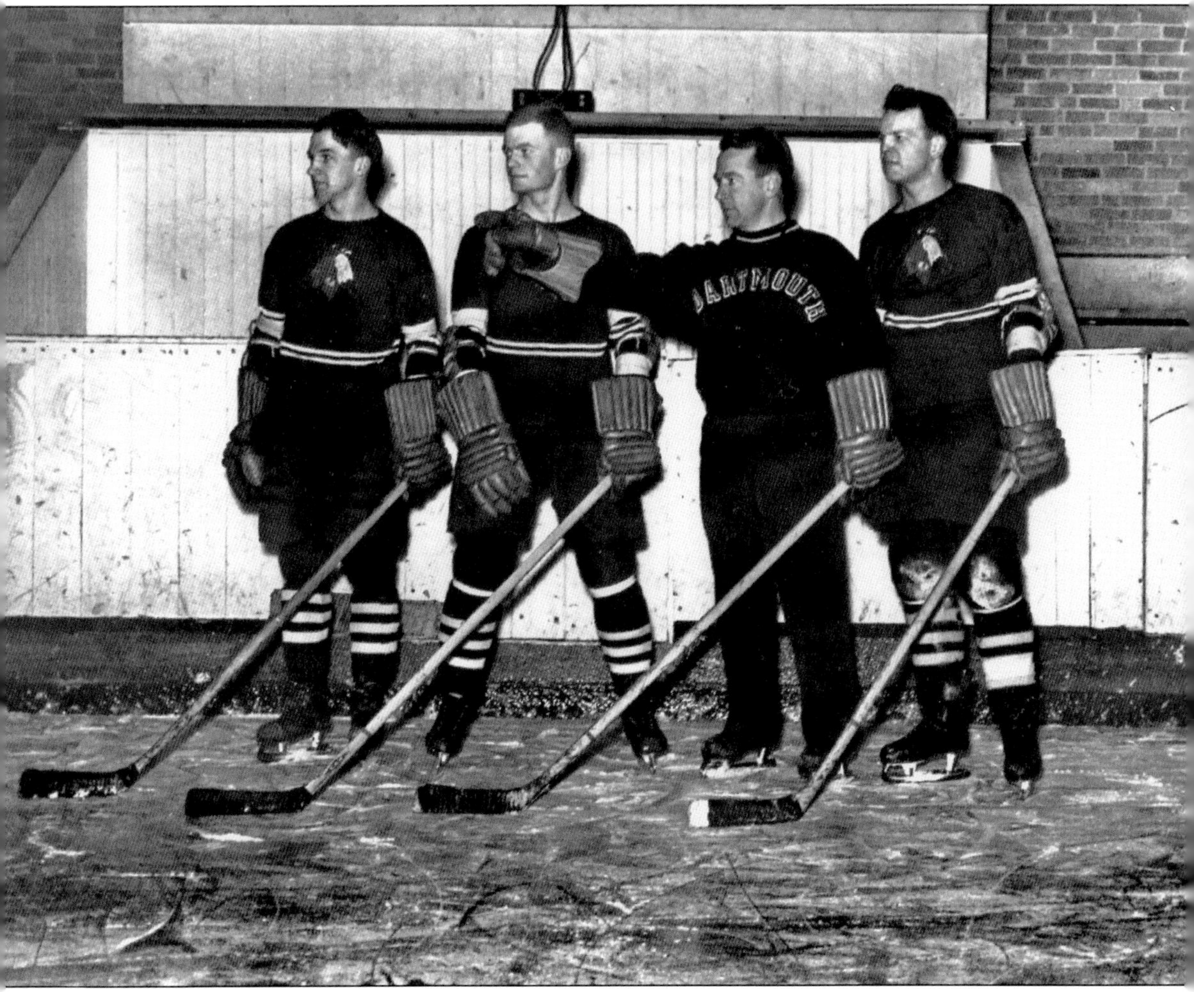

CHARLES "HAFEY" ARTHUR '34. In many respects, Hafey Arthur was instrumental in the great success that coach Eddie Jeremiah's teams enjoyed through the early 1950s. Arthur prepped for Dartmouth at Hebron Academy (the school had one of the few indoor prep school rinks), and played for the Green from 1931 to 1934. He was an innovative hockey coach at Hebron from 1935 to 1941, and many of his Hebron players later played at Dartmouth. During the 1943–44 and 1944–45 seasons, he was Dartmouth's coach, and he remained as a physical education instructor for another decade. His two Dartmouth teams won 12 games without a loss, bringing the Green's unbeaten streak to 45-0-1 (Yale ended the streak with a 6-4 win in New Haven in the first game of the 1945–46 season). With Arthur, second from right in this photograph, are the first line of the 1944–45 team that was built from scratch during the last year of World War II. From left to right are Ralph Warburton (U.S. Navy), Bruce Cunliffe (U.S. Marine Corps), Arthur, and Charlie Holt '45 (U.S. Army). Holt was captain of the 1945–46 team, while Warburton and Cunliffe remained after the war to play for two seasons, graduating in 1947.

GEORGE PULLIAM '45. A 190-pound defenseman in hockey, George Pulliam was also an outstanding football player (he kicked a 32-yard field goal as Dartmouth beat Holy Cross 3-0 in 1946). An honored athlete at Cranston (Rhode Island) High, he earned the nickname "the Cranston Crusher" for his superb play in 1947 as Dartmouth, despite a 2-2 tie with the University of Toronto, was awarded the Thompson Trophy as the North American intercollegiate champion.

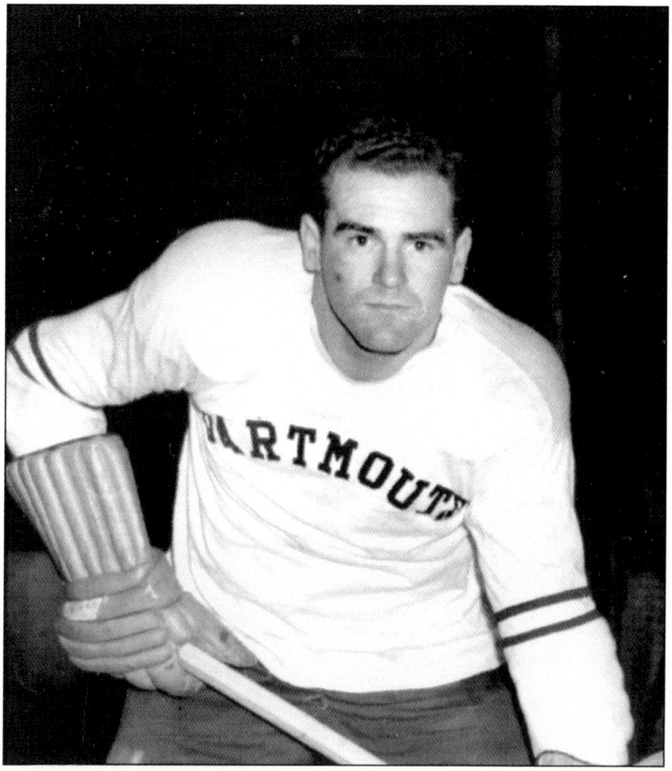

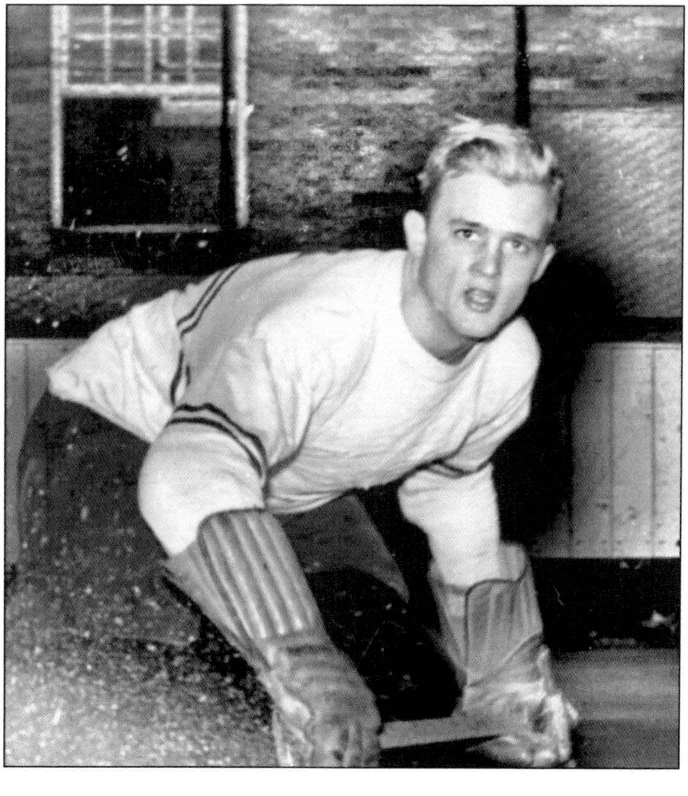

CRAWFORD "WHITEY" CAMPBELL '46. After serving with the Army Air Corps in the Burma-China theater during World War II, Whitey Campbell returned to play three seasons for Dartmouth. A wing who shifted to defense during the 1946–47 and 1947–48 seasons (paired with Mike Thayer '46), Campbell was a member of the AAU team that was fated to watch, not play, in the 1948 Winter Olympics (see page 46).

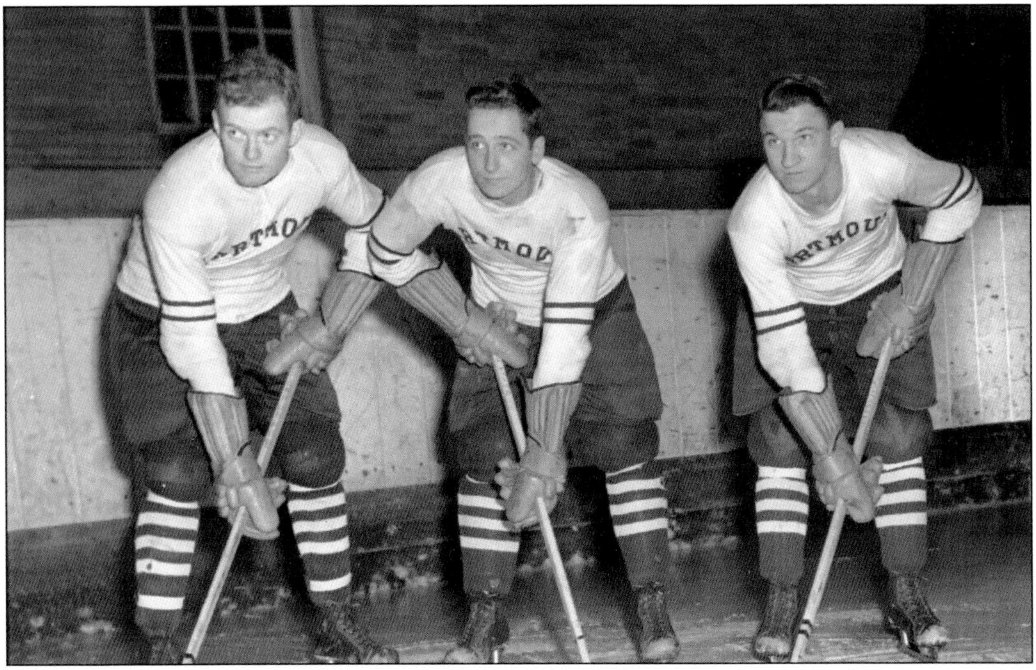

FIRST LINE IN 1945–46. With World War II over, Eddie Jeremiah returned as Dartmouth's coach. His top line that season (and again in 1946–47) would later compete as a line for the United States in the 1948 Winter Olympics. From left to right are Bruce "Knobby" Cunliffe '47, Bruce Mather '47, and Ralph Warburton '47. Cunliffe had a career total of 96 points (52 goals). Mather, a center, played in 1943–44 and one game in 1944–45. He was then Dartmouth's leading scorer in 1945–46 and 1946–47, helping the Green build a combined record of 22-3-2 in those seasons. He is a member of the U.S. Hockey Hall of Fame. Warburton later said, "What a treat to be on the ice with my two Bruce linemates." With Jack Riley '44, Warburton was co-captain of the 1946–47 team that finished 16-1-2.

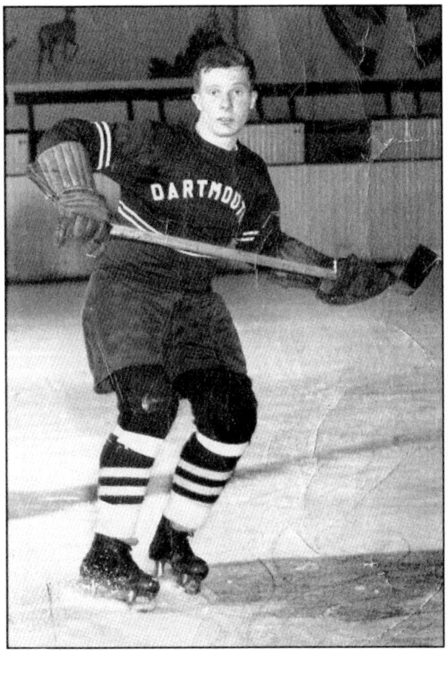

BOB MERRIAM '48. A steady wing on outstanding teams from 1946 to 1948, Bob Merriam declined an invitation to the 1948 Olympic Games. Merriam was also a standout player and captain in soccer and lacrosse. His brother, Lou (better known as Junie), was a member of the class of 1939's "Grand Old Men" contingent that compiled a record of 35-8 from 1937 to 1939.

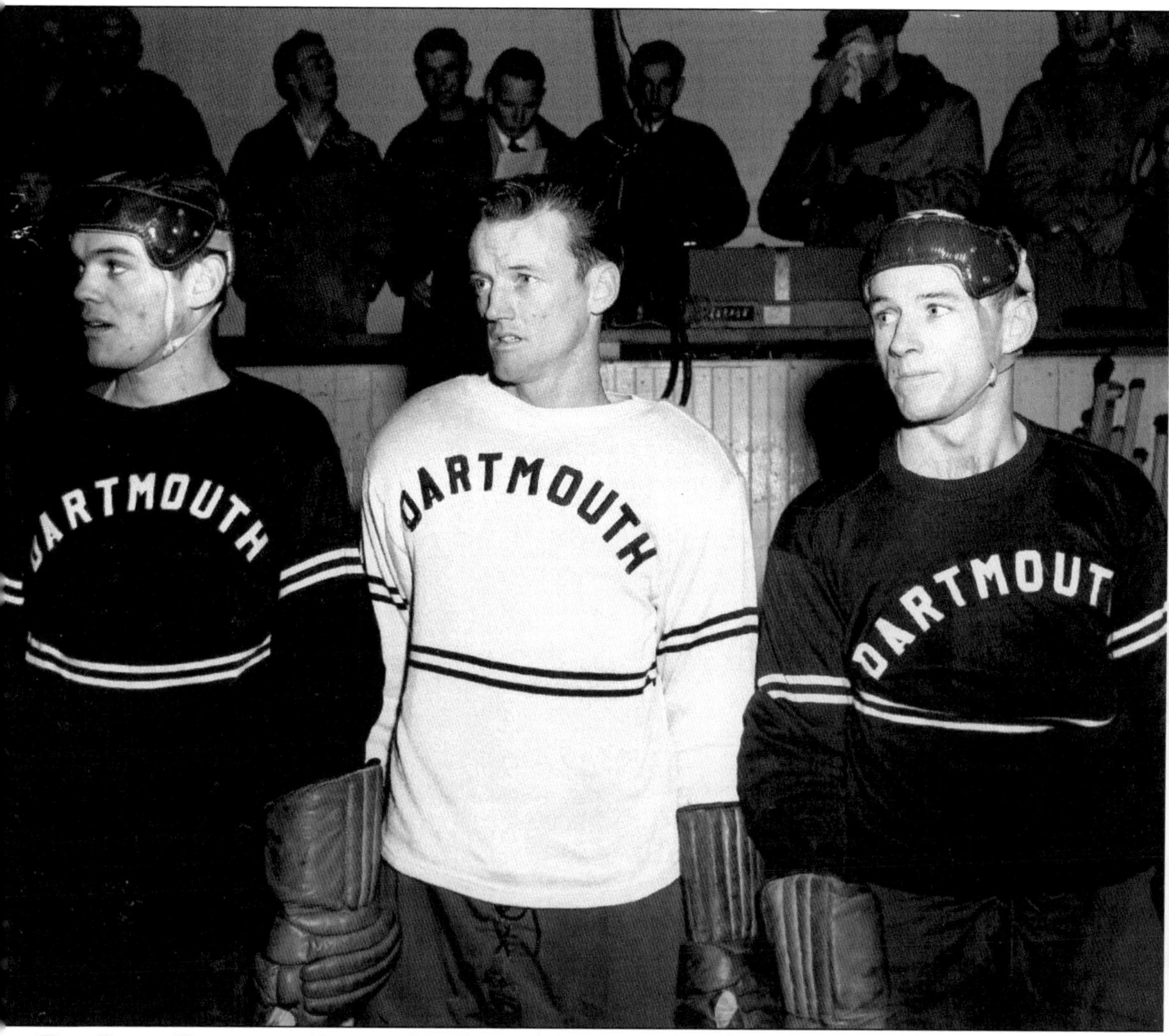

THE RILEY BROTHERS. During the 1940s, the Riley brothers (from left to right), Joe '49, Jack '44, and Bill '46, became legends in Dartmouth hockey annals. They all are enshrined in the U.S. Hockey Hall of Fame. One of the rare instances when they were together on the ice in Dartmouth uniforms was for this photograph, taken at the varsity-alumni game in 1948. They came to Dartmouth from Medford, Massachusetts. Jack was a standout on the 1941–42 team that was mythical national champion and played with Bill during the 1946–47 season. Bill and Joe played together on the 1947–48 and 1948–49 teams that reached the finals of the first NCAA tournaments (Joe was voted the most valuable player in the 1948 tourney). Bill played in 71 games over four seasons and ranks as Dartmouth's all-time scoring leader with 228 points—his 118 goals and 110 assists are also career records. Joe shares the record for goals in a season (45) with Dick Rondeau '44. During five seasons in the 1940s when there was at least one Riley on the ice, Dartmouth had a record of 90-14-3.

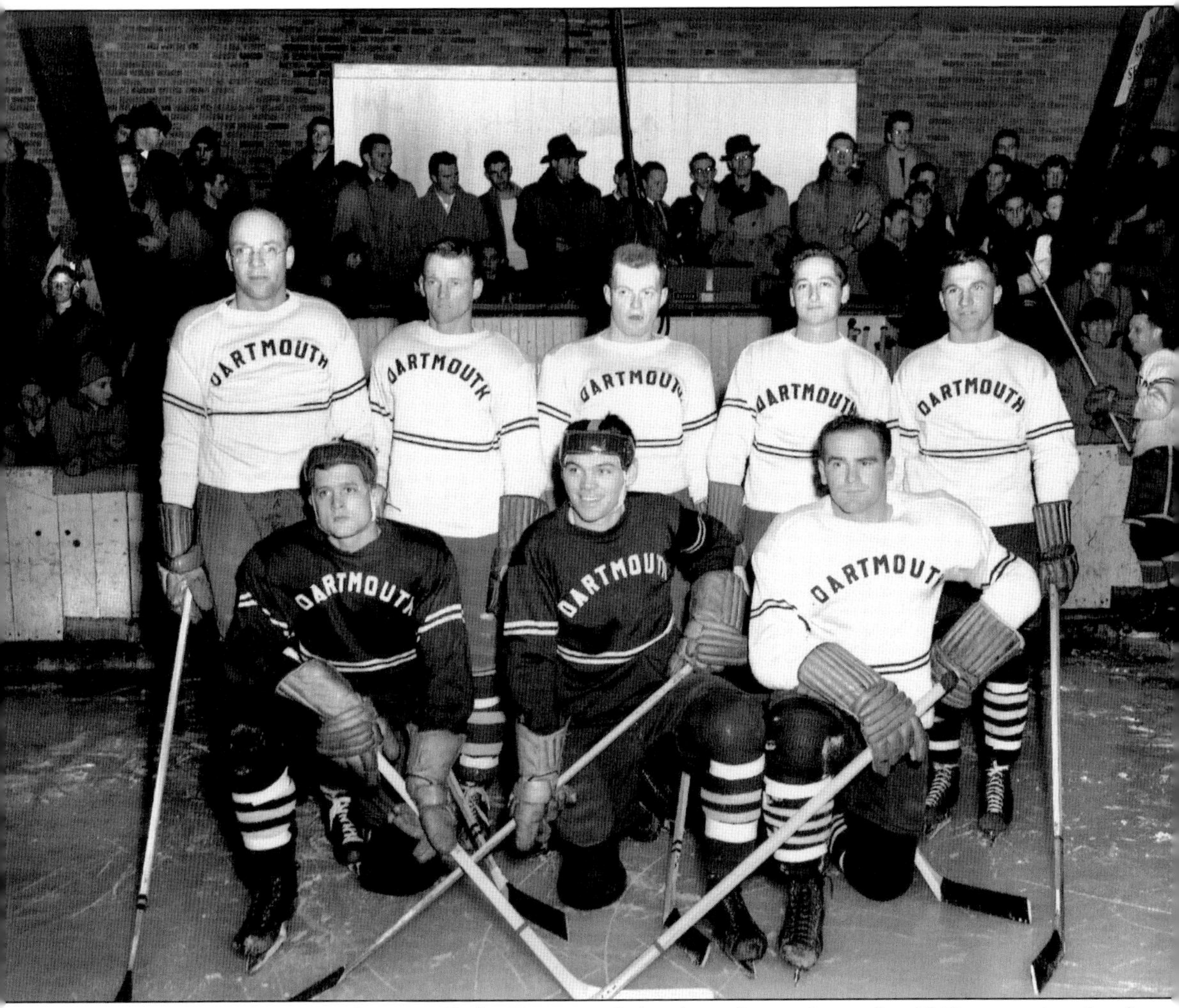

THE 1948 OLYMPIC GAMES. Eight Dartmouth hockey players from the 1940s were involved in an extraordinary episode in hockey history. They are, from left to right, as follows: (front row) Whitey Campbell '46, Joe Riley '49, and George Pulliam '45; (back row) Stan Priddy '43, Jack Riley '44, Bruce Cunliffe '47, Bruce Mather '47, and Ralph Warburton '47. Bill Riley '49 and Bob Merriam '48 were invited by the AAU but declined. Two organizations, the Amateur Hockey Association (AHA) and the Amateur Athletic Union (AAU), selected teams to represent the United States in the 1948 Winter Games at St. Moritz, Switzerland. Both teams went to Switzerland as the AAU and AHA dueled with the Olympic leadership to determine which team would play. On the eve of the games, it was announced that the AHA team (including Priddy, Mather, Cunliffe, Warburton, and Jack Riley) would play. The AAU team (including Campbell, Pulliam, and Joe Riley) was left to watch as the AHA team won five of nine games in the round-robin and finished fourth. This photograph was taken prior to the first Alumni-Varsity game on March 12, 1948. The Alumni, a veritable who's who of Dartmouth hockey, won 8-4. The benefit game for the Mary Hitchcock Memorial Hospital Building Fund was a warm-up for the first NCAA tournament a week later.

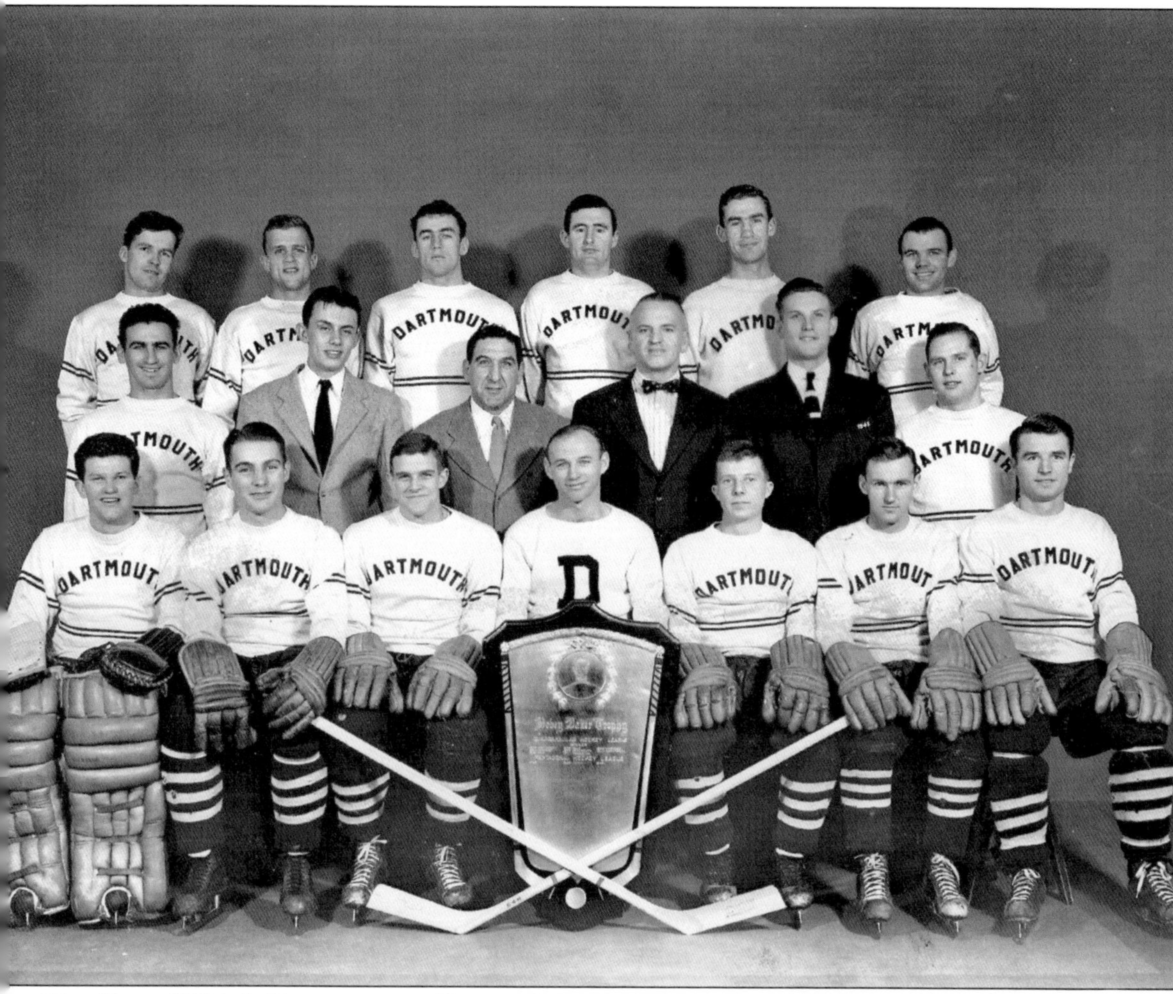

THE FIRST NCAA TOURNAMENT TEAM, 1947–48. Surrounding the 1948 Winter Olympics, the 1947–48 season was one of Dartmouth's best ever. With Bill and Joe Riley combining for 52 goals (Bill had 30), Dartmouth built a 21-3-0 record. The Green's only regular season loss was at Boston College 4-3. After an exhibition loss to the Alumni, the University of Toronto regained the Thompson Trophy 5-0 at Montreal. Dartmouth then flew to the NCAA tournament in Colorado and beat Colorado College 8-4 in the semifinals. Michigan beat Boston College in the other semifinal game. The Michigan-Dartmouth championship game was colored with controversy. Dartmouth led 4-3 late in the second period when Michigan scored. But the goal was disallowed. During the intermission, Michigan's goal was reconsidered and allowed. Coach Jeremiah called it "the most unusual exhibition of officiating I've ever seen." Michigan scored four unanswered goals in the third period to beat the deflated Green 8-4.

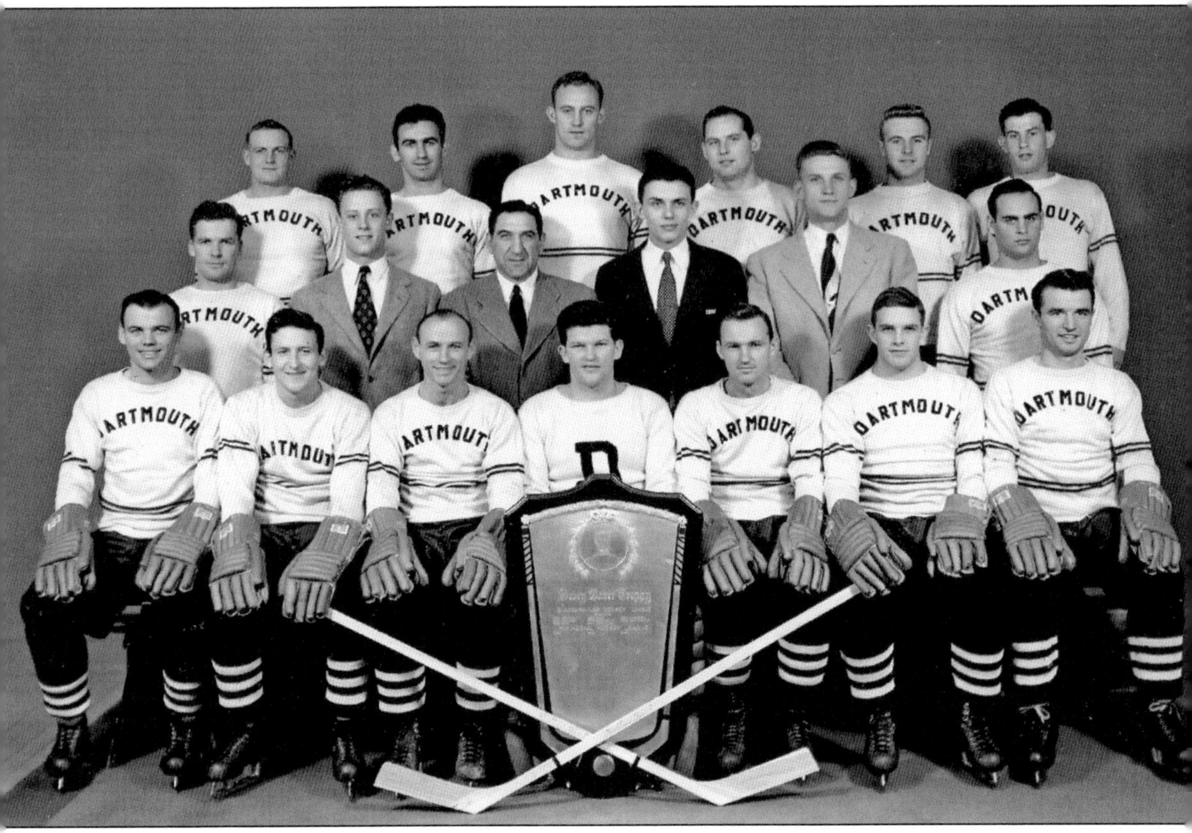

THE SECOND NCAA TOURNAMENT TEAM, 1948–49. The Riley era ended with the 1948–49 season but not before Bill and Joe joined Cliff Harrison '51 (brother of Bill '44) and four-year goalie Dick Desmond '49, the captain, to produce an 18-6-0 record and another trip to the NCAA tournament. One writer opined, "The Rileys are to Dartmouth hockey what eggs are to bacon." The Riley-Riley-Harrison line combined for 98 goals, including Joe Riley's 45. Desmond, a member of the U.S. Hockey Hall of Fame, had a pair of shutouts, over Clarkson (coached by Bill Harrison) and Yale. In the NCAA tournament at Colorado Springs, Colorado, Desmond earned most valuable player honors as Dartmouth avenged its loss to Michigan in the 1948 title game with a semifinal win 4-2 but lost the championship to Boston College 4-3 (the teams had split regular season decisions).

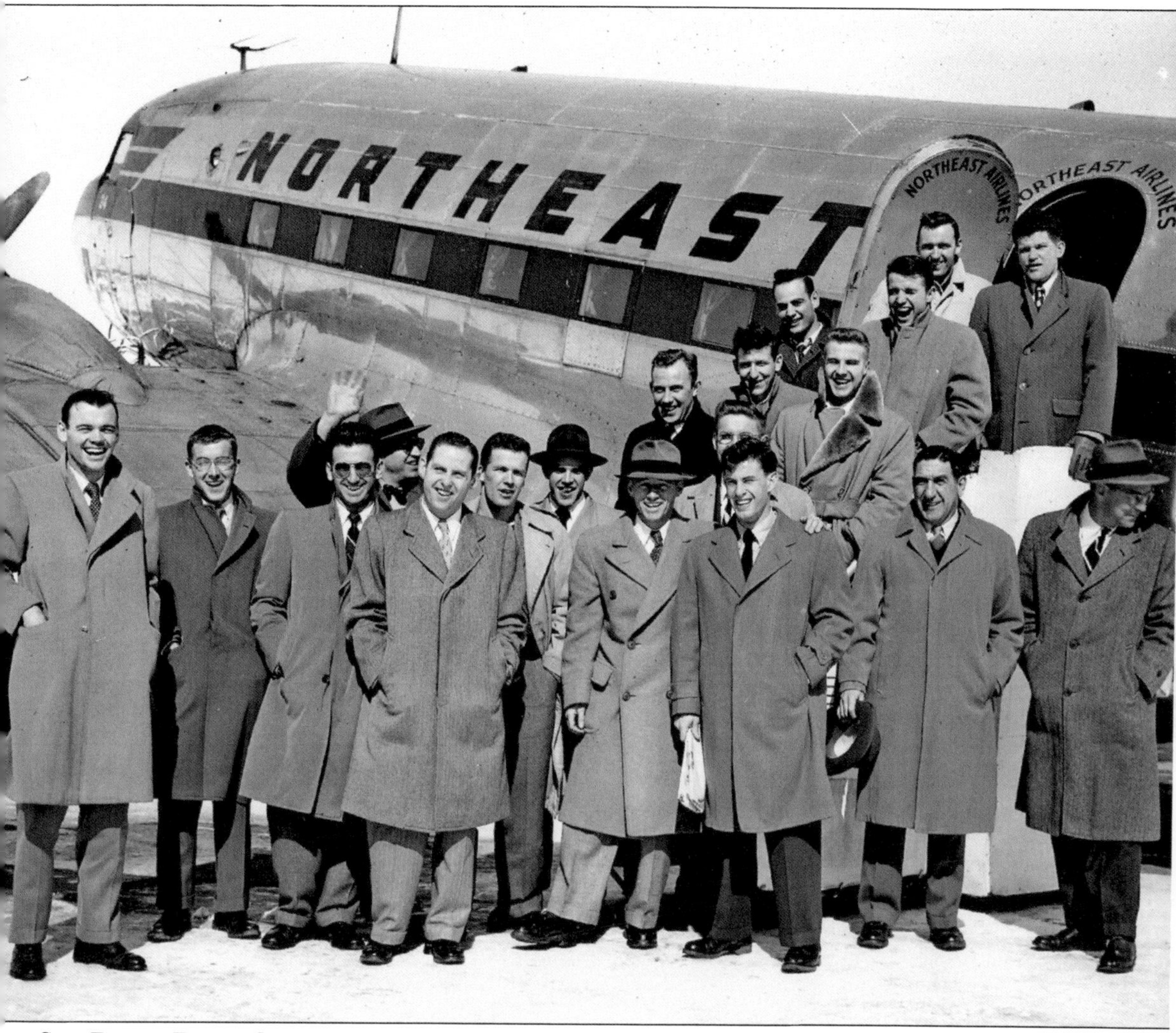

SIX DAYS, FOUR GAMES, 6,000 MILES. During a remarkable era from 1941 to 1949, Dartmouth won 108 games, lost 16, and tied 3. There was nothing, however, that quite compared with the exceptional journey that concluded the 1948–49 season. After beating the Alumni 11-8 in an exhibition at Hanover on March 12, the team beat Harvard 7-2 in a Pentagonal League playoff at Boston on March 14. A day later, at Montreal, Dartmouth lost the Thompson Trophy game to the University of Montreal 4-3. The team is shown as it boards the flight from Montreal to Colorado for the NCAA tournament (the Boston College and Michigan teams became traveling companions). By the time they returned to campus after the NCAA title game with Boston College on March 19, publicist Roger Wolbarst reported that the team had traveled nearly 6,000 miles to play four games in six days.

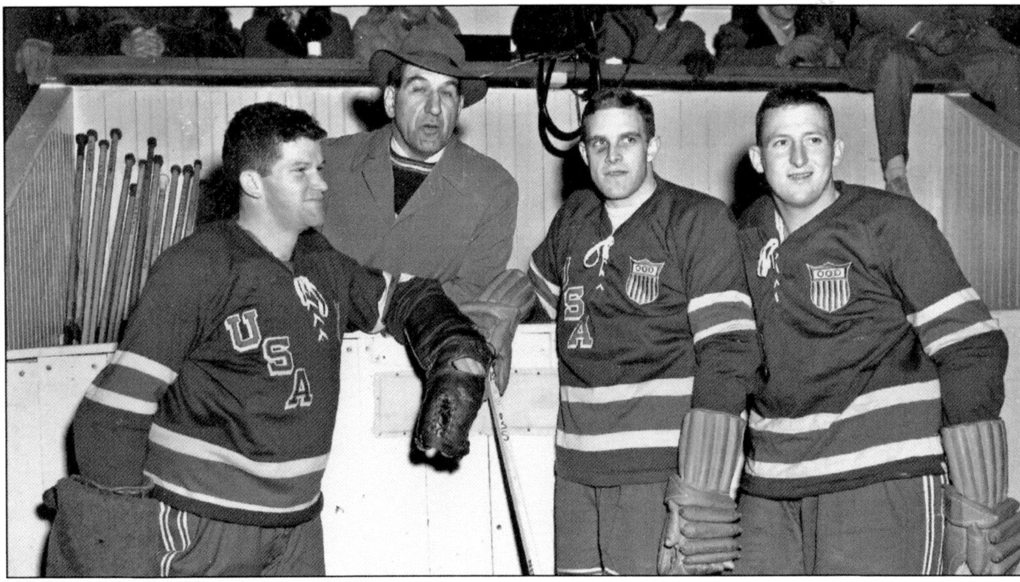

OLYMPIANS, 1952. Just as in 1948, though without the controversy of two U.S. teams, Dartmouth was well represented on the U.S. Olympic hockey team that won the silver medal at Oslo, Norway, in 1952. With coach Eddie Jeremiah are, from left to right, goalie Dick Desmond '49, center-wing Arnie Oss '50, and center Cliff Harrison. Desmond was captain of the 1948–49 Dartmouth team and most valuable player in the 1949 NCAA tournament and had a career goals-against average of 2.98 during four seasons in the nets. Oss had 98 career points over three seasons, including a team-leading 55 points (36 goals) as a senior in 1949–50, the same year his father, Arnie Sr., was voted the outstanding athlete of the half-century in Minnesota (he was a three-sport star at the University of Minnesota in the 1920s). Harrison ranks fourth all-time among Dartmouth scoring leaders. He was captain of the 1950–51 team and finished with 138 points (54 goals, 84 assists) from 1948 to 1951.

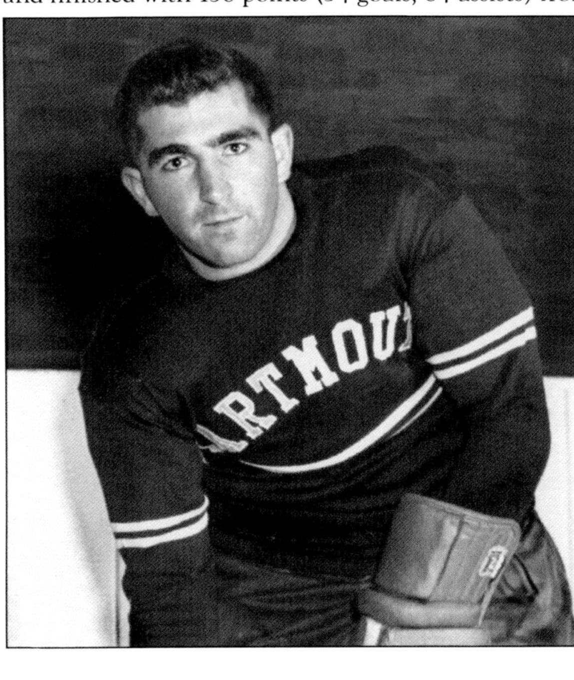

JOHN GROCOTT '52. An outstanding defenseman from 1949 to 1952, John Grocott came from Melrose, Massachusetts, and was captain of the 1951–52 team. His consistent play earned him a place on the All-American team in 1952.

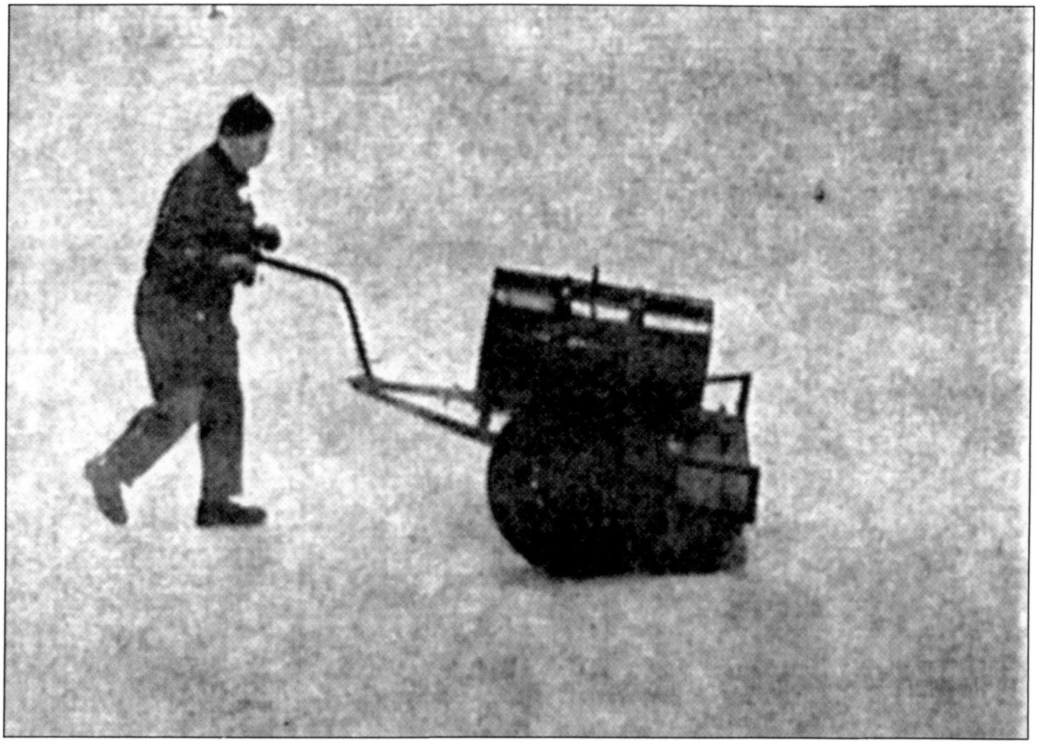

NICK PELTON. Nick Pelton probably would have won 12 letters in football, basketball, and baseball by the time he graduated from Hanover High School in 1932. He won 11—because Hanover High did not have a football team until his sophomore year. A lifelong Hanover resident, Pelton returned from wartime service in the navy and, in 1949, joined the Dartmouth athletic grounds crew. He was a fixture on the hockey scene, resurfacing the ice in Davis Rink (above) with a 200-pound rig featuring a 55-gallon drum of hot water. When artificial ice came to Davis Rink in 1954, he became the first Zamboni driver to don a top hat and tuxedo for the annual Winter Carnival game. Pelton, the quiet giant with an easy smile, served Dartmouth's team for most of three decades until he retired in the late 1970s.

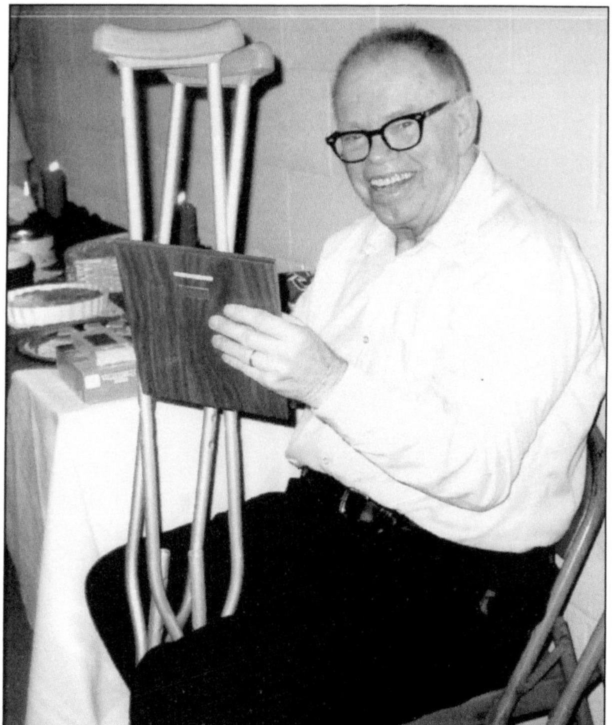

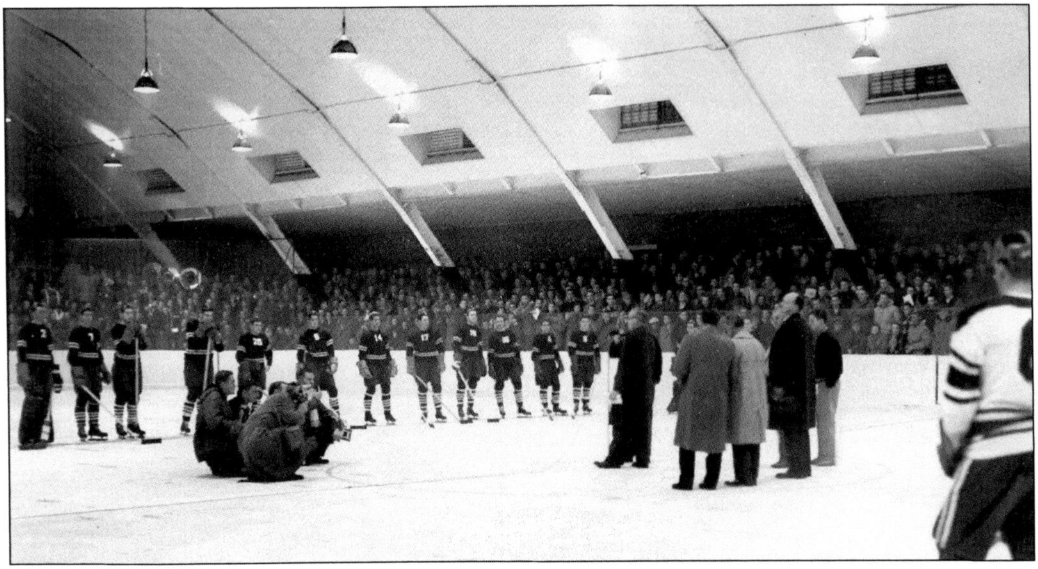

ARTIFICIAL ICE COMES TO DAVIS RINK. Twenty-four seasons after Davis Rink opened, an artificial ice system was installed. A bronze tablet near the rink entrance bore an inscription in Latin: *Melior machina quam natura* (The machine is better than nature). On December 4, 1953, after the speeches (above), Dartmouth president John Sloan Dickey dropped the ceremonial puck between the opposing captains—Dartmouth's Seaver Peters '54 (right) and Norm Wood of Harvard. Dartmouth celebrated with a 5-1 victory over the Crimson. In 1953–54, Dartmouth played 30 games (including exhibitions with the Alumni and the Boston Bruins), a first. In 1967, Peters began a 16-year tenure as Dartmouth's director of athletics.

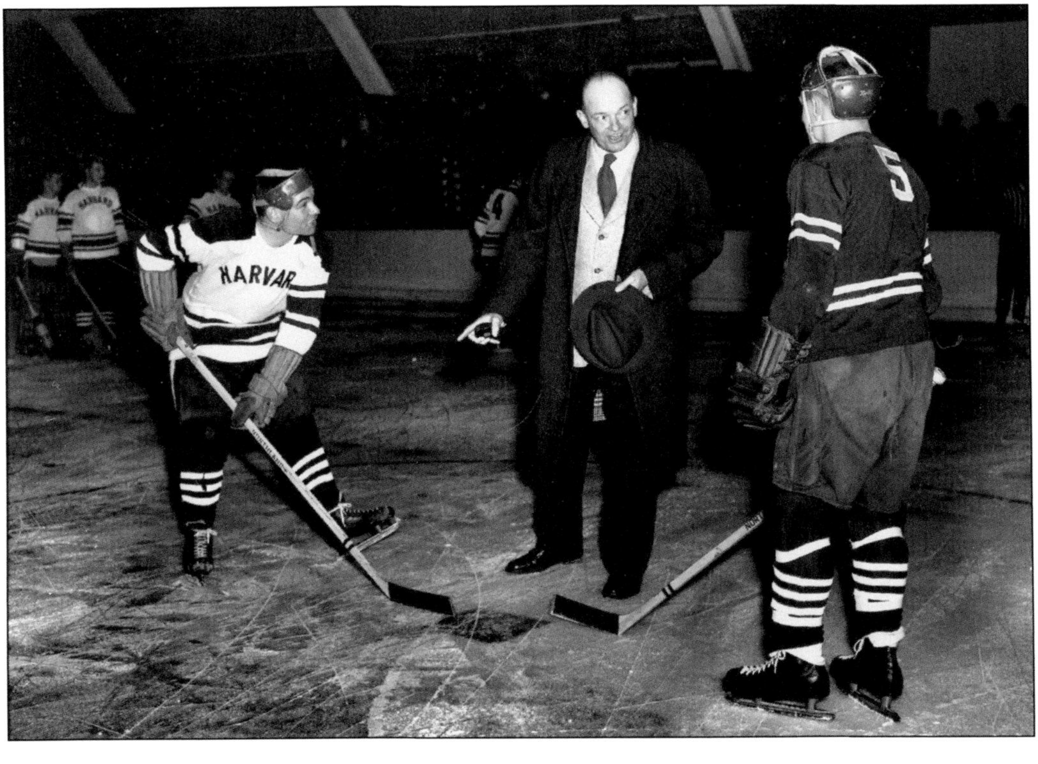

JOHN TITUS '54. The right wing on a line centered for three seasons by his classmate Seaver Peters was John Titus; they had played since the early days of youth hockey with the Green Street Reds in Melrose, Massachusetts. Titus led Dartmouth in scoring and finished with 101 career points. It was a performance that earned Titus a place on the U.S. national team from 1955 to 1957 and on the U.S. Olympic hockey team in 1956.

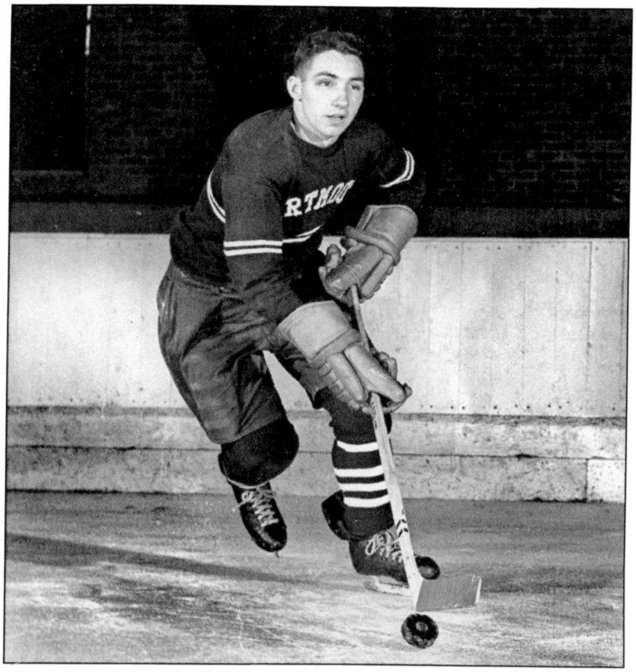

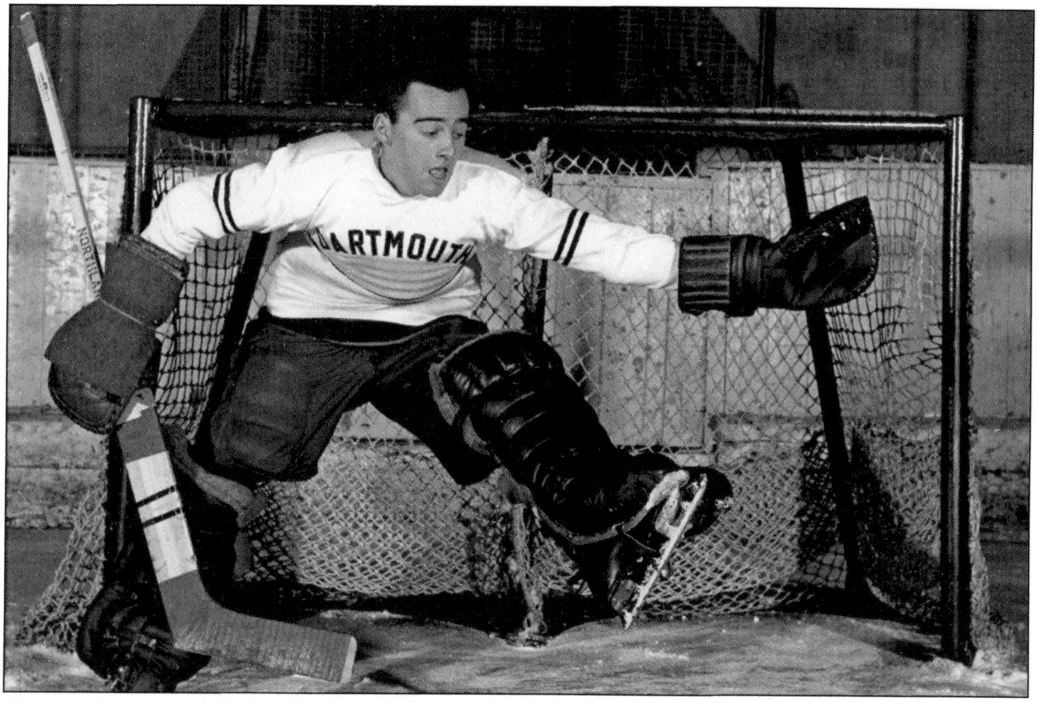

GORDIE RUSSELL '55. In the days before molded face masks and helmets became vogue, wrist shots were as daunting as they are today. Gordie Russell learned that when the Boston Bruins came to Davis Rink for an exhibition game in 1954. A Bruins shot nearly took off his ear. In 1953–54, he set a Dartmouth record for saves (746 in 28 games) that stood for more than 20 years. Russell has carved a remarkable career in venture capital management and has been one of Dartmouth's most generous benefactors.

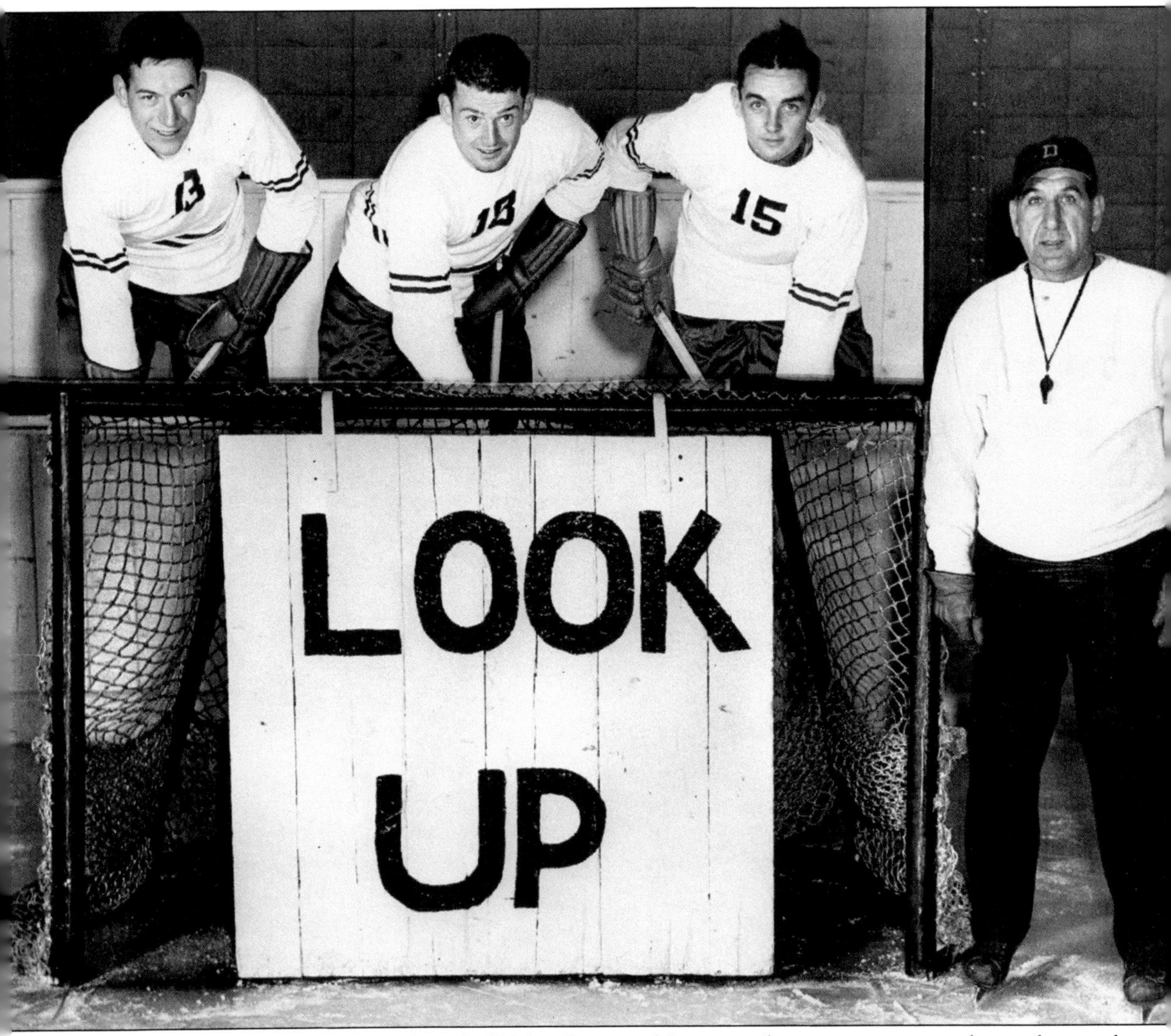

"Heads-Up Hockey." Coach Eddie Jeremiah's contributions as a teacher of sound, fundamental hockey skills to players included his books *Ice Hockey* and *Heads-Up Hockey*, which were "must haves" for players and coaches at all levels. His credo to Dartmouth players was "Look up and keep fighting," though Mike Choukas '51, a sophomore center for the Green on the NCAA tournament team in 1949 and later head of alumni relations at Dartmouth, admitted, "Behind his back, the motto became, 'Keep up and look fighting.' " It was impossible for Jerry's players not to get the "look up" message during practice. The coach is shown here with three members of the 1954–55 team, from left to right, Chet Gale Jr. '55, son of Dartmouth's standout goalie in 1920 (see page 16) and the leading scorer; captain and center Dana Hennigar '55; and junior wing Dave Tonneson '56.

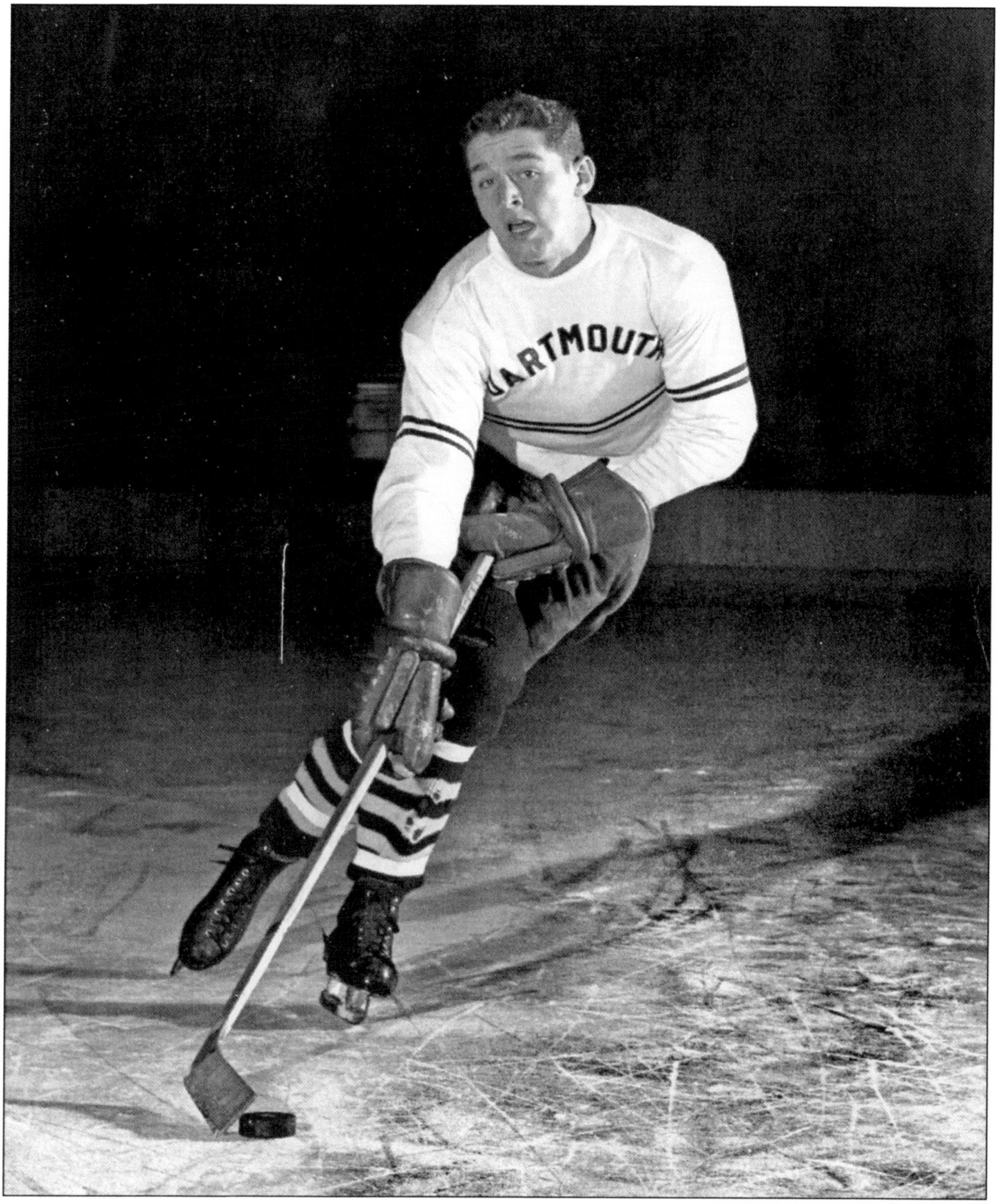

TIM ELLIS '55. Coach Eddie Jeremiah called Tim Ellis "a big, friendly St. Bernard. He had limited ability but unlimited love for the game." He scored three goals during his junior season. On September 11, 1955, shortly before he was to begin studies at Dartmouth Medical School, Ellis drowned while fishing alone on Lake Erie. The Alumni-Varsity game, on March 10, 1956, was called the Tim Ellis Memorial Game. That year, his family, teammates and classmates established the Timothy Wright Ellis Award, which is given annually to the Dartmouth senior who exemplifies the qualities of personality, friendliness, loyalty, and perseverance that made Tim Ellis an inspiration to his associates.

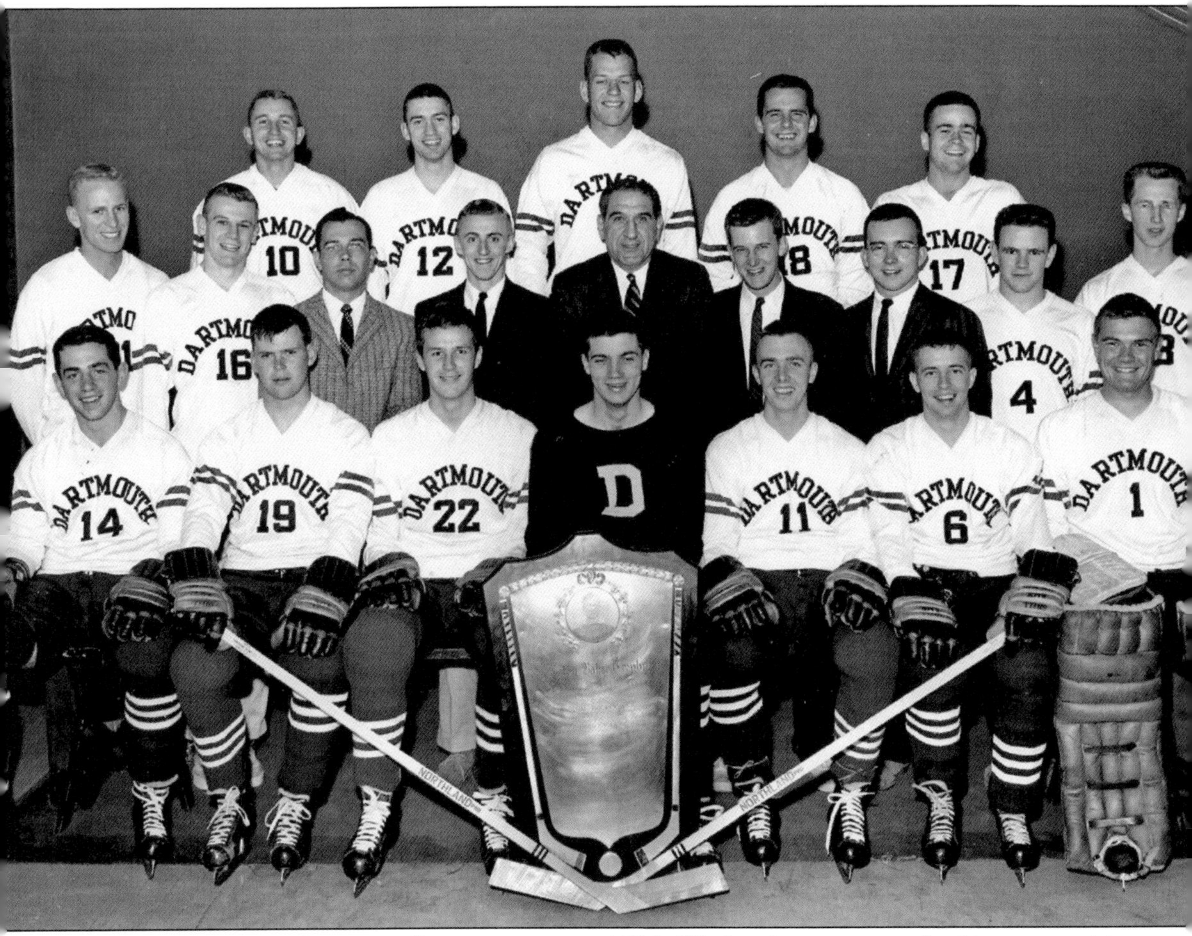

The First Ivy League Championship, 1958–59. Ivy League round-robin competition began in 1955. The hockey round-robin grew to include Brown, Cornell, Dartmouth, Harvard, Princeton, and Yale by the 1958–59 season, and Dartmouth made it a perfect campaign. Led by captain Rod Anderson '59, the Green posted a 10-0-0 record in Ivy games (17-8-0 overall). The reign continued into the 1959–60 season as Dartmouth split decisions with runner-up Harvard to finish 9-1-0 (14-5-1 overall). The 1959–60 team advanced to the NCAA tournament for the first time since the 1949 team's appearance but lost to Boston University 4-1 in the quarterfinals. On another rink (in Squaw Valley, California) in the winter of 1960, Jack Riley '44 coached the U.S. Olympic hockey team to a gold medal.

ROD ANDERSON '59. A center, Rod Anderson began leading the drive to the Ivy League title in 1958–59, when he led Dartmouth in scoring as a sophomore with 38 points (20 goals). He was also the Green's top scorer (41 points, 28 goals) and an All-Ivy selection as a senior and finished with 101 career points. Anderson was also an outfielder in baseball.

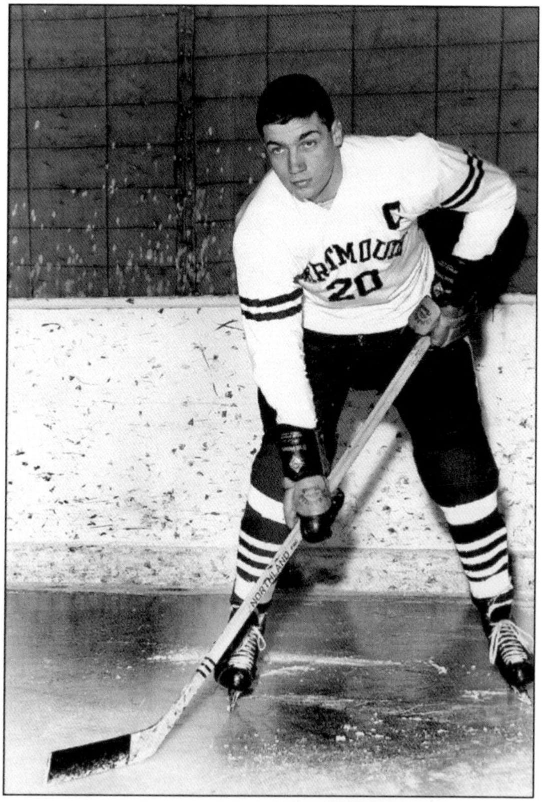

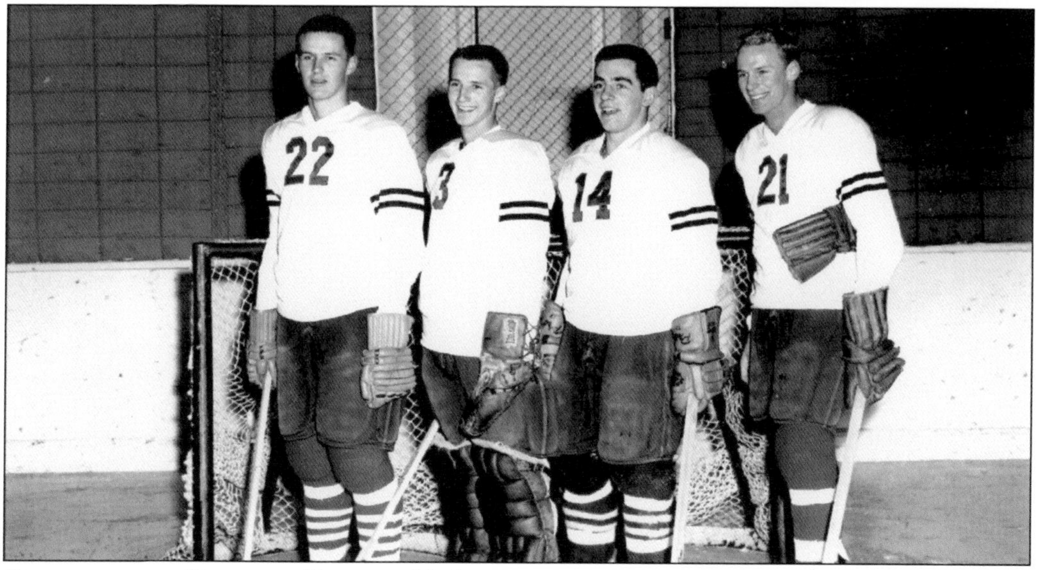

CHAMPIONSHIP QUARTET. Dartmouth's drive to successive Ivy League titles in 1959 and 1960 was helped significantly by this quartet, from left to right, defenseman Ryan Ostebo '60, goalie Tom Wahman '60, defenseman Russ Ingersoll '60, and center-wing John Wadman '59. Ostebo and Ingersoll were two-time All-Ivy League choices, and Wahman, called "the goalie who wants to play forward," was the All-Ivy netminder in 1960. Wadman was second to captain Rod Anderson among Green scorers in 1958–59 and finished with 90 career points (35 goals).

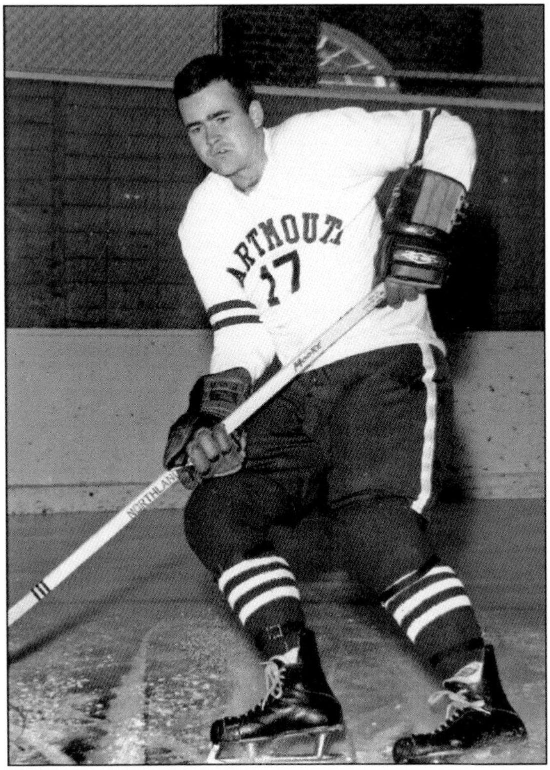

BOB MOORE '61. Known as "the Rocket," Bobby Moore needed four points in his last game to share the Ivy League scoring title in 1961 with Princeton's John Cook. Moore, a right wing from Duluth, Minnesota, notched a goal and three assists in an 8-3 win at Princeton to retain the scoring title he shared with teammate Jake Haertl '61 in 1960. Called "the best clutch player on our squad" by coach Eddie Jeremiah, Moore was captain of the 1960–61 team. He had 113 career points, including 65 goals.

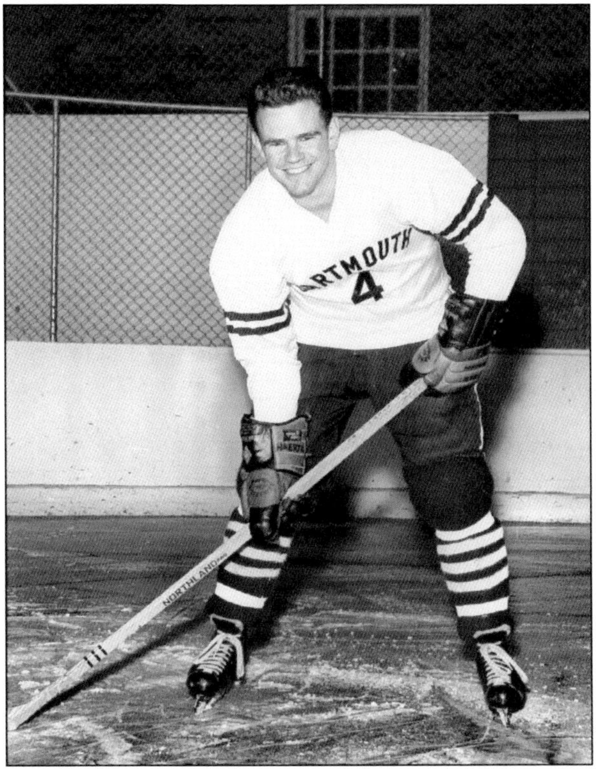

JAKE HAERTL '61. Left wing Jake Haertl followed his brother Bruce '54 onto the ice at Dartmouth. For two seasons (1959 to 1961), Haertl joined Bob Moore as the Green's 1-2 scoring threat (both earned All-Ivy honors in 1961). Haertl closed his career with 97 points (35 goals).

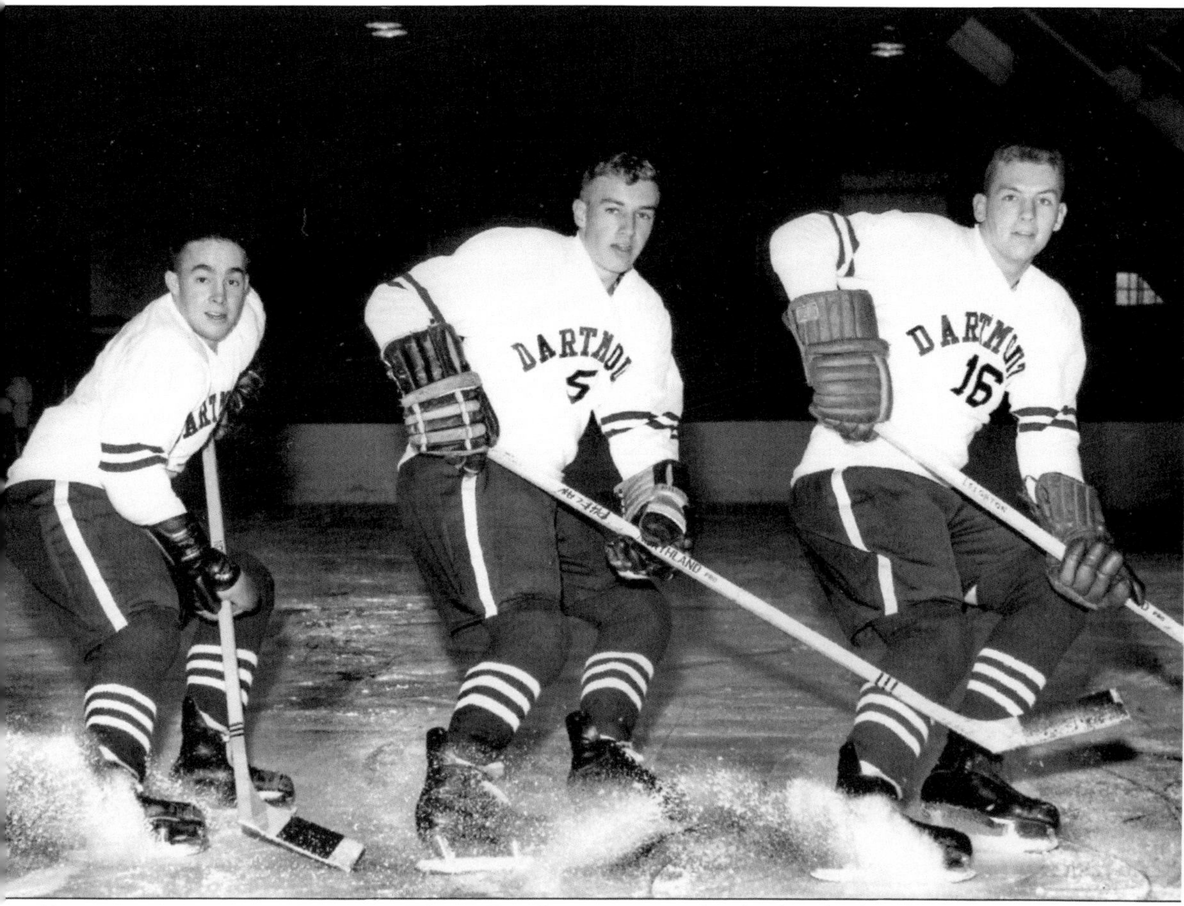

REBUILDING TOWARD ANOTHER TITLE. For three seasons after back-to-back titles in 1959 and 1960, Dartmouth regrouped, largely around this trio, from left to right, Warren Loomis '62, left wing John Phelan '63, and right wing Dave Leighton '63. Loomis was a sophomore wing on the 1960 title team and scored 20 points (14 assists) as a senior defenseman. As a junior and senior, Phelan was runner-up to Leighton in scoring and finished with 84 career points (32 goals). Leighton was All-Ivy and led the league in scoring as a junior and joined the list of 100-point career scorers with 102 points (66 goals).

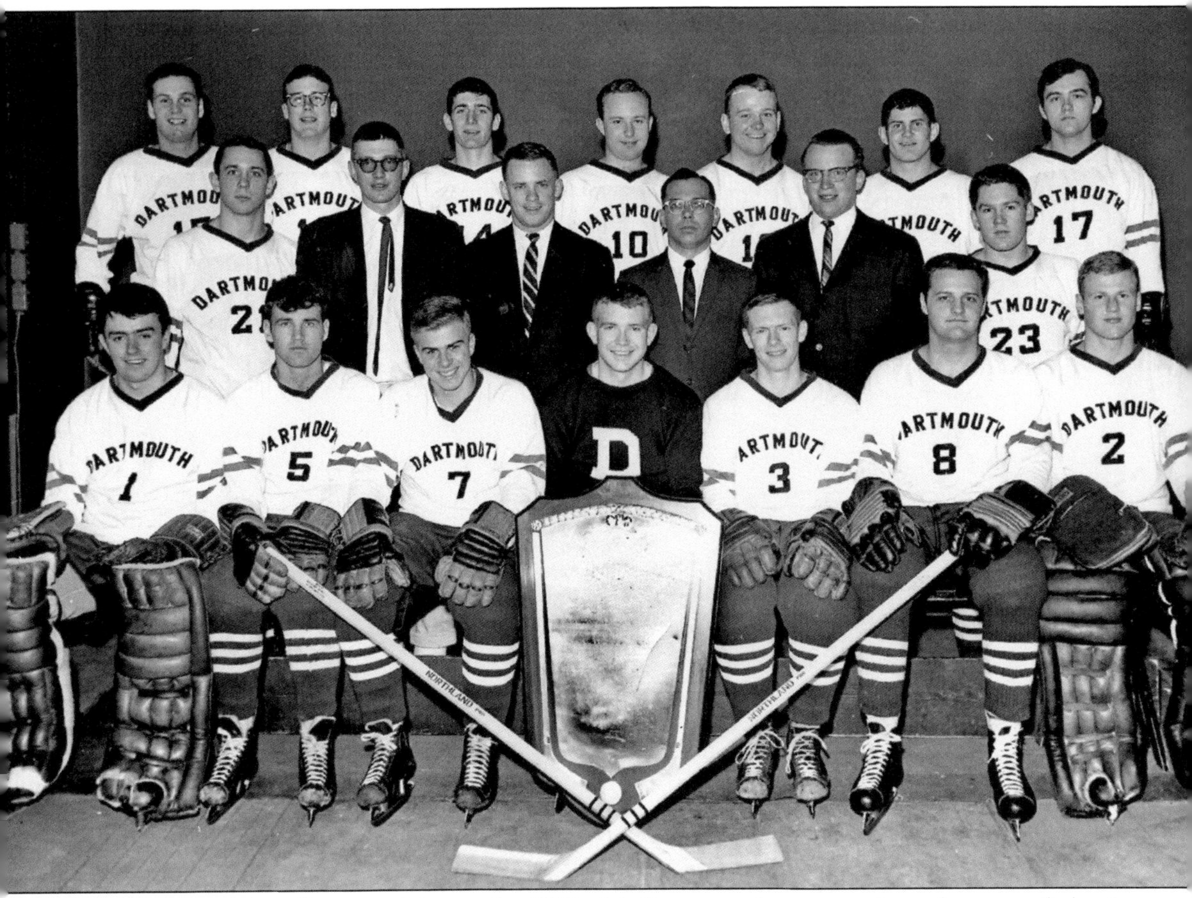

ANOTHER IVY LEAGUE TITLE. In 1963–64, Dartmouth returned to the top of the Ivy League—without coach Eddie Jeremiah. Abner Oakes '56, captain of the 1955–56 team and Jerry's assistant, took charge while Jeremiah coached the U.S. Olympic hockey team at Innsbruck, Austria. Dartmouth had an overall record of 14-7-0 and took the Ivy crown with an 8-2-0 record. The team was led by captain John Carpenter '64, a center and also a standout in soccer. The top scorer was center Doug "Chip" Hayes '65 with 35 points (23 assists). A key to Dartmouth's success was Brewster "Budge" Gere '66, who was named the All-Ivy goaltender as a sophomore. Gere's goals-against average (3.11) included a 2.90 effort in Ivy games. In this photograph, Carpenter holds the championship plaque. Hayes is to Carpenter's right. Gere is extreme right in the front row.

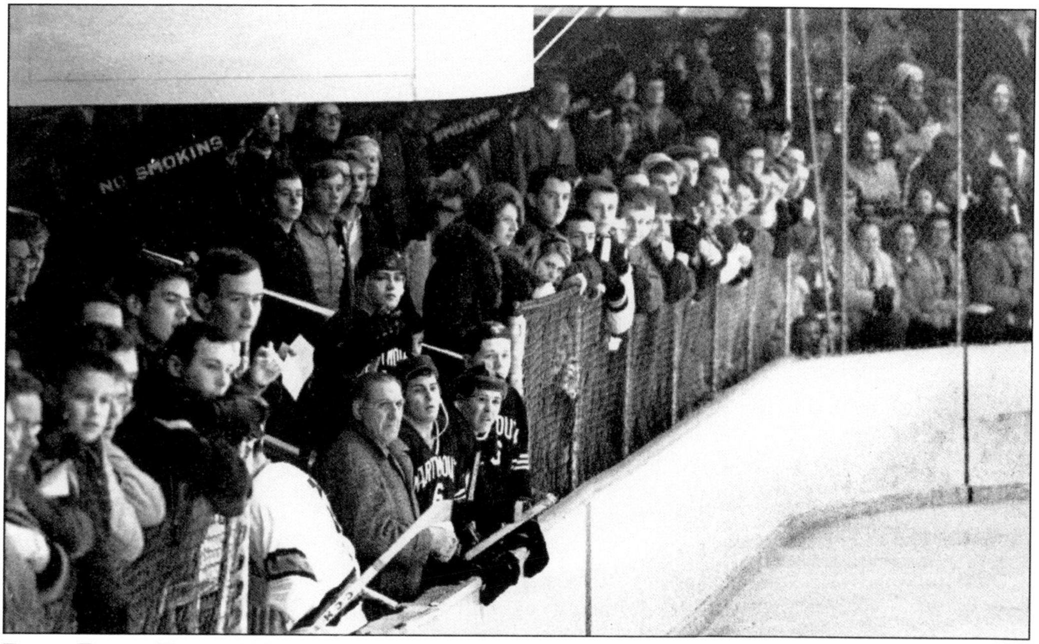

DAVIS RINK, TRULY "HOME" ICE. There isn't an opposing team in the history of Dartmouth hockey that enjoyed coming to Davis Rink. Except for a reserved seating area at the rink's east end, it was standing room only. As soon as the doors opened, Dartmouth students rushed to get preferred locations along the wire fencing that surrounded the ice. By game time, the crowd usually numbered about 2,000 fans—and those draped over the fencing were the loudest. While its successor, Thompson Arena, is one of the nation's finest collegiate rinks, Davis Rink was truly a hockey "pit."

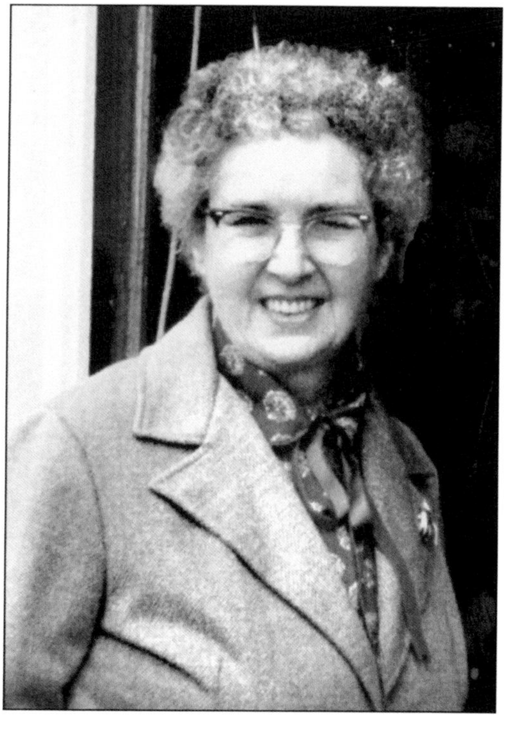

MARY WESBROOK. From the day she arrived as a secretary in the sociology and anthropology departments (1948 to 1979), Mary Wesbrook ranked among Dartmouth's most loyal fans. Mary worked for many years with professors Bob McKennan '25 (the 1924–25 team's manager and later the timekeeper for Dartmouth games) and Elmer Harp. Seated directly behind the Dartmouth bench in Davis Rink and wearing her signature tuque, Mary was hit at least twice by errant pucks. (Courtesy of Margaret Wesbrook, Mary's sister.)

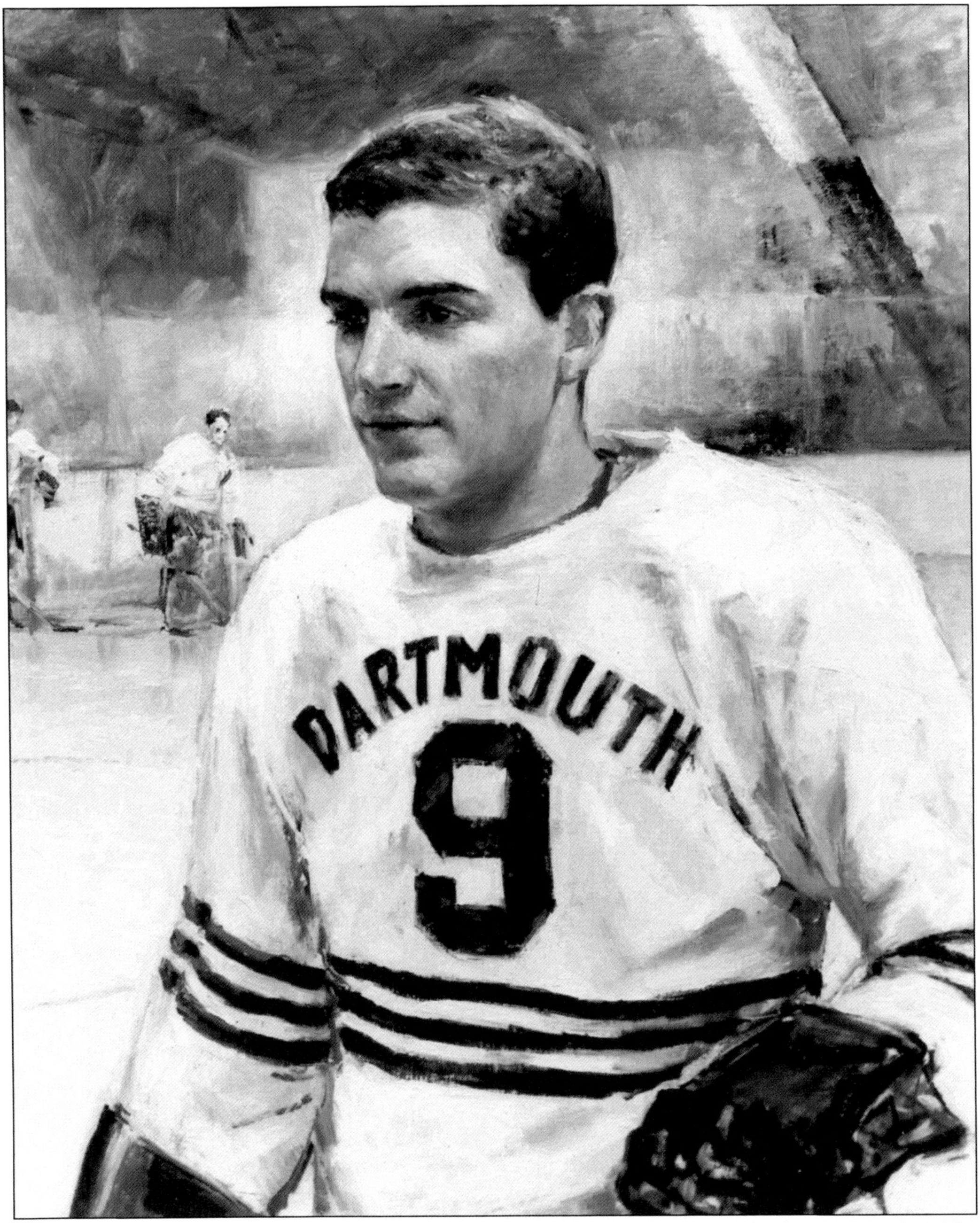

BILL SMOYER '67. As a junior and senior, Bill Smoyer was the scoring leader on coach Eddie Jeremiah's last two Dartmouth hockey teams. He followed his father, Stan '34, and brother Dave '63 (a nine-letter winner in soccer—he was an All-American goaltender, squash and tennis) to Dartmouth. Upon graduation, Bill began service in the Marine Corps. Barely a year later, he died in action in Vietnam. When Thompson Arena opened in 1975, Smoyer Lounge in the arena was made possible by the Smoyer family's gift in memory of Bill Smoyer. This painting of Bill Smoyer hangs in the lounge.

JACK RILEY '44, HALL OF FAME. Had there been an All-American hockey team when he helped Dartmouth to the mythical national championship in 1942, Jack Riley would have been on it. As a player, coach, and administrator, Riley has spent a lifetime in the game of hockey. During 29 years (1951 to 1980) as coach at Army, Riley's team had a record of 390-266-16. He was a member of the U.S. Olympic team in 1948 and coached the U.S. Olympians to their first gold medal in 1960. With his brothers, Bill '46 and Joe '49, he is in the U.S. Hockey Hall of Fame.

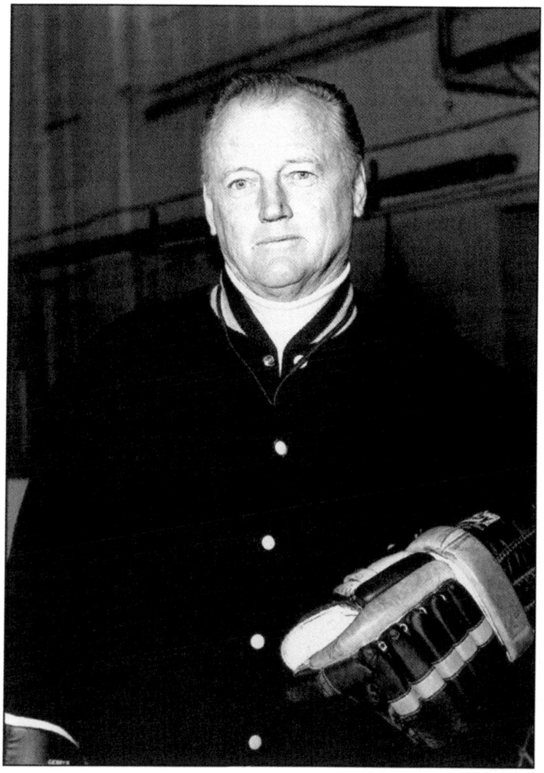

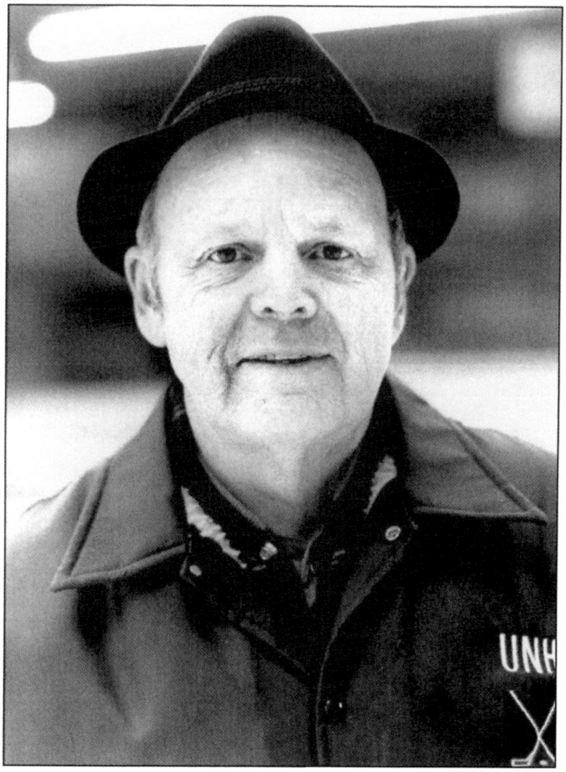

CHARLIE HOLT '45, HALL OF FAME. After serving in the army during World War II, Charlie Holt was captain of the Green in 1945–46. His career as a hockey coach spanned four decades. After six years (1962 to 1968), 65 wins, and a Division II national title at Colby, Holt spent 18 years (1968 to 1986) as coach at the University of New Hampshire. His record at UNH was 347-232-18 and he was national coach of the year three times. He was elected to the U.S. Hockey Hall of Fame in 1997.

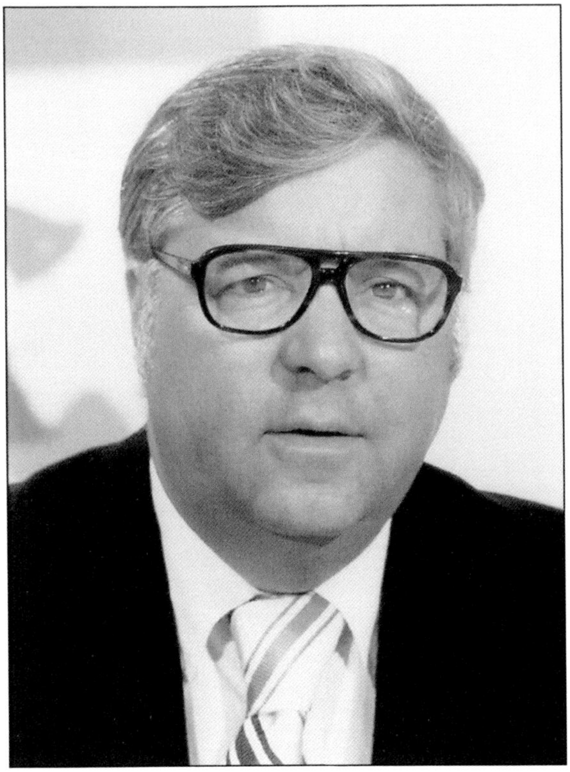

WALTER BUSH '51, HALL OF FAME. Walter Bush played freshman hockey at Dartmouth and, over the past half-century, played a vital role in the growth and development of amateur and professional hockey in the United States. Bush has held numerous leadership positions with the Amateur Hockey Association and the U.S. national team. He was instrumental in bringing the National Hockey League to his home state as primary founder of the Minnesota North Stars. In 1980, Bush was elected to the U.S. Hockey Hall of Fame. In 2000, he was elected to the Hockey Hall of Fame in Toronto.

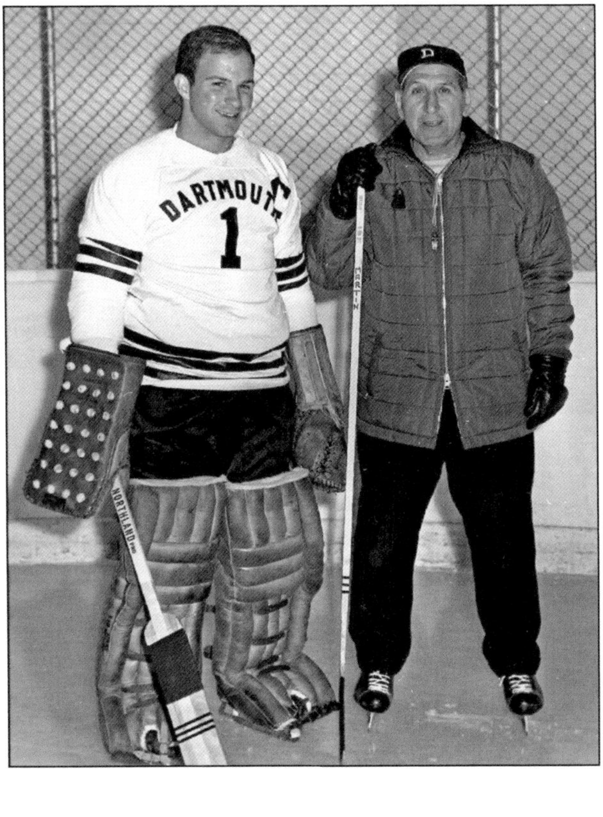

EDDIE JEREMIAH '30, HALL OF FAME. Shown with Warren Cook '67, captain and goalie on his last team, Eddie Jeremiah retired from coaching in 1967. Including alumni and other exhibition games, his Dartmouth teams over 26 seasons had a record of 308-246-10. Jeremiah coached his last game at Davis Rink on March 4, 1967. Barely three months later, he lost his battle with cancer. As a coach and teacher, Jeremiah's name is inseparable from hockey and Dartmouth College. In 1973, he was Dartmouth's first inductee into the U.S. Hockey Hall of Fame.

FOUR

The Davis Rink Era Ends 1967–1975

These were the in-between years at Dartmouth. Between coaches—Eddie Jeremiah and George Crowe. Between presidents—John Sloan Dickey and David T. McLaughlin (bracketing John G. Kemeny, the overseer as coeducation came to Dartmouth). Between a hockey scene that for 70 years was all-male and one that was, on the varsity level, about to become half male and half female.

And, as befits an in-between era, the record was mixed. Some terrific individual performances. Some good but also some disappointing team finishes. These teams played good hockey—and they played fearsome foes. Years later, some of them would identify themselves as members of a Dartmouth team that was frustrated by goalie Ken Dryden and Cornell's two-time national champions. Others would brag they were part of a team that won the ECAC Holiday Tournament at the old Boston Garden and that bid farewell to Davis Rink—well loved, to be sure, but a facility that outlived its era.

These were tough years: student unrest, Vietnam, economic distress. Dartmouth hockey was full of tough men, including coaches Ab Oakes '56 and Grant Standbrook and players such as Ken Davidson '71, Mike Turner '72, Peter Proulx '73, and Fred Riggall '73.

At the center of these years was a group of men who would play in their college years and then build a future for their game and their college. Years after leaving the ice, they would appreciate more than many the construction of the sparkling new Thompson Arena. They would help to elevate Dartmouth hockey to the premier position it occupies today in the winter sporting scene. Then, as now, they would make Saturday night at the rink the place to be. They were hockey men.

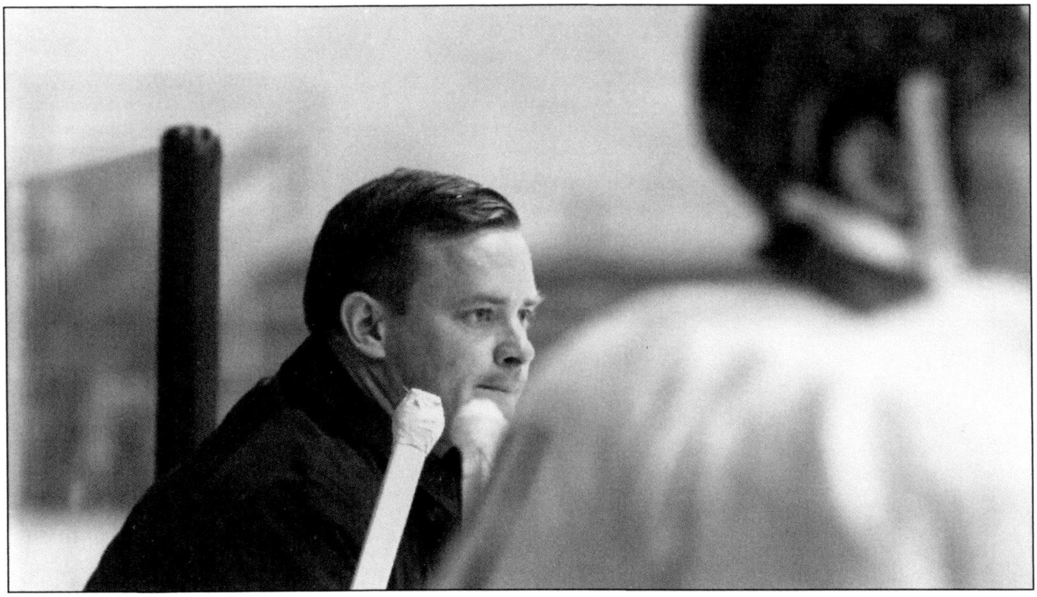

COACH ABNER OAKES III '56. Ab Oakes was captain of Dartmouth's hockey team in 1955–56. He became freshman coach in 1960, served as head coach of the Ivy League title team in 1963–64 (when Eddie Jeremiah was coaching the U.S. Olympic team), and succeeded Jeremiah as the head coach from 1967 to 1970. His four-season coaching record was 35-55-2. The Oakes family name is famous in Dartmouth athletic lore. In 1881, Ab's grandfather, Charles Oakes '83, scored the first touchdown in the history of Dartmouth football.

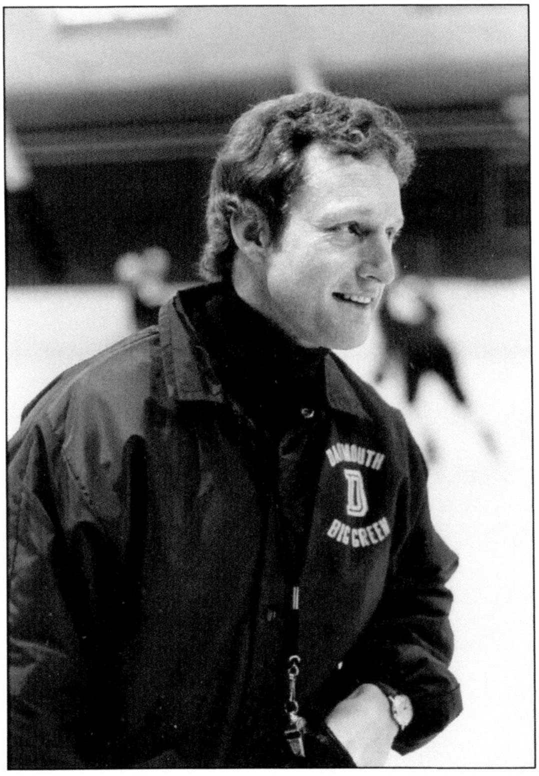

COACH GRANT STANDBROOK. From 1970 to 1975, Grant Standbrook produced three winning seasons (1971–74) but resigned after a disappointing 5-19-0 record in 1974–75. He became an assistant coach at the University of Wisconsin for 12 years. Since 1988, Standbrook has been an assistant coach at the University of Maine. He helped coach eight teams at Wisconsin and Maine to the NCAA tournament championship game, including three titles at Wisconsin and two at Maine.

KEN DAVIDSON '71. From 1968 to 1971, Ken Davidson collected 100 career points (48 goals). The fiery center, who would go on to play professional hockey for several years, was the scoring leader as a sophomore. He was the Green's most valuable player in 1971. In this photograph, Davidson is between shifts, watching the action with Dick Donohue '72, the team manager.

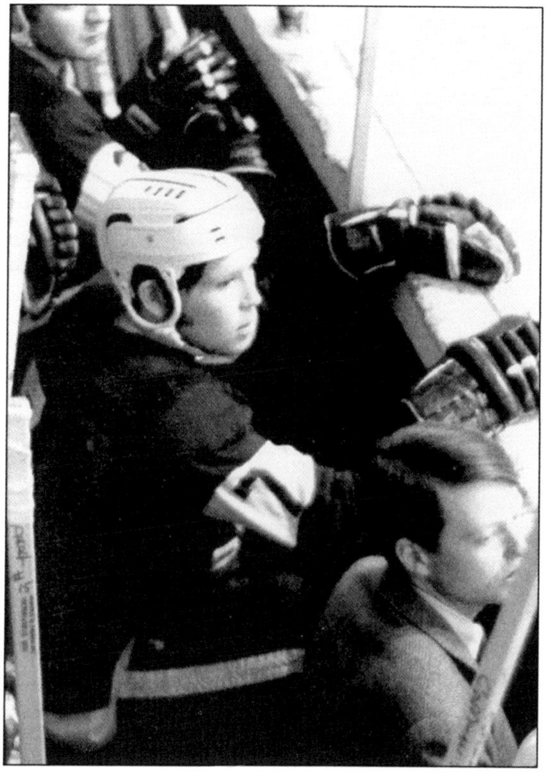

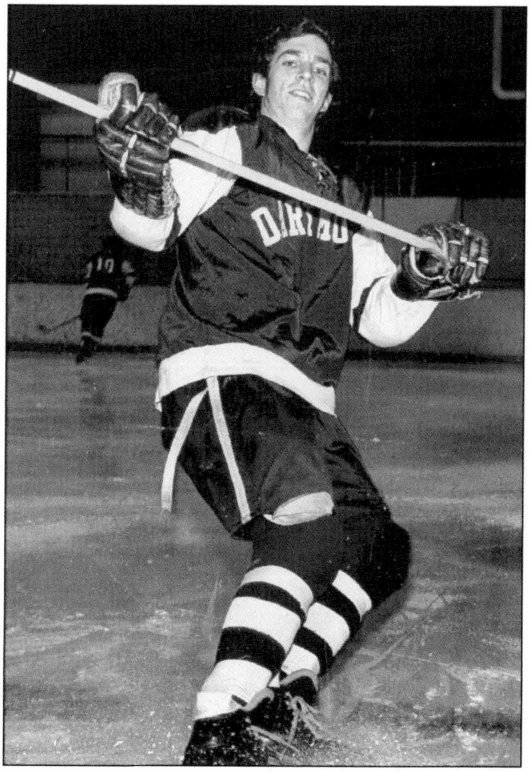

MIKE TURNER '72. In 1971–72, center Mike Turner became the 10th player from Melrose, Massachusetts, to be elected captain of hockey at Dartmouth. For three seasons (1969 to 1972), Turner led the Green in scoring. He ranks ninth all-time in scoring at Dartmouth with 124 points (48 goals, 76 assists). His son Mike '04 was a four-year skater at Dartmouth from 2000 to 2004.

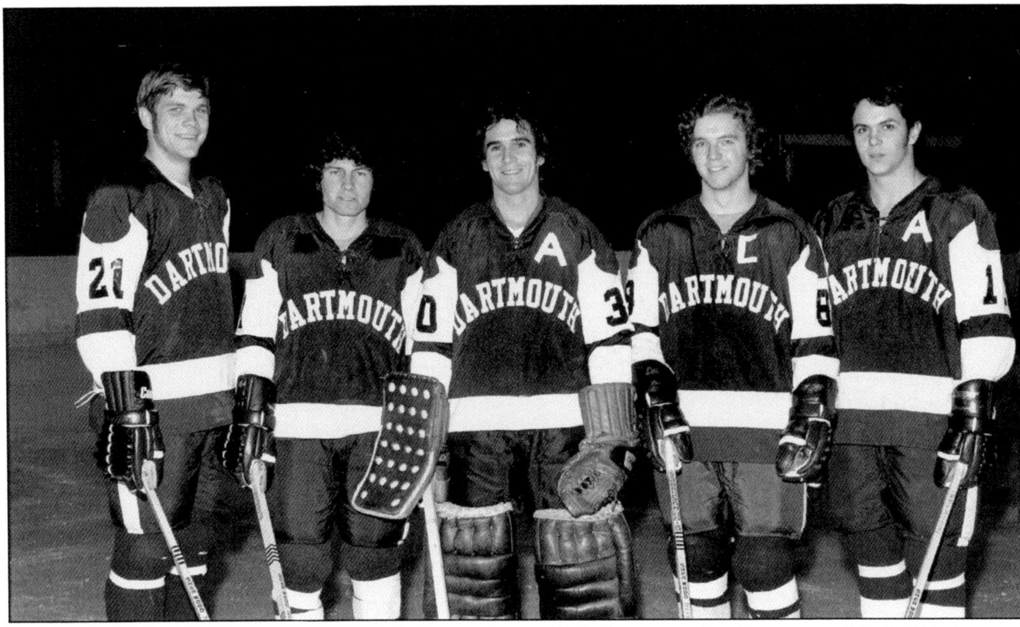

SENIORS, 1972–73. This quintet of seniors provided the core for Dartmouth's 12-11-1 record in 1972–73. Shown from left to right are defenseman Jim "Duke" Edgeworth, center Dave Walkom, goalie Peter Proulx, captain and defenseman Dana Johnson, and wing Fred Riggall. Riggall was the team's scoring leader with 41 points (26 goals). Edgeworth, Walkom, and Johnson combined for another 15 goals and 51 assists.

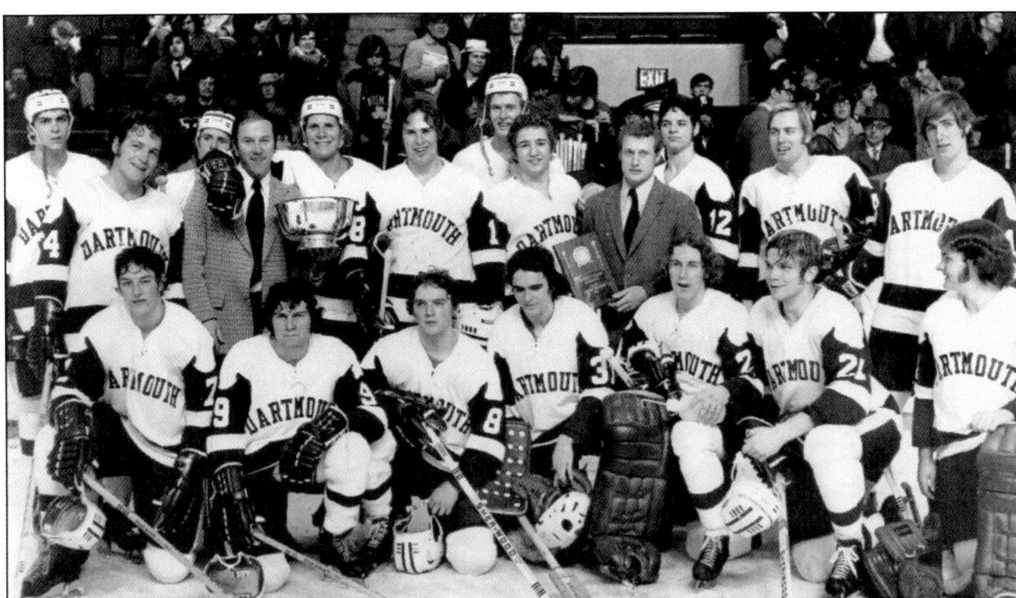

HOLIDAY CHEER AT BOSTON GARDEN. Christmas came early in 1972 for Dartmouth's 1972–73 team. On December 18, at the ECAC Holiday Tournament in Boston Garden, the underdog Green stunned the University of New Hampshire 5-4. The game was decided with a goal by defenseman Jim Johnston '73 (it was his only goal of the season). Two nights later, the Green pulled another upset over Boston College 8-5. Here, the team celebrates its holiday success.

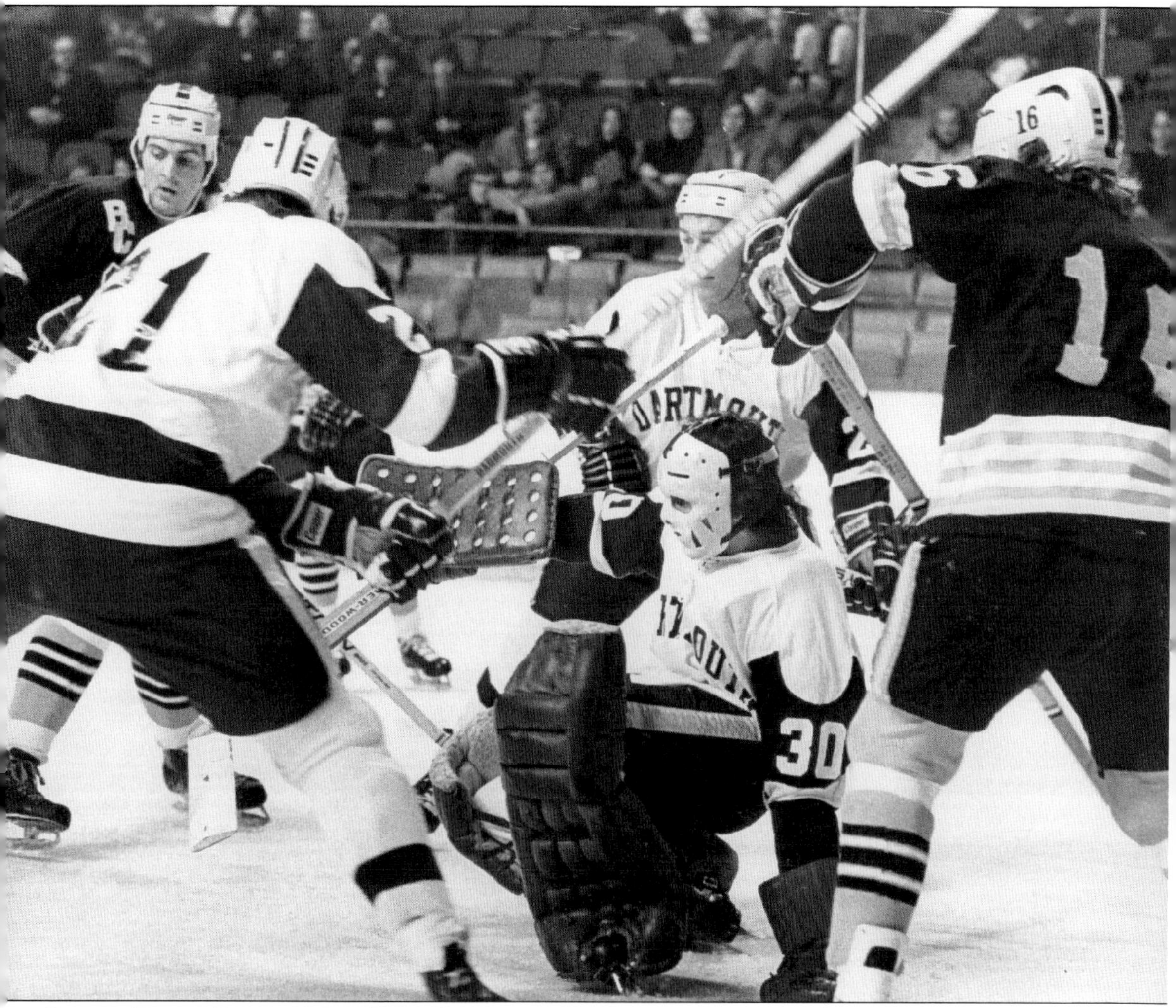

GOALIE PETER PROULX. Proulx made 41 saves against Boston College in the ECAC Holiday Tournament. Proulx, who was the All-Ivy League goalie a year earlier, had 79 saves in two games at the Boston Garden and was the tournament's most valuable player. (Photograph by Danny Goshtigian, the *Boston Globe*.)

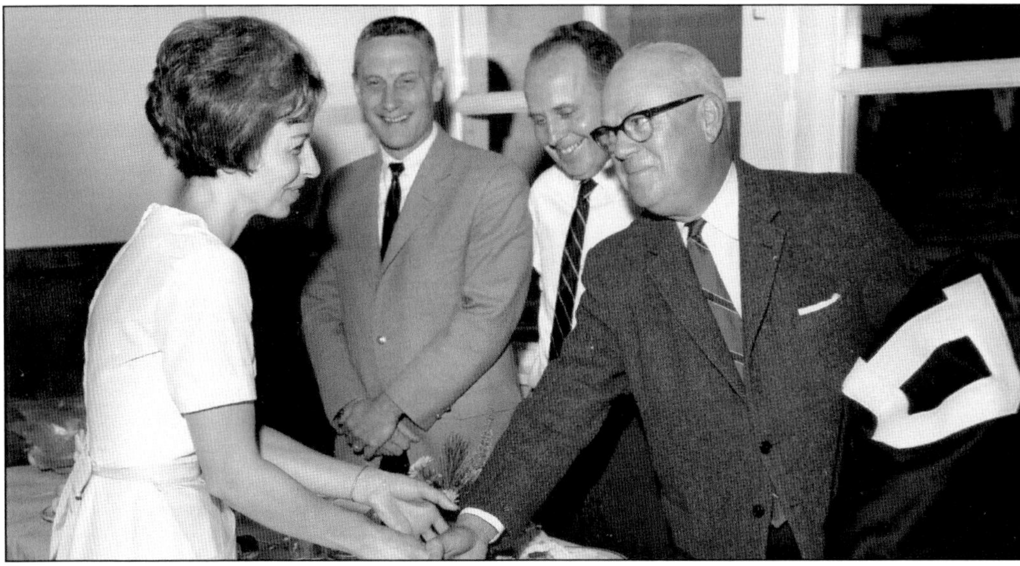

John Manser '26. After a long career in business, John Manser (right) retired to Hanover in the late 1960s and became instrumental in creating the Friends of Dartmouth Hockey. Manser, from Melrose, Massachusetts, was captain of the Green's 1925–26 team. He was Dartmouth's scoring leader as a junior. Manser is shown receiving a birthday cake and *D* blanket in 1972 at Lou's Restaurant in Hanover. Sharing the moment are, from left to right, waitress Nettie Blanchard; Seaver Peters '54, a former hockey captain and Dartmouth's director of athletics from 1967 to 1983; and Lou Bressett, the restaurant owner and one of Hanover's greatest civic leaders.

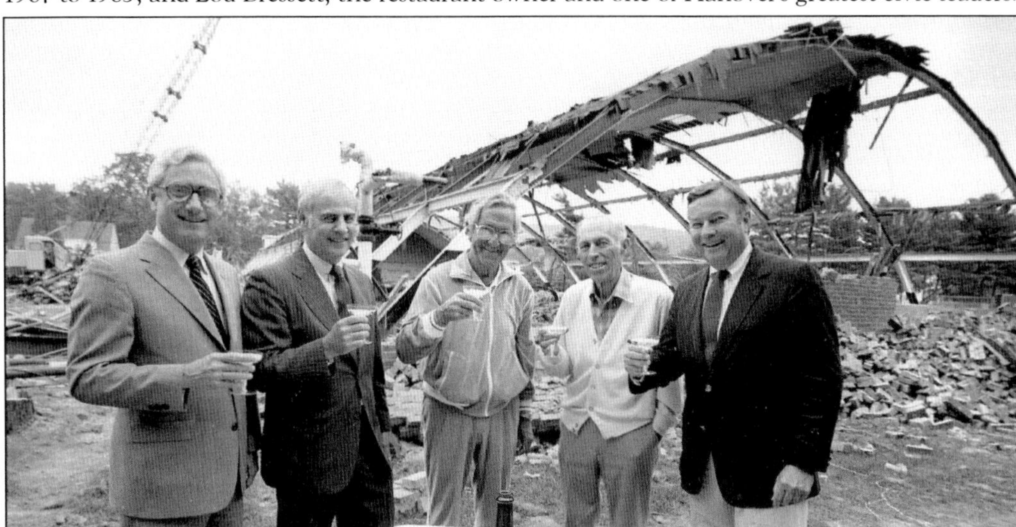

Davis Rink Adieu. In 1985, Davis Rink was demolished after 55 years to make way for the John W. Berry Sports Center. It prompted a nostalgic champagne toast by four former Dartmouth players and a manager. From left to right are Seaver Peters '54, the 1953–54 captain; Michael Choukas '51, a three-year center from 1948 to 1951; All-American Paul Guibord '36; Jack Manchester '33, a forward from 1930 to 1933; and Addison Winship '42, manager of the 1941–42 team that was the mythical national champion. Guibord retired to Hanover, and Manchester was a longtime local business leader. Peters, Choukas, and Winship had long tenures in Dartmouth administrative positions. (Photograph by Stuart Bratesman '74.)

FIVE

Thompson Arena and Crowe's Men 1975–1984

The period between 1975 and 1984 belongs to no individual, whether in hockey sweater or coaches' regulation blazer and tie, but to a concrete structure. This period is defined by Thompson Arena.

The miracle of the building is that, three full decades later, it stands as a metaphor for Dartmouth hockey; it seems forever new. Five men have been president of the United States, and three have ascended to the presidency of Dartmouth since Thompson had its inaugural event, and yet the place still gleams, the ice still shimmers, the stands still rock the way they did in that first year. The contrast with Dartmouth's last ice hut could not be more dramatic.

Thompson was not only for games. In its very first season, an insurgent Republican presidential candidate, former governor Ronald Reagan of California, gave a rousing New Hampshire primary speech inside Thompson. Two decades later, torrential rains during commencement weekend forced the proceedings inside, and so some parting memories of Dartmouth became intertwined with the concrete triangles of Thompson.

But Thompson was, for much of those early years, Crowe's nest. George Crowe brought his special brand of hockey, an admixture of what he saw in the pro, prep, and proletariat levels, the latter being no joke; Soviet hockey had its day, or at least its strains could be seen, on the Hanover ice. These teams were always in contention, often in unassailable leads, sometimes in the NCAA championships. They melded strong individual performances with spirited team play. One of them (Jeff Sollows '77) even merited a sculpture. Fittingly, it was made of ice and melted after Winter Carnival in the winter of 1977.

These were strong teams in their own right, producing strong records in their own right. But, like Thompson Arena itself, they created a strong foundation. A generation later, the leading goalie of the period, Bob Gaudet '81, would be standing in street shoes behind the Dartmouth bench, one of the leading coaches in the land. On his team would be a son of this era, Nick Johnson '08, whose father, Kevin Johnson '77, was a scoring machine (his uncle, Dana Johnson '73 was a Dartmouth captain in the pre-Thompson era). The place was built to endure and from its first day has produced enduring memories.

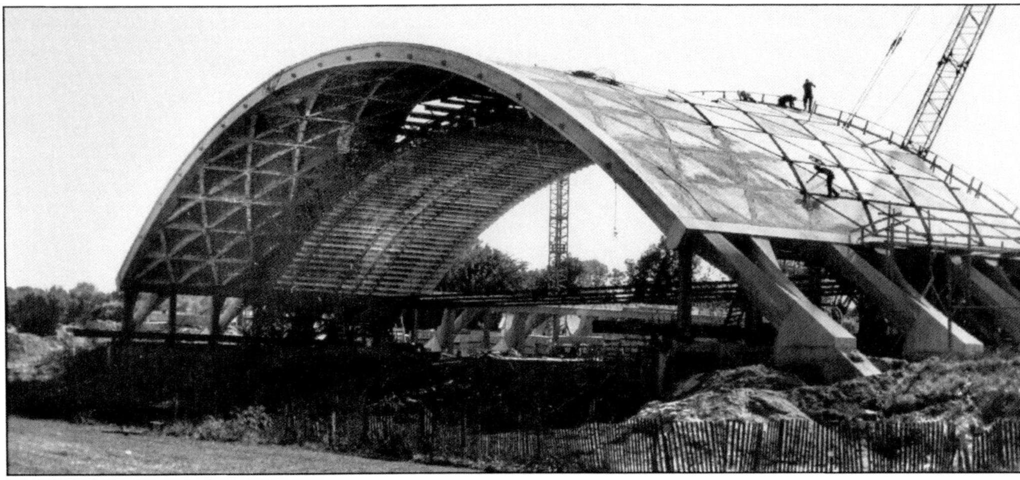

RUPERT THOMPSON ARENA. Pier Luigi Nervi, the Italian architect whose 1960 Rome Olympiad structures inspired Dartmouth administrators to bring his innovative use of concrete to the Hanover campus, led to two athletic landmarks: Leverone Field House, opened in 1962, and Thompson Arena, opened in November 1975. Nervi's design features about 1,000 pre-cast, pie-shaped concrete wedges, each weighing one ton, that create an attractive clear-span vault over the ice surface and 3,520 seats. The ceiling was installed wedge-by-wedge, using a centered metal arch system that traveled on rails. The process was flawless. Today, the arena is as magnificent as when it opened. The building bears the name of Rupert C. Thompson Jr. '28, the major donor who served as chair of Dartmouth's Third Century capital campaign in the late 1960s.

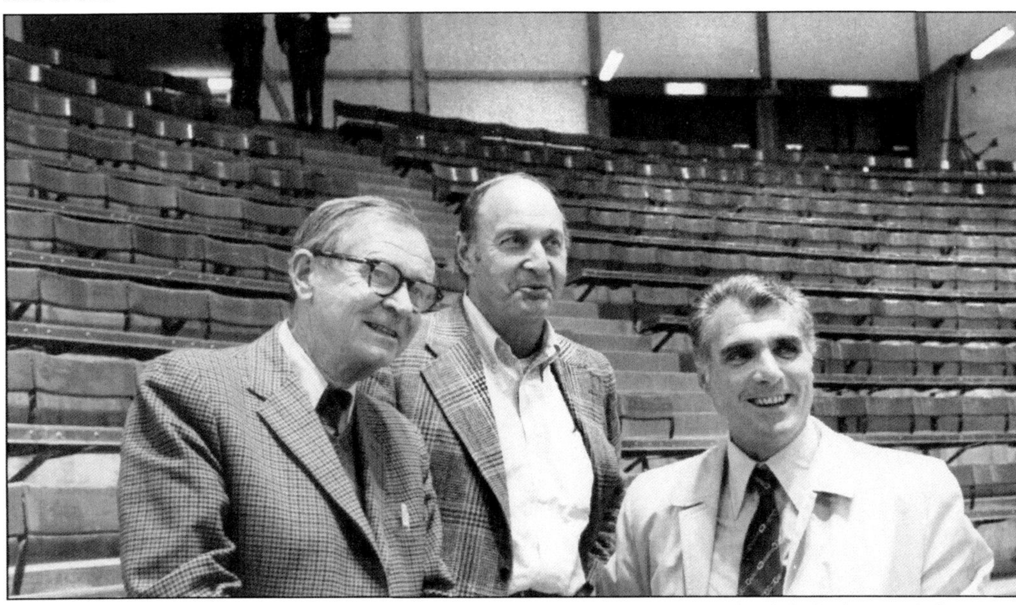

PRIME MOVERS. Less than two months before the first event was scheduled, three of the prime movers in the construction of Thompson Arena watched the continuous pouring of nearly 20,000 square feet of concrete, the base for the ice surface. From left to right are Dick Olmsted '32, Dartmouth's director of facilities planning; Phil Jackson '43, president of the construction firm that built the arena; and Antonio Nervi, son of the Rome-based architect Pier Luigi Nervi. (Photograph by Adrian Bouchard.)

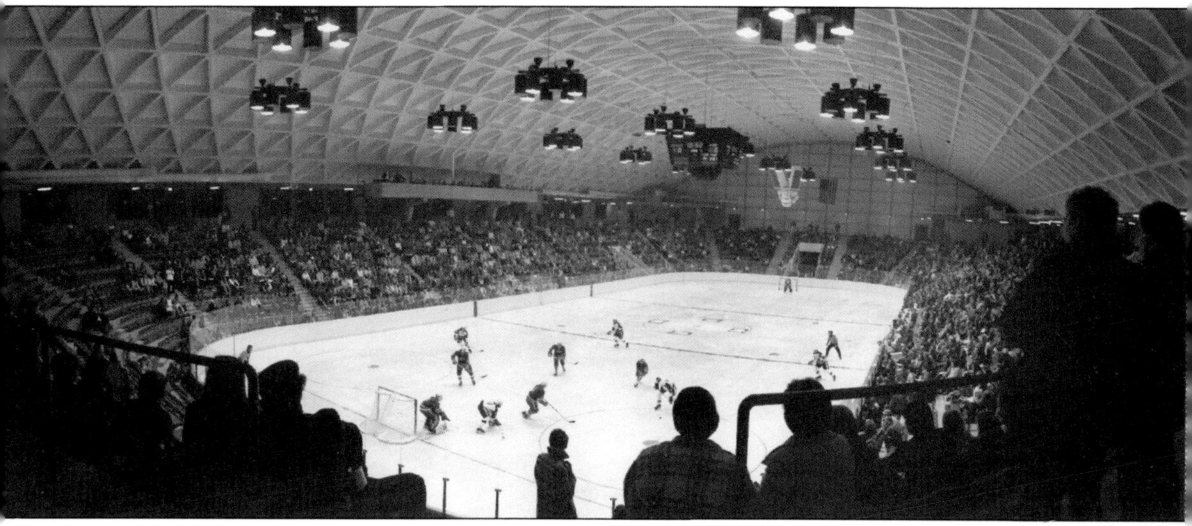

FULL HOUSE. Dartmouth hockey teams usually played to a full house in Davis Rink. When Thompson Arena opened as the new home of Big Green hockey in 1975, there were twice as many fans. Standing-room crowds of more than 4,000 spectators made Thompson a mecca for raucous students. Youth hockey had gained a firm foothold in the area, and Hanover High School's fine hockey team brought an ever increasing number of fans to the building. Ivy League hockey was as strong as ever, and the Eastern College Athletic Conference (ECAC) had created a hockey conference in 1962 that included the Ivy League among 20 Division 1 teams in the Northeast. In its early years, Thompson Arena was also the home for basketball. (Many Dartmouth hockey players manned the crew of work-study students who converted the rink for basketball.) The first intercollegiate contest in Thompson Arena was not a hockey game. On November 22, 1975, three days before the first hockey game, the men's basketball team won an exhibition game against a team from Yugoslavia.

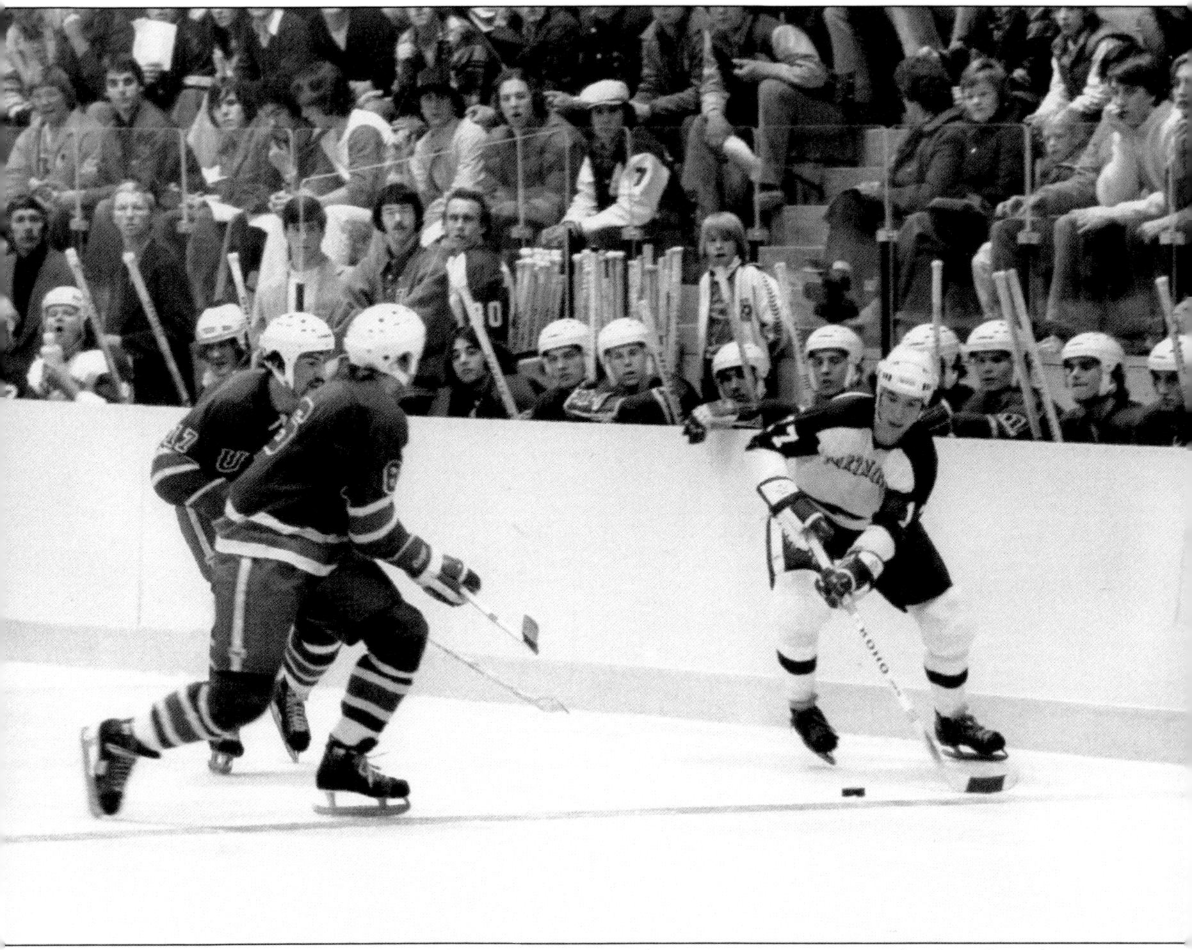

THOMPSON'S FIRST HOCKEY GAME. On November 25, 1975, Dartmouth played its first game in Thompson Arena, an exhibition game with the U.S. Olympic team that ended in a 3-3 tie. In this photograph, wing Dan Leigh '76 crosses the blue line. Dartmouth's first goal on the new ice was netted by wing Joey Tomlak '79 from Thunder Bay, Ontario; it was the first season that freshmen were eligible to play varsity hockey. Dartmouth unveiled the style of play that George Crowe, the new coach, had taught during his years at Phillips Exeter Academy. Crowe combined his own philosophy with elements made fashionable by teams from the Soviet Union and, minus the violence, the NHL's Philadelphia Flyers. Crowe utilized three sets of five-man units with a fourth line ready to plug holes. The five-man forecheck system meant that forwards had to learn the defensemen's duties and vice versa. After a 5-19-0 record in 1974–75, the 1975–76 team finished 16-11. It was the start of a new era in every respect for Dartmouth hockey. The arena was dedicated on February 14, 1976, with a 9-7 win over Cornell.

COACH GEORGE CROWE. Crowe grew up playing junior and senior hockey in New Brunswick, Canada. He graduated from Springfield College, where hockey was discontinued after his freshman year (he turned to soccer, tennis, and track). Fourteen years of college and prep school coaching, including a 94-44-1 record in seven seasons at Phillips Exeter Academy, preceded his arrival at Dartmouth in 1975. When he was hired, many people said, "George who?" After his first season, a 16-11 record and a trip to the ECAC Tournament earned Crowe honors as the New England coach of the year.

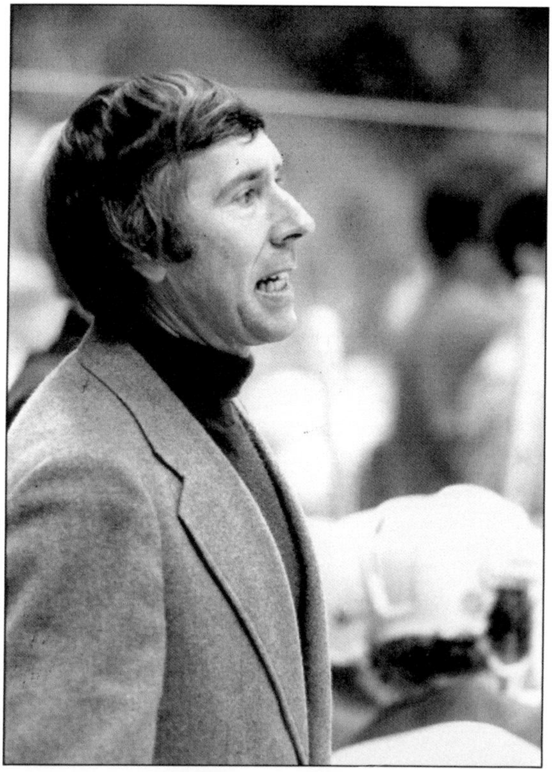

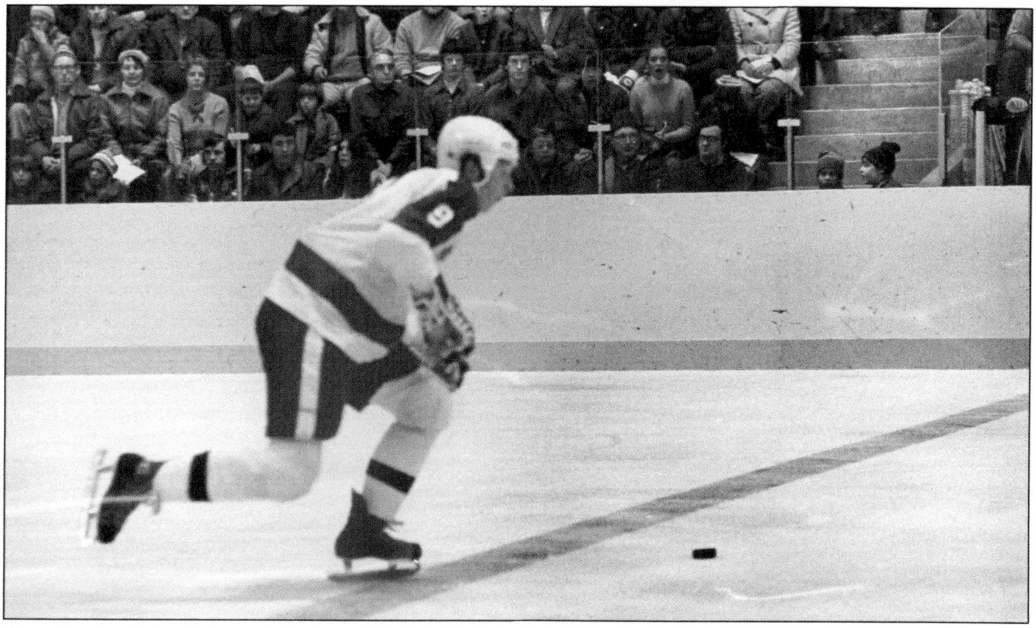

TOM FLEMING '76. A three-sport standout, Tom Fleming ranks among Dartmouth's finest all-around athletes. He shared in records as a sprinter in track and had a record 98-yard kickoff runback (against Columbia, 1973) as a split end-return specialist in football. For three hockey seasons (1973–76), Fleming, a center, was Dartmouth's scoring leader, finishing with 133 points (60 goals, 73 assists).

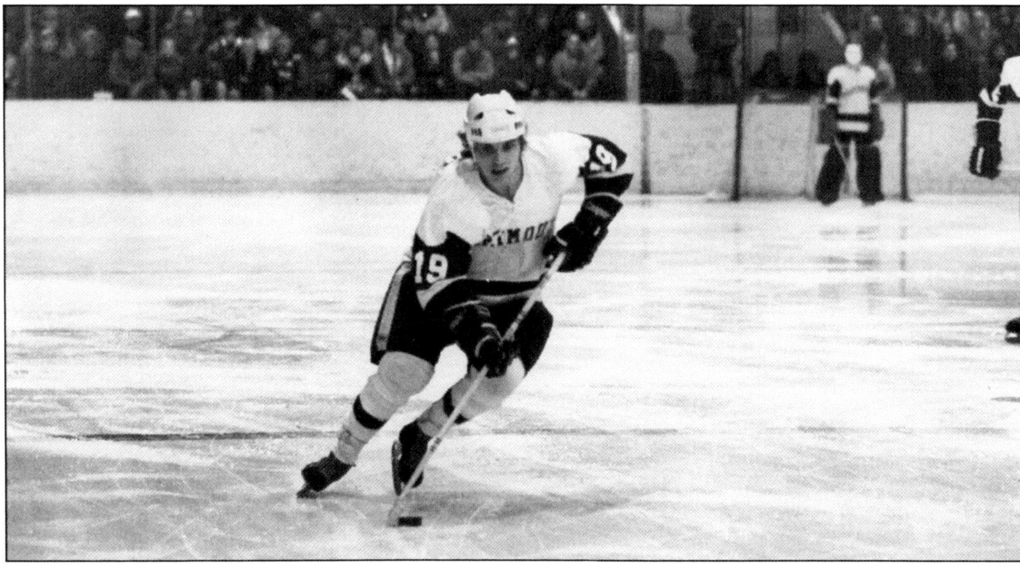

KEN PETTIT '76. As captain of Dartmouth's 1975–76 team, center Ken Pettit was the Green's most versatile player. "He played in man-up and penalty-killing situations and even moved to defense when needed," said coach George Crowe. For three seasons, Pettit was runner-up to classmate Tom Fleming among Dartmouth's scorers, finishing with 103 career points (49 goals).

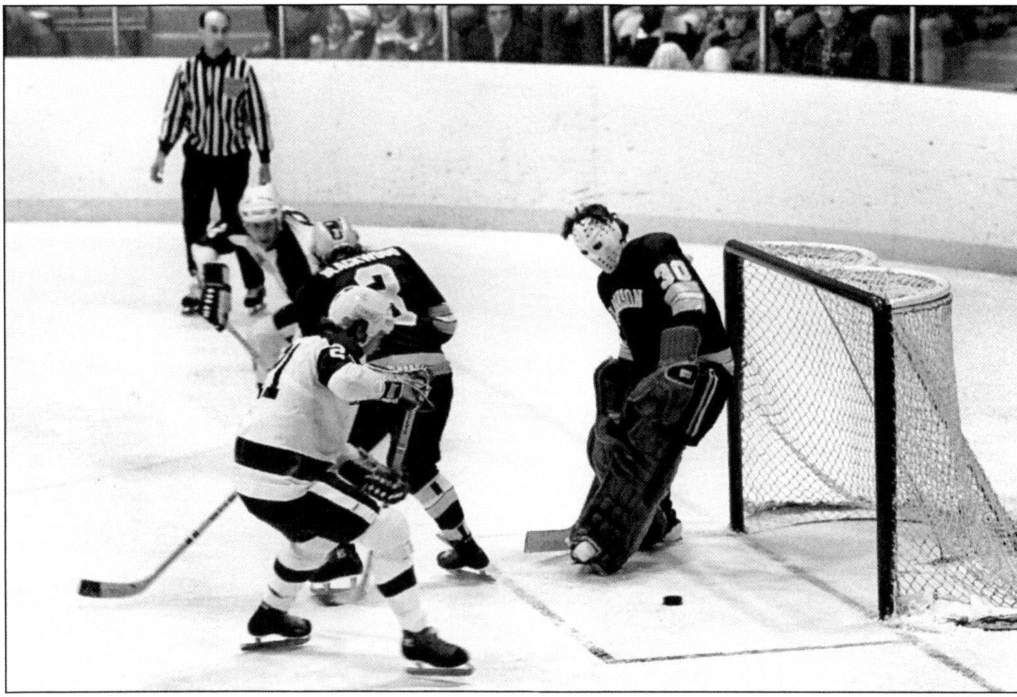

KEVIN JOHNSON '77. He was known as "Dr. J" (he has gone on to become a physician). Kevin Johnson, shown scoring against Clarkson, had four successive two-goal games (six overall) as he led the Green in scoring in 1976–77 with 42 points (26 goals) and had 83 career points. His brother Dana '73 was Dartmouth's captain in 1972–73, and his son Nick '08 is one of the Green's top current-day players (page 127).

JEFF SOLLOWS '77. During three seasons (1974 to 1977), goalie Jeff Sollows was the mainstay in Dartmouth's nets. He was the Green's most valuable player in 1975–76, when he broke the Dartmouth record for saves in a season (865, finally eclipsed by Nick Boucher '03 with 867 in 2000–01). Sollows ranks sixth all-time in career saves (1,812) and had a .860 save percentage over 51 games.

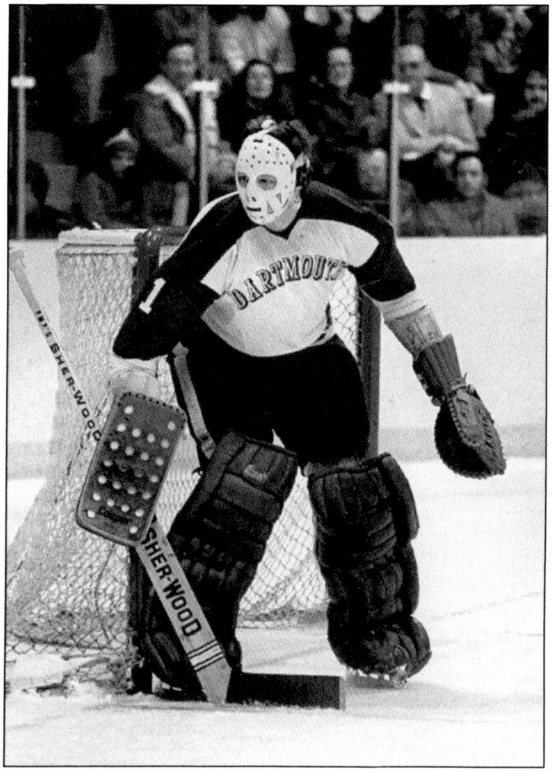

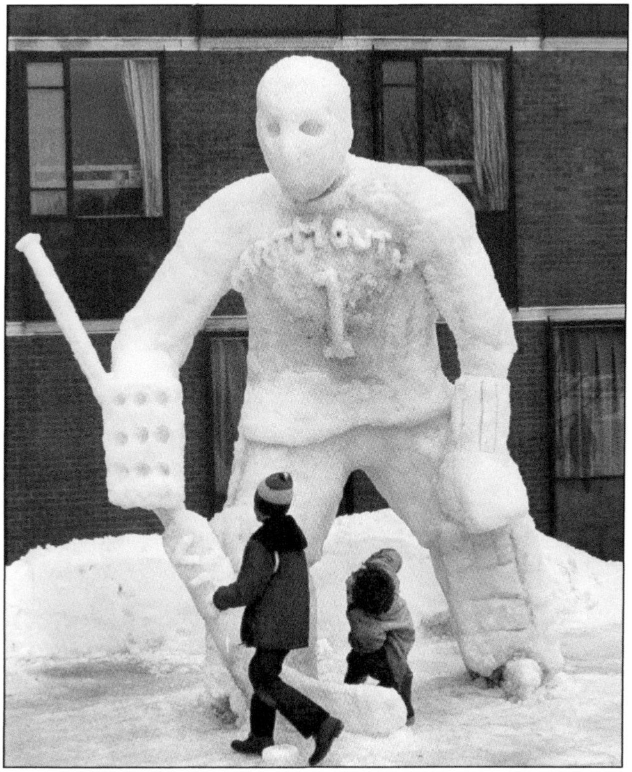

ICE IN HIS VEINS. Ironically, Dartmouth played at Cornell on Winter Carnival weekend in 1977. That did not deter student sculptors from recognizing Jeff Sollows. They carved a 10-foot ice sculpture to honor the Green goalie who backstopped Dartmouth to five wins in the last six games of a 12-12-2 campaign.

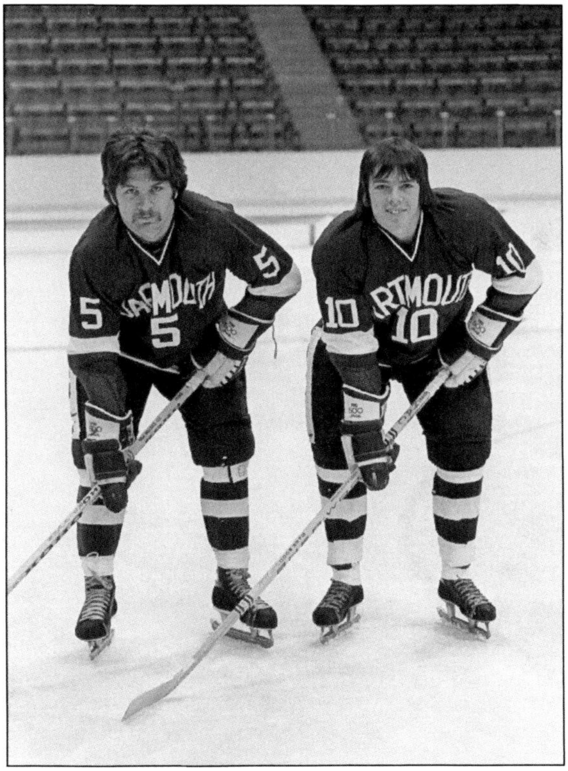

THE 1976–77 CO-CAPTAINS. Ron Dove '77 (left), a defenseman, and wing Brian McCloskey '77 were tenacious captains of the 1976–77 team and integral to the resurgence of Dartmouth hockey. Dove, only five feet seven inches tall, was two inches taller than McCloskey. Dove won All-Ivy honors as a junior and had 71 career points (62 assists). McCloskey, now the head coach of women's hockey at the University of New Hampshire, had 92 career points (62 assists).

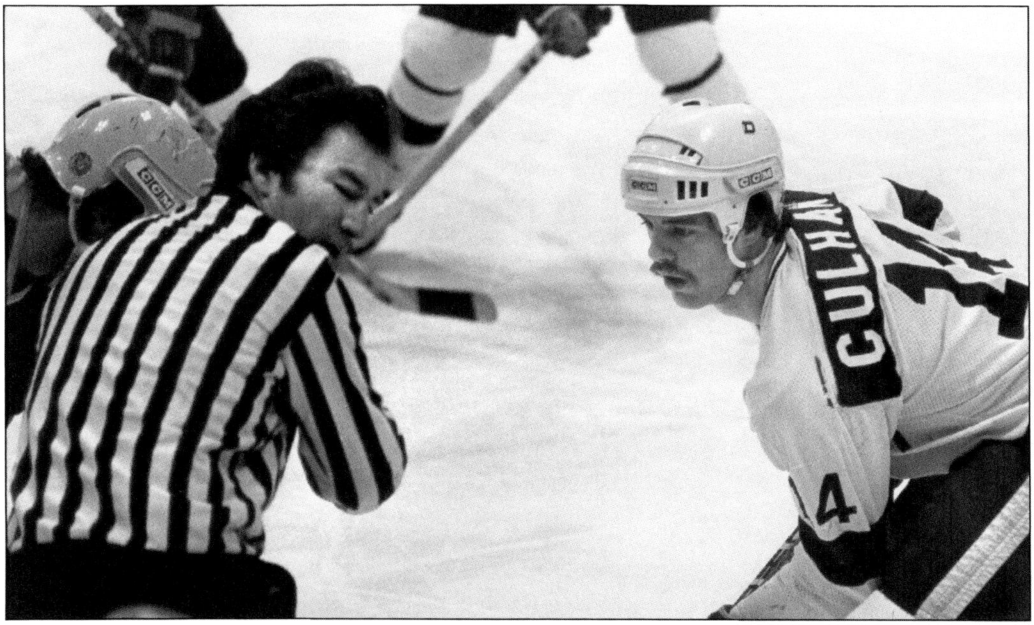

MARK CULHANE '79. The captain of Dartmouth's 1978–79 team, Mark Culhane is about to take a faceoff against Clarkson. The linesman, coincidentally, is Bill Riley Jr., son of Dartmouth legend Bill Riley '46. Culhane's two power-play goals ignited a 7-3 win over New Hampshire in the third-place game of the NCAA tournament in 1979, capping a career that included 44 goals among 103 points.

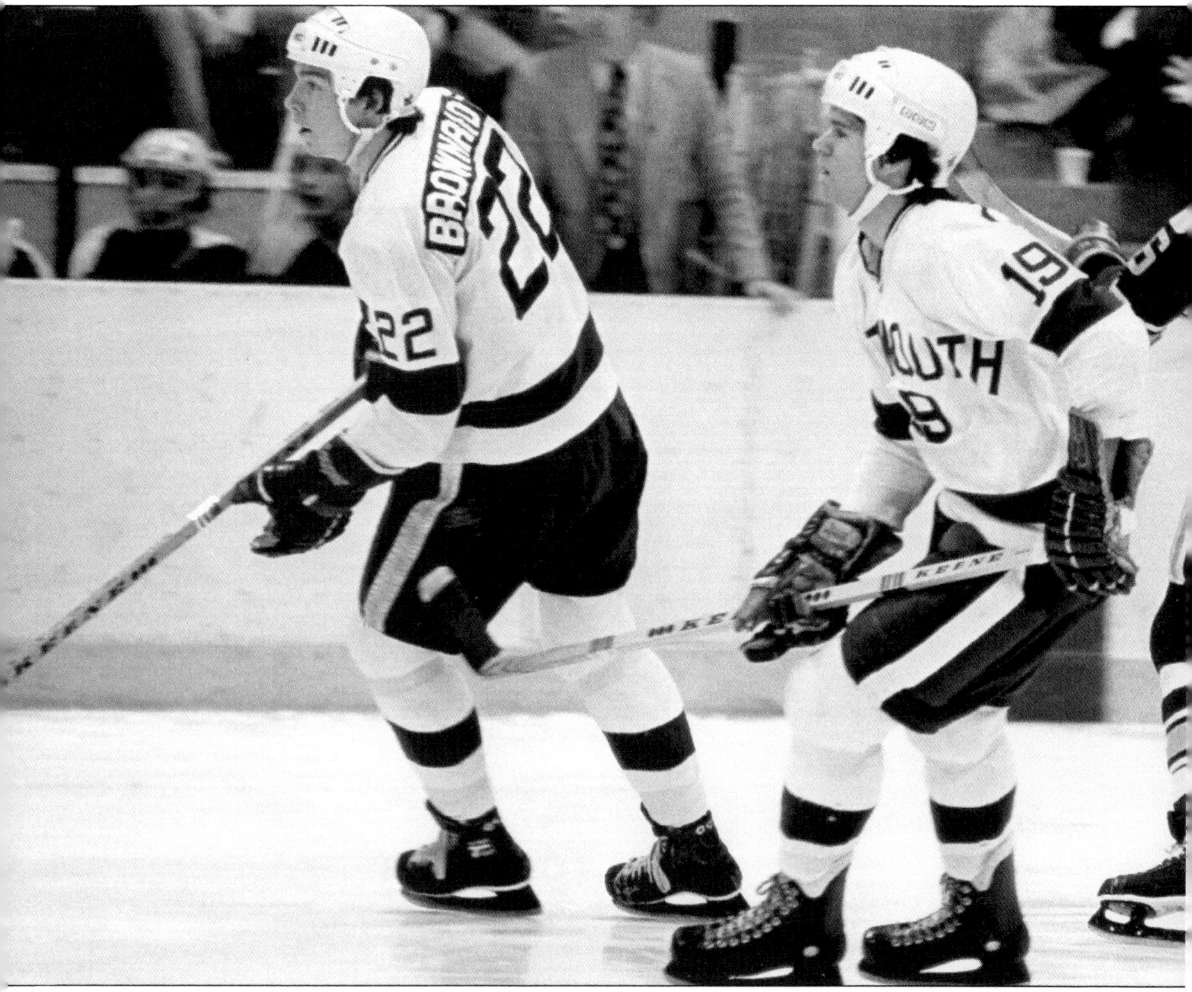

ROSCOE AND MURPH. Ross "Roscoe" Brownridge '80, the center, and right wing Dennis Murphy '80 ranked as Dartmouth's most explosive scoring tandem in three decades as they paced the Green to successive NCAA tournament appearances. As a sophomore and a senior, Brownridge was Dartmouth's scoring leader, and Murphy was next. They reversed places as juniors when Murphy had 48 points (Brownridge had 46). Brownridge ranks third among Dartmouth's all-time scoring leaders. He finished with 166 points, including 70 goals; 30 of them came in 1979–80. Brownridge was a two-time All-Ivy pick. In 1980, he was All-ECAC and an All-American. With 136 career points (80 assists), Murphy ranks sixth among the Green's all-time scorers. Since graduating, Murphy has played and coached hockey in Europe. He played one season in Denmark and has been in France, as a player, coach, and director of club sports programs, first in Briancon and, since 1994, in Villard de Lans.

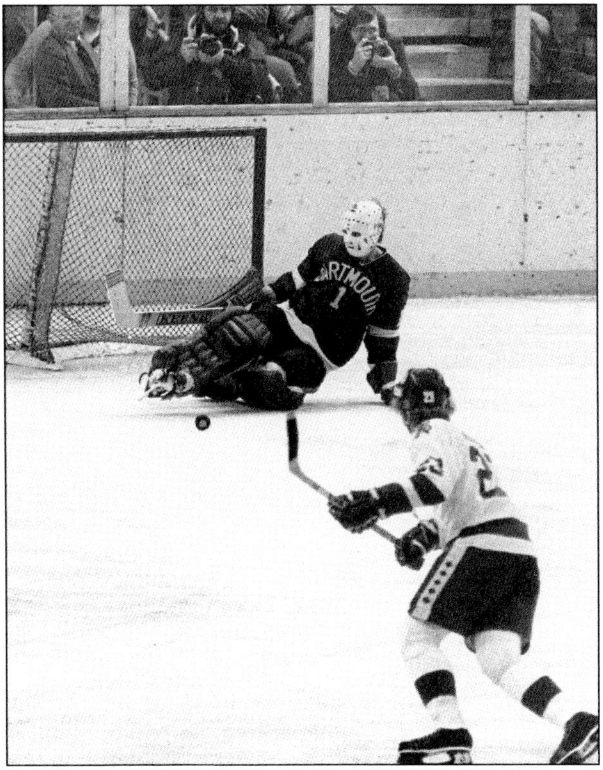

Bob Gaudet '81, the Player. As a freshman, Bob Gaudet was the backup goalie to his classmate Jim Jankowski. For the next three seasons, the Dartmouth net belonged to Gaudet. He was the All-Ivy goaltender as the Green won the Ivy League title and advanced to the NCAA tournament in 1979 and 1980. Gaudet ranks third all-time in career saves (2,129) and career wins (40). He was co-captain of the 1980–81 team and soon after launched his career in coaching.

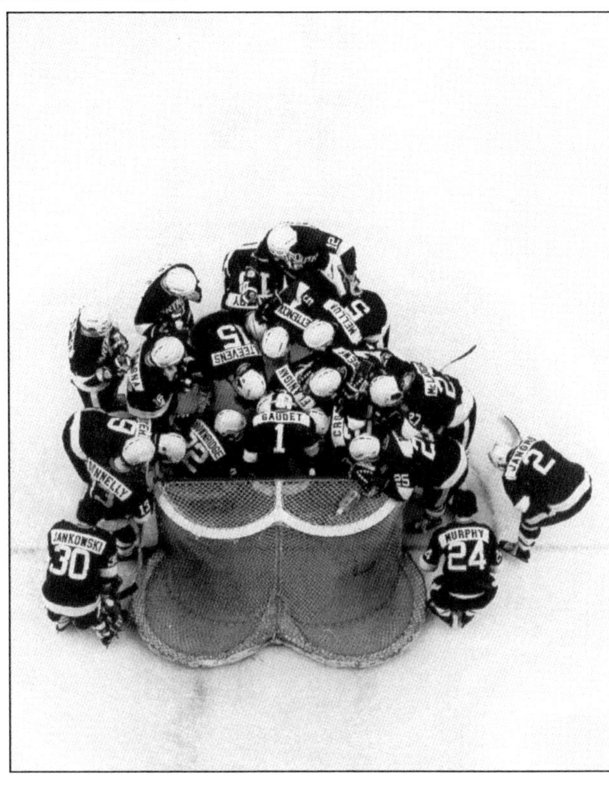

Pregame. The 1979–80 team surrounds goaltender Bob Gaudet (1) and co-captain Ross Brownridge (22) for a pep talk prior to the Green's NCAA tourney action at Providence in 1980. In both 1979 and 1980, Dartmouth lost to the University of North Dakota in the NCAA semifinals and then rebounded to take the third-place games, beating New Hampshire and Cornell, respectively.

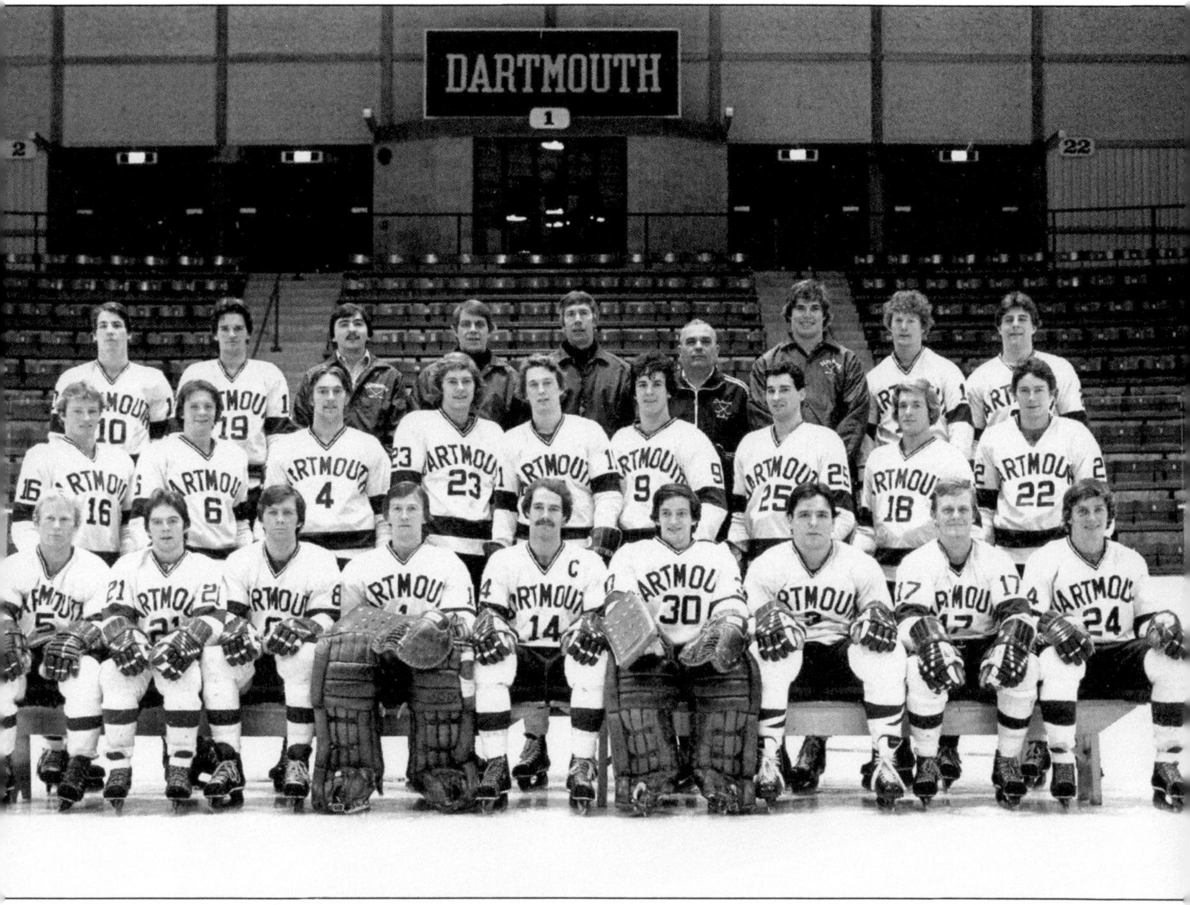

ANOTHER NCAA TOURNAMENT APPEARANCE. Dartmouth's 1978–79 team posted a 19-9-2 record, the most wins for a Green hockey team since the 1947–48 team finished 21-3-0. Led by captain Mark Culhane '79, Dartmouth won the Ivy League title for the first time since 1964. In the ECAC Tournament, Dartmouth beat Clarkson in overtime 2-1 with Dennis Murphy's goal. The Green stopped Boston University 5-3 in the ECAC semifinals at Boston Garden but fell to New Hampshire 3-2 for the ECAC title. Dartmouth beat UNH a week later in the NCAA third-place game at Detroit's Olympia rink. "We had good 'team' players, not stars. There were few players who hadn't been on the jayvee team in their early years," said coach George Crowe. That included high-scoring Ross Brownridge '80. Culhane was one of eight seniors on this team who were completing four seasons with Crowe—defensemen Bob Grant, Dennis Hughes, and Chris Sosnowski and wings Joey Tomlak, Mark Mile, Steve Higgins, and Buddy Teevens (front row, extreme right). Teevens led Dartmouth to the Ivy League football title in 1978 and is now Dartmouth's head football coach.

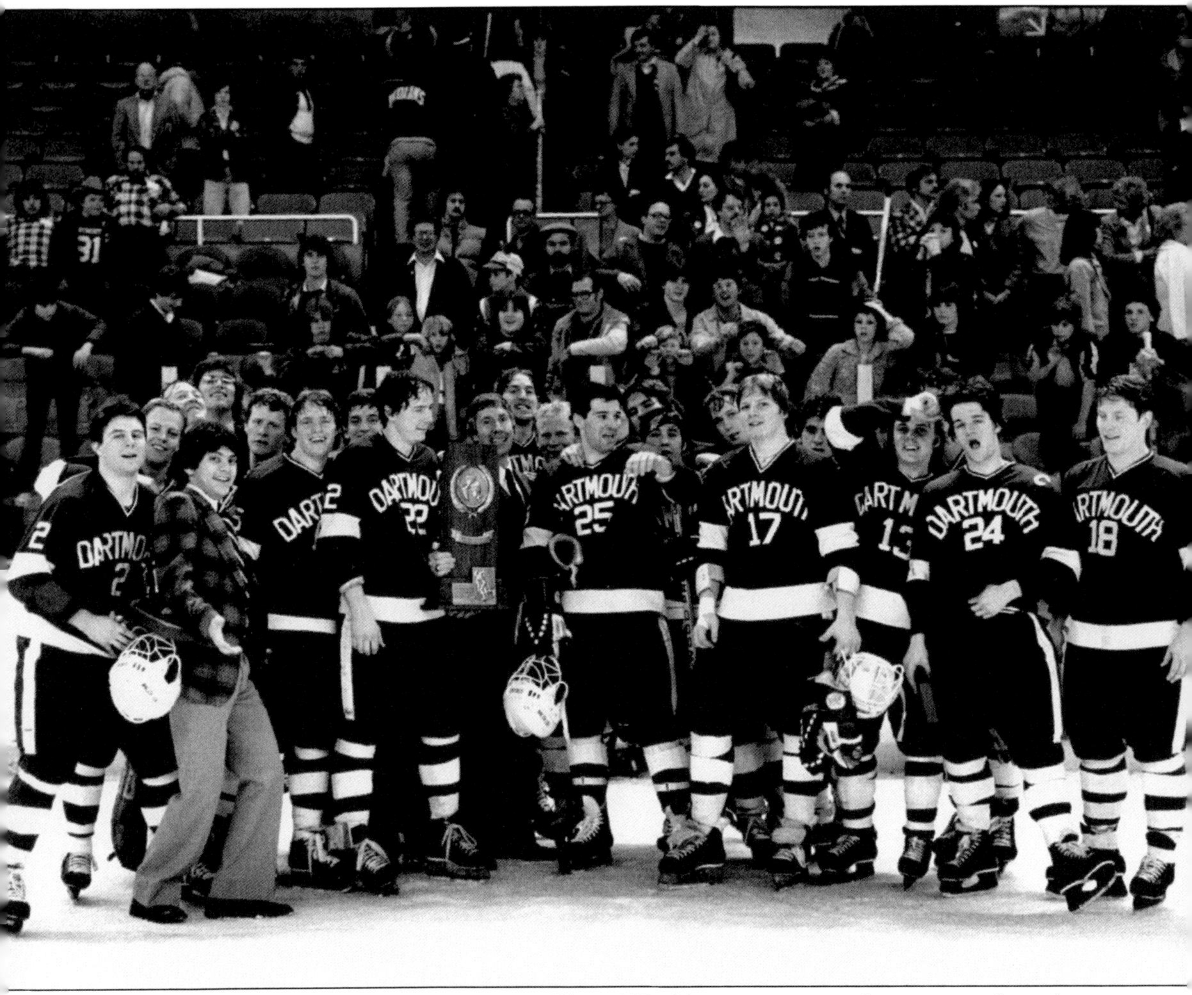

BACK TO THE NCAA TOURNAMENT. The 1979–80 team wrote a fitting sequel to the prior season's success. Dartmouth repeated with 19 wins (19-11-1) and another Ivy League title. The Green swept past RPI and Clarkson to reach the ECAC Tournament final at Boston Garden, where they lost to Cornell 5-1. The team lost to North Dakota in the NCAA tourney semifinal but is shown here celebrating its 8-4 win over Cornell in the third-place game at the Providence Civic Center. Co-captains Ross Brownridge and Dennis Murphy set the scoring pace on a team that had four other seniors—forwards Rich Ryerson and Ric Mellum and defensemen Don O'Brien and Barry Ryan. O'Brien is an interesting story. When he was being recruited to Dartmouth, an inquiry was made to the admissions office, "Can we consider Don O'Brien because he's dyslexic?" The one-sentence reply: "Nelson Rockefeller (class of 1930 and later vice president of the United States) was, too." In 1980, Crowe was named the national coach of the year.

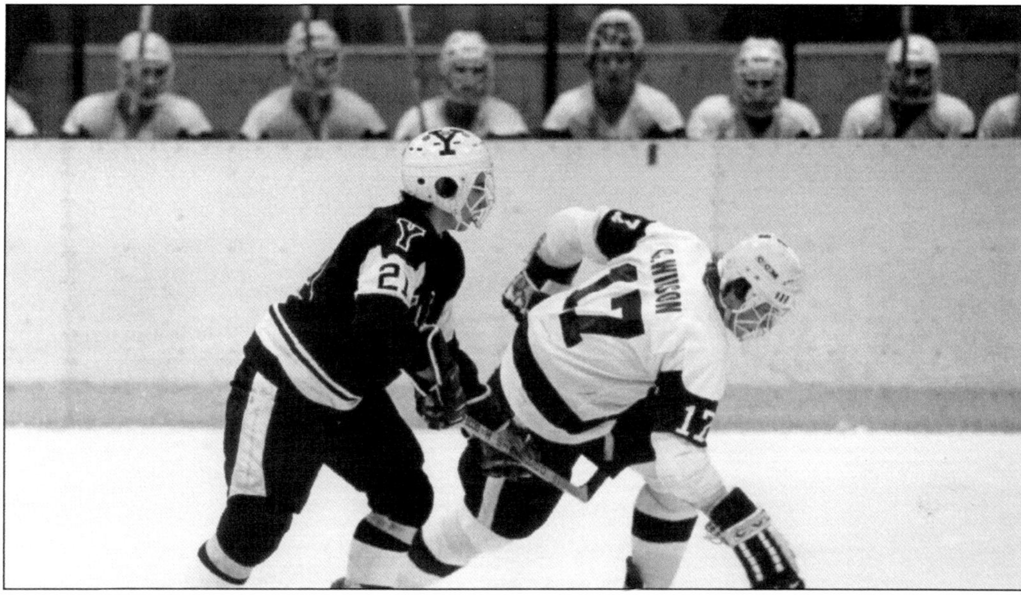

CAREY WILSON '83. As a freshman in 1979–80, Carey Wilson, a center, trailed Ross Brownridge and Dennis Murphy among Dartmouth's scorers. As a sophomore, he was third behind All-Ivy wing Rick Wilson '81 and captain Mark Bedard '81. Wilson's hockey future was at a higher level. Though he returned to complete his education over time, Wilson went on to a 12-year career in the National Hockey League with Calgary, Hartford, and the New York Rangers. He was also a member of Canada's Olympic team in 1984.

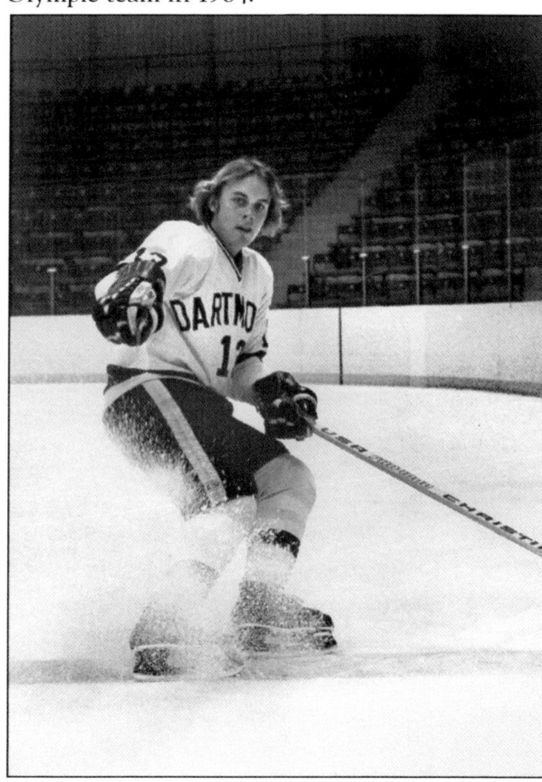

JOHN DONNELLY '83. From 1979 to 1983, John Donnelly became Dartmouth's all-time scoring leader among defensemen. The diminutive Donnelly fit perfectly into coach George Crowe's style of play. Donnelly set a record for points by a Dartmouth freshman with 28 in 1979–80. He holds the Dartmouth career record for assists by a defenseman (83), and his career total of 116 points equaled the scoring of Hall of Fame wing Joe Riley '49.

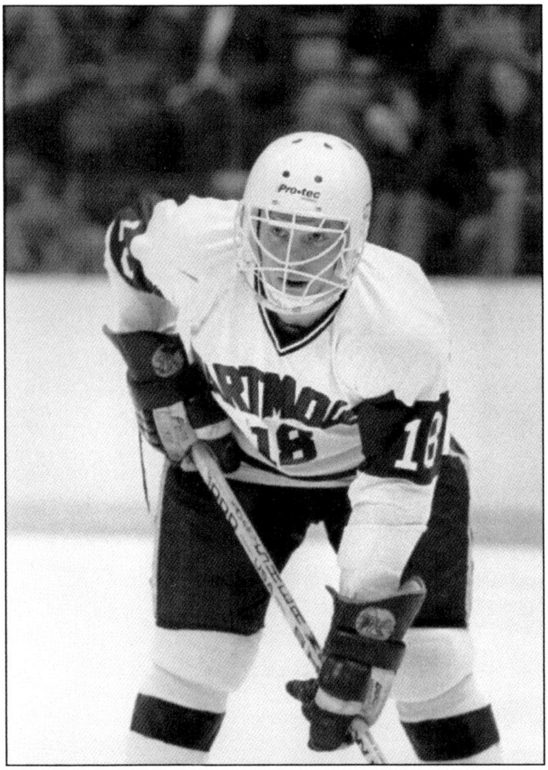

PETER LAVERY '83. One of three brothers (Pat '84 and Jim '86 also marked the Dartmouth athletic scene in the early 1980s), Peter Lavery earned 11 letters (four in hockey and baseball, three in football) from 1979 to 1983. He played 75 games as a hockey wing (35 career points) at Dartmouth after being a halfback and return specialist in football. He was captain of the 1983 baseball team (his brothers were teammates) and won the Archibald Prize as Dartmouth's outstanding student-athlete in 1983.

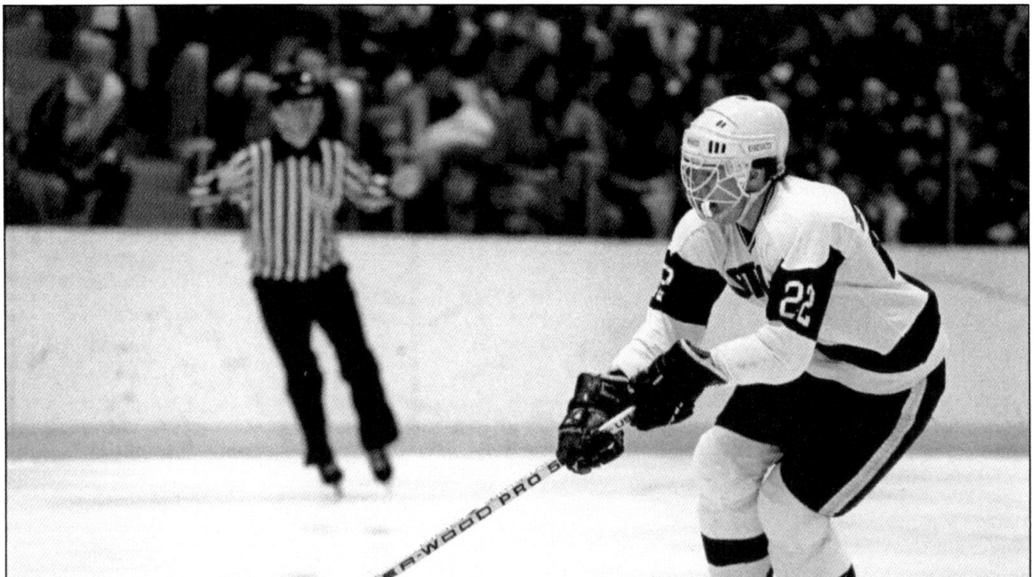

BRUCE CULLEN '84. During four seasons (1980 to 1984), Bruce Cullen was on the ice for 103 of Dartmouth's 104 games. The wing finished with 107 points (48 goals). The low point: he was the team's scoring leader in 1983–84 as the Green struggled to a 3-23 record. Changes in admissions standards in the Ivy League in the early 1980s (applied immediately at Dartmouth—the other colleges used a rolling schedule) put George Crowe at a recruiting disadvantage. He left coaching after the 1983–84 season.

SIX

Crowe's Women 1986–1998

George Crowe's striking success coaching men's hockey at Dartmouth was a prelude to his enormous success coaching women's hockey. He attributed it to their attitude, but it was more that Crowe's turn of mind was more attuned to the women's game. Foremost, Crowe was a teacher. At the heart of his ethos were two elements: skill and flair. These were the elements that Dartmouth's women of this era possessed in surplus. He harnessed them, he refined them, he transformed them from ore to precious mettle. In some cases, that meant a gold medal in the Olympics.

In many ways, the women's teams eclipsed the men's in these years. Their players were more colorful, their style of play more sophisticated, their achievements more memorable. Judy Parish '91 was the sort of athlete Dartmouth produced in the era when Dartmouth athletes were all male—and dominant All-Ivy. She held court on the ice both as a player and a coach, with spectacular results in each role. Gretchen Ulion '94 was perhaps the dominant Ivy player of her time. She collected Olympic gold in 1998. So, too, did Sarah Tueting '98. She is remembered today as perhaps the best Dartmouth goalie since Bob Gaudet. Sarah Hood '98 was Dartmouth's first female hockey All-American and a member of the U.S. national team. Sarah Devens '96 may be the greatest tragic figure in all of Dartmouth sports history, a standout in hockey, field hockey, and lacrosse who collected three All-Ivy laurels and twice was selected an All-American in lacrosse. Her suicide in 1995 sent shivers through all who knew her at Hanover, and ripples across all of sports.

In an odd way, the Devens tragedy marked the sport at Dartmouth and helped propel women's hockey to another level. The torch was passed to others who held it high. Players like Sarah Howald '96 and Michelle Erickson '96 led Dartmouth to its first 20-win season. Before Crowe completed his mission in Hanover, he had won four Ivy women's championships.

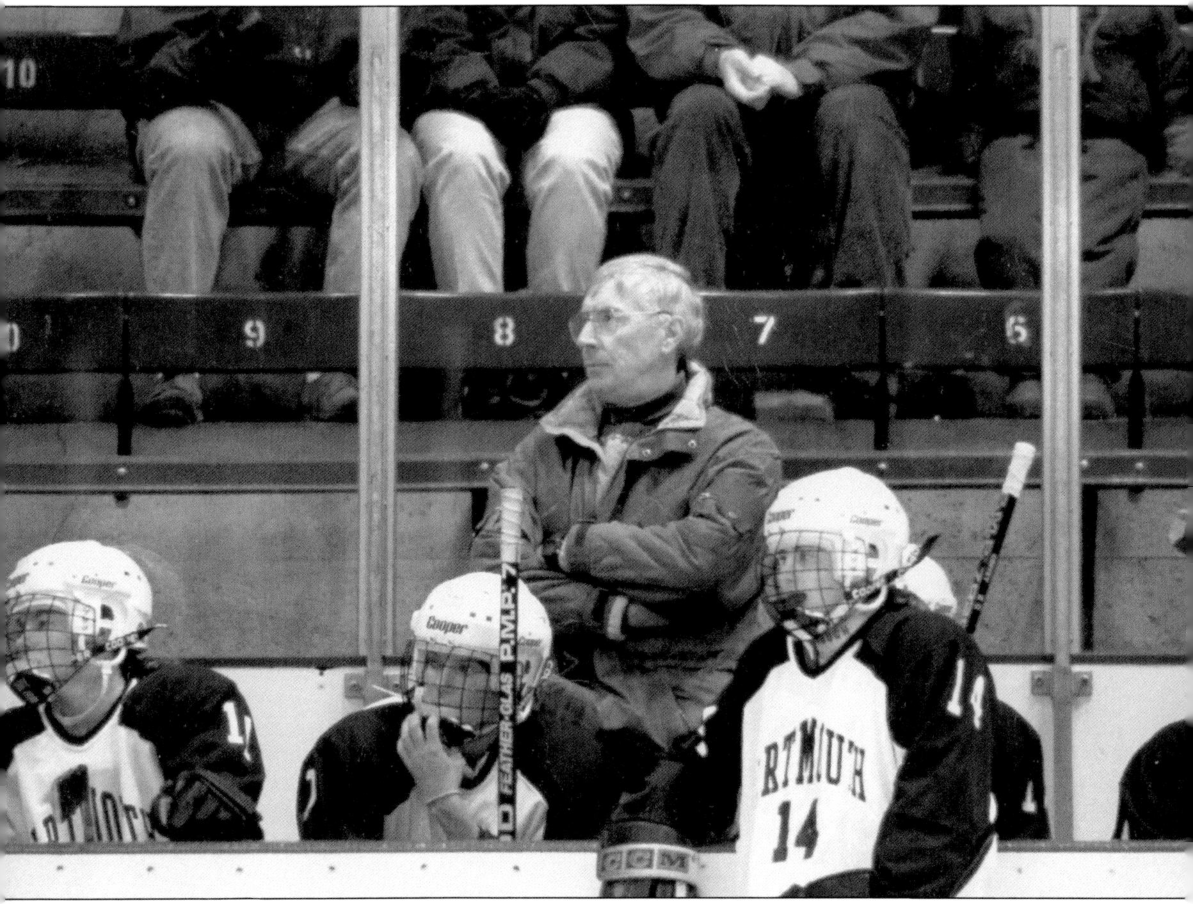

George Crowe, the Women's Coach. Over nearly a quarter-century of coaching prep and college men's teams, Crowe decided, in 1984, to devote full attention to the Elite Sports Camps he had developed. He had a 109-127-8 record as the Dartmouth men's coach (1975 to 1984). Including four years at Oswego State (55-23-3), his overall college coaching record was 162-150-11. When Crowe left coaching in 1984, so did Mark Panella '78 after six years as the Dartmouth women's coach. Panella's assistant for five seasons was Bob Ceplikas '78, who assisted Chuck Metz with the Green women in 1984–85 but declined the head coaching post due to his job in the Dartmouth admissions office. In the summer of 1986, after one season with Amy Crafts at the helm, director of athletics Ted Leland asked Crowe to coach the women's team. Crowe agreed to try it for a year. He stayed for 12 winning seasons. When he finally retired from coaching in 1998, Crowe had led the Dartmouth women to a record of 196-107-20 and four Ivy League championships and had established women's hockey at Dartmouth as one of the nation's preeminent programs.

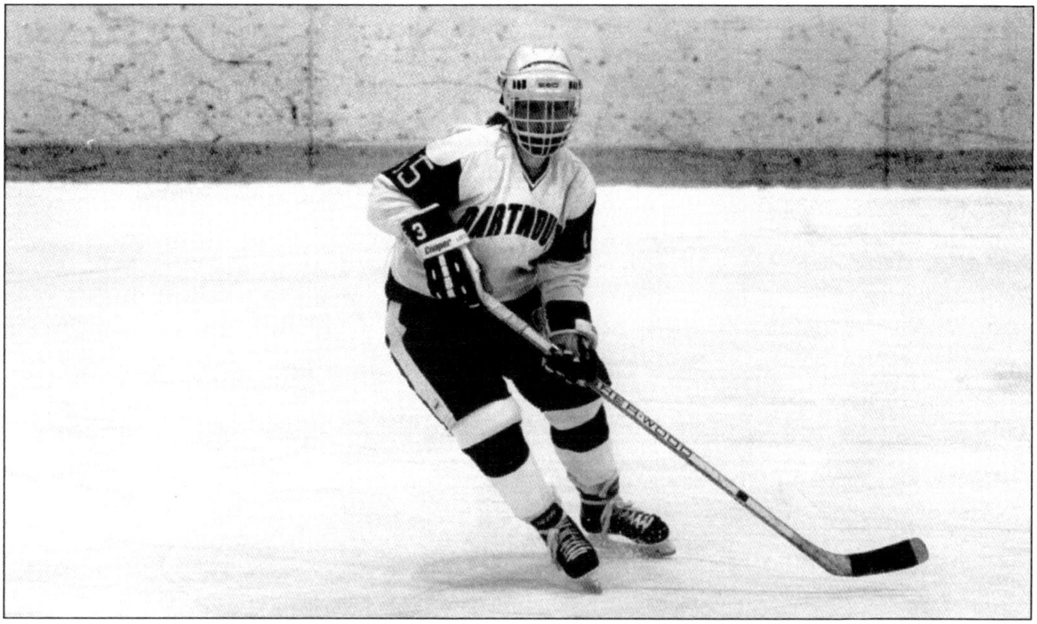

GINA GUALTIERI '89. When her four-year career ended in 1989, Gina Gualtieri ranked second to Estey Ticknor '85 in scoring with 109 points (64 goals, 45 assists). The center was Dartmouth's top scorer as a sophomore and junior. She grew up chasing pucks with her brother Joe '90, a four-year defenseman for the Dartmouth men's team. In 1986–87, Gualtieri was Dartmouth's most valuable offensive player.

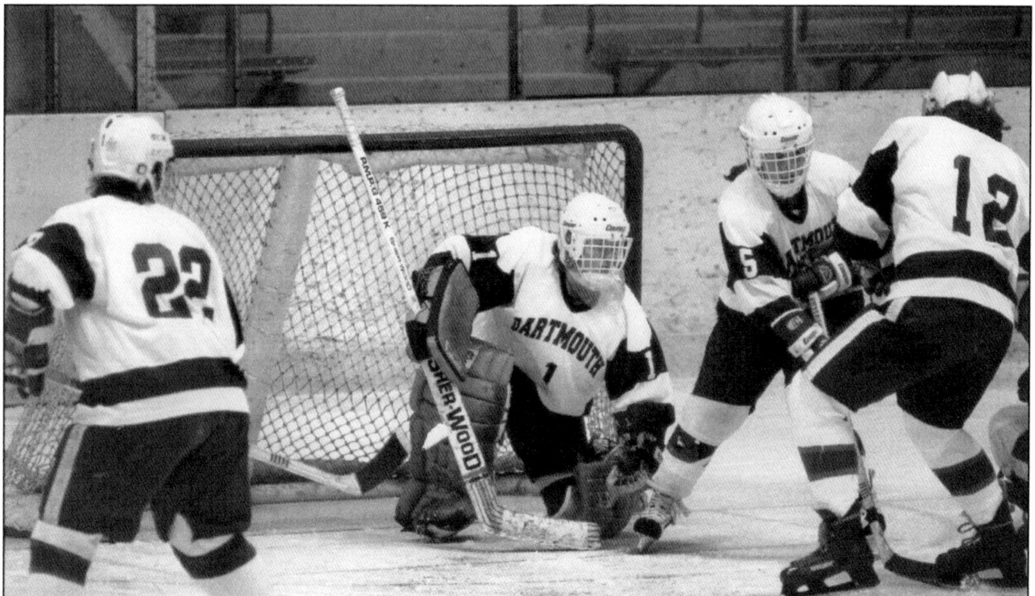

KELLEY COYNE '90. As a freshman, and again as a senior, Kelley Coyne was named the All-Ivy League goaltender. Coach George Crowe had only 15 skaters in 1986–87. He said, "Kelley made a big difference." Coyne defended Dartmouth's goal in 96 of 98 games (the Green won 54 times). Coyne's single-season save percentage of .931 (twice) and her career save percentage (.929, 2,479 saves) are Dartmouth records.

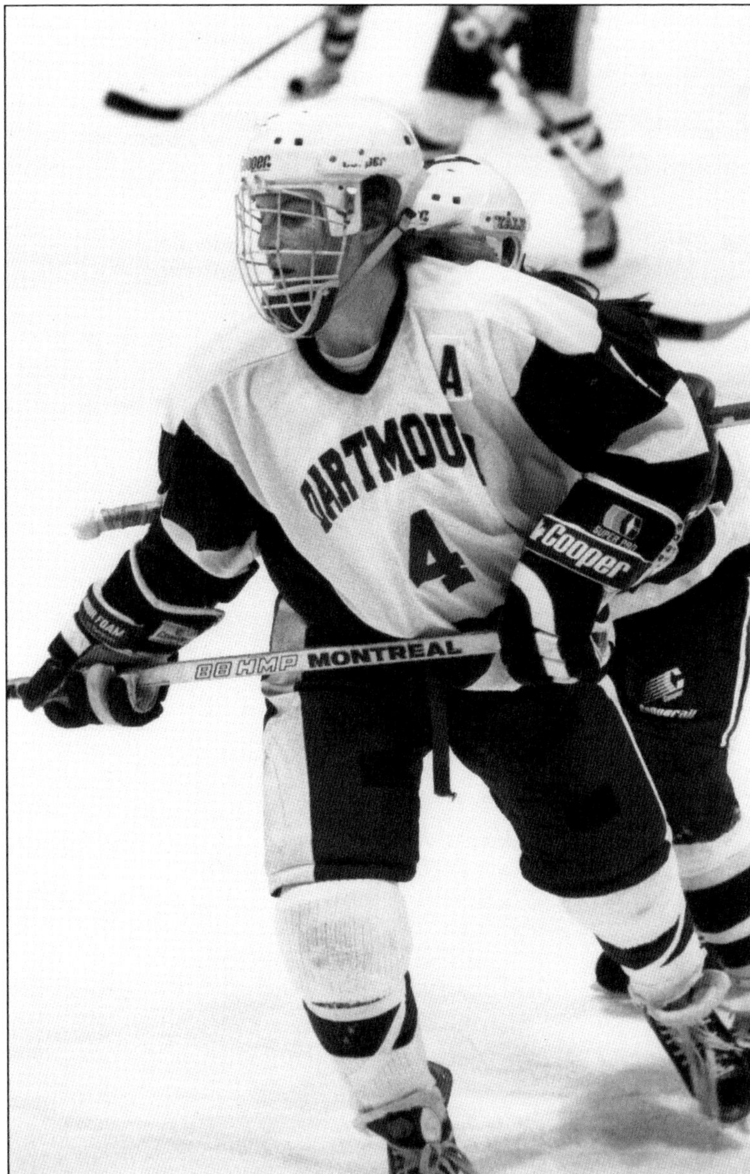

JUDY PARISH '91, THE PLAYER. In the 1980s, only three New England college women's hockey teams (New Hampshire, Providence, Northeastern) were scholarship programs. But women's hockey was exploding, and through his summer camps and watching the all-star programs in Massachusetts and Connecticut, George Crowe knew where the promising talent was located. In 1987, one of Dartmouth's greatest skaters, Judy Parish, arrived from West Hartford, Connecticut. Parish played defense for two seasons and then became a forward as a junior and senior. She was All-Ivy League three times and holds the Dartmouth records for points in a game by a forward (12) and a defenseman (8). Parish had 215 career points (89 goals), second only to Gretchen Ulion '94. In 1990, Parish was a member of the first U.S. women's national hockey team that won the silver medal in the inaugural World Ice Hockey Tournament. Parish became Crowe's assistant and then associate head coach before succeeding him in 1998.

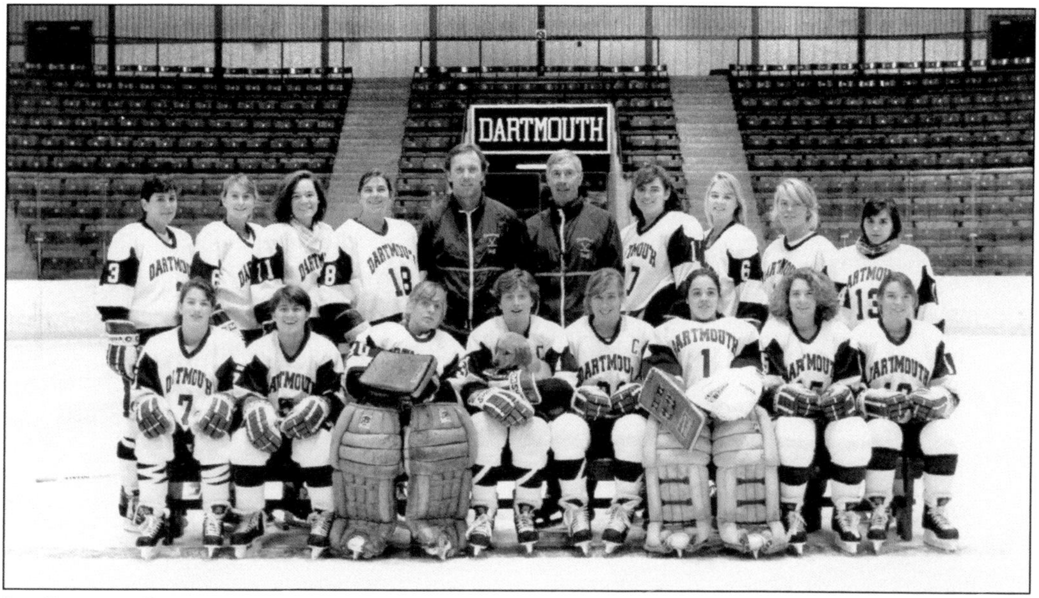

IVY LEAGUE CHAMPIONS, 1990–91. "Women are more coachable and more fun to work with than men," said coach George Crowe. "They're no less competitive but they have a better perspective." That atmosphere produced Dartmouth's first Ivy League title in 1990–91. Led by co-captains Judy Parish and Robin Chandler, the Green posted the best record in their history (19-7-0) and swept to a 10-0-0 record in Ivy games. The Green outscored their 26 opponents 149-59.

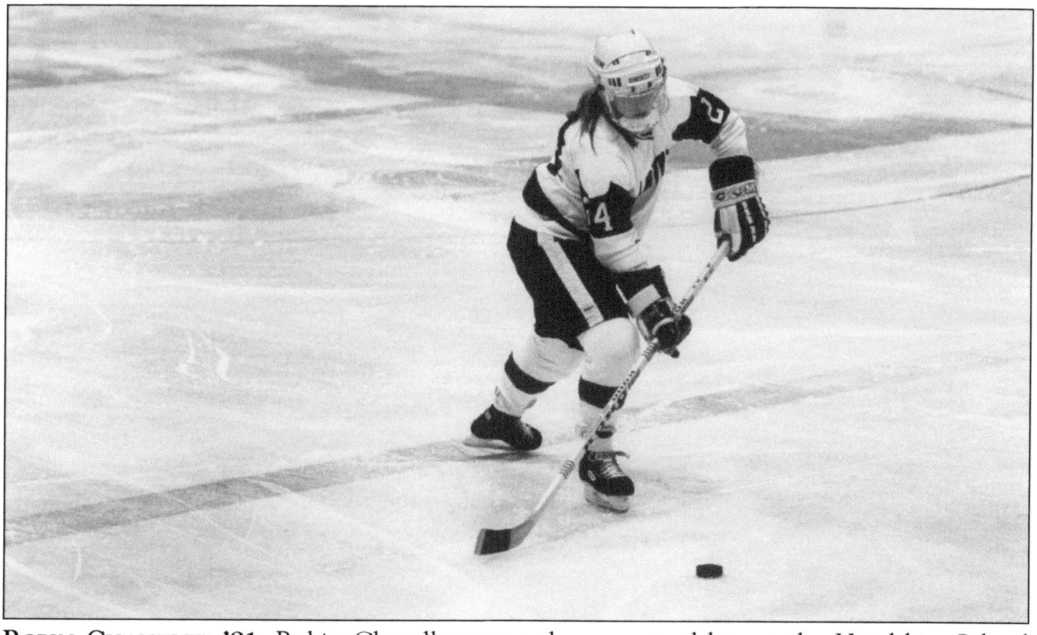

ROBIN CHANDLER '91. Robin Chandler was a three-sport athlete at the Hotchkiss School in Connecticut. She was a co-captain with Judy Parish of the Ivy League championship team in 1990–91 and the team's most valuable defensive player. She was the first female athlete to win 12 varsity letters at Hotchkiss, where she is now the director of athletics, one of several Dartmouth women who have become prep school and college coaches and administrators.

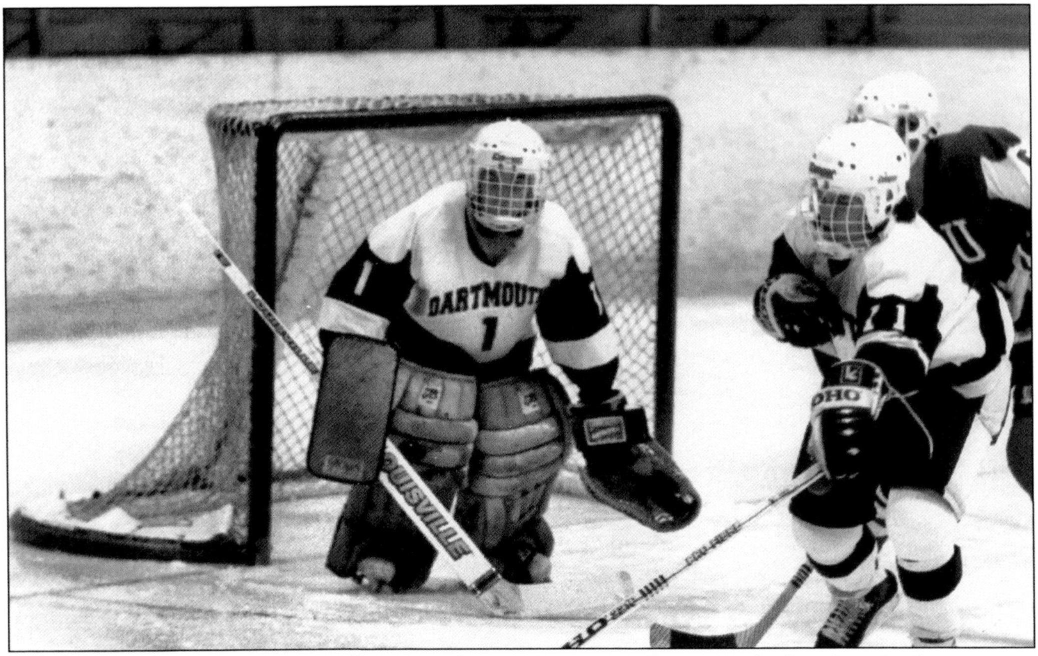

Sarah Millet '95. Sarah Millet played two seasons at Dartmouth, but her freshman year was memorable in 1991–92. In an 18-8-0 campaign, Dartmouth posted eight shutout wins, and Millet was in the Green goal for seven of them, a record. Her sister Elizabeth '92 was a wing and defenseman for the Green from 1988 to 1992.

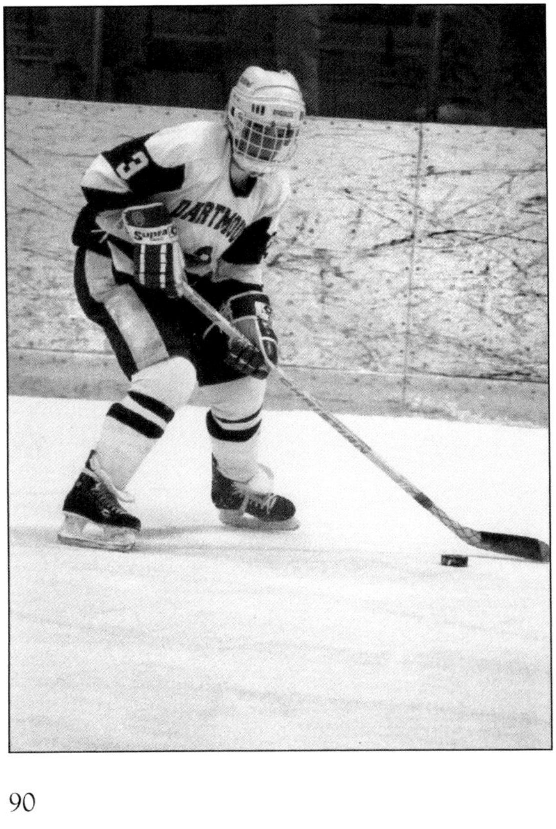

Lori Jacobs '92. Lori Jacobs ranks fourth all-time among Dartmouth's all-time scorers with 200 points (104 goals), but none of her goals were more memorable than her hat trick against Northeastern on January 14, 1992. The wing triggered a first-ever win over the Huskies, who came into the game as the nation's top-ranked team. Two weeks later, Jacobs had another three-goal game as the Green scored another first; they beat New Hampshire 4-1.

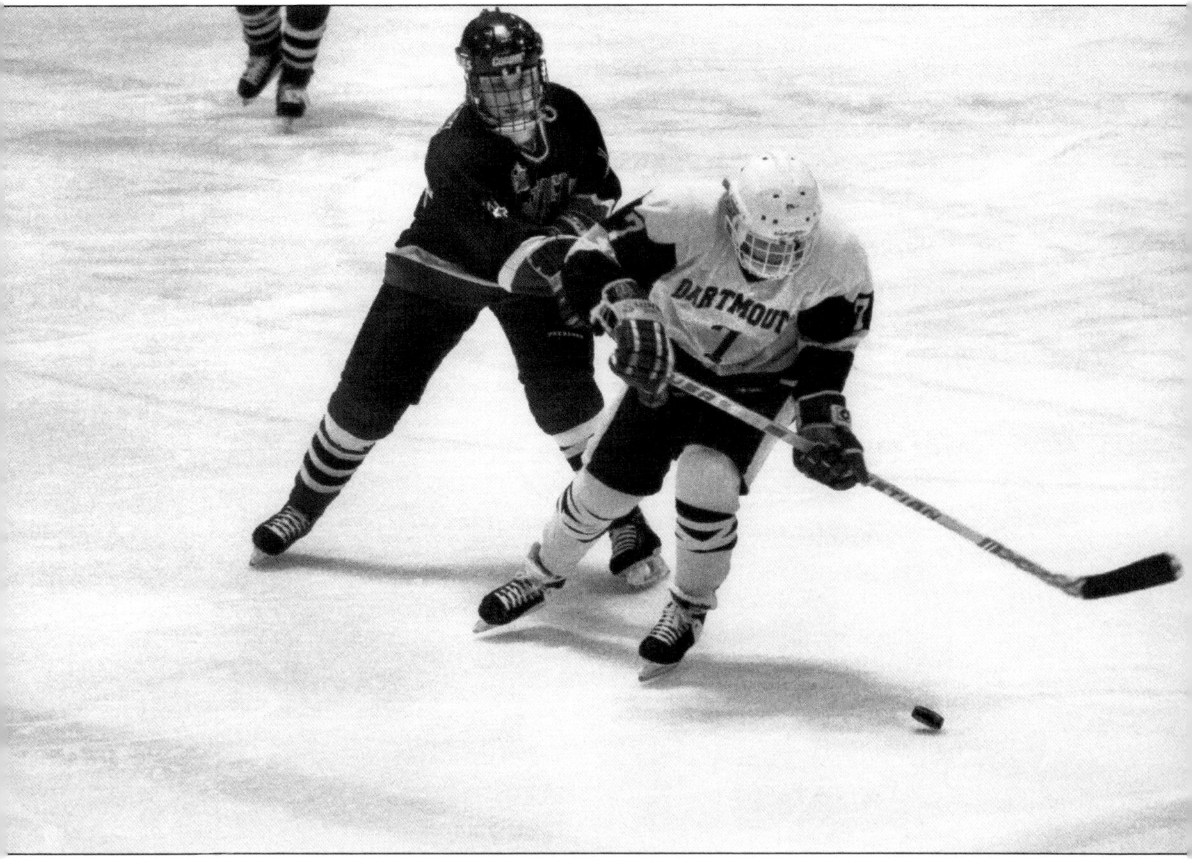

GRETCHEN ULION '94, "THE GREAT GRETA." "If we needed to make something happen," said coach George Crowe, "we sent Gretchen onto the ice. She was a natural scorer with great instincts." That sums up the role of Connecticut's Gretchen Ulion, who played four years as a center—and the center—of Dartmouth hockey from 1990 to 1994. By nearly 100 points (312 to 215 by Judy Parish '91, including 189 goals and 123 assists, both records), Ulion is the all-time women's scoring leader. Her numerous records include these that reflect her diversity: hat tricks in a season (seven, four times); power play goals in a season (11) and career (34); short-handed goals in a season (4) and career (12). She had a record eight goals in a 14-1 romp at Yale in 1994. Ulion was the Ivy League rookie of the year in 1991 and a unanimous All-Ivy selection three times. As a junior and senior, she was the Ivy League player of the year. She helped the Green to Ivy League championships in 1990–91 and again in 1992–93. Her achievements with the U.S. Olympic women's hockey team are recorded on page 96.

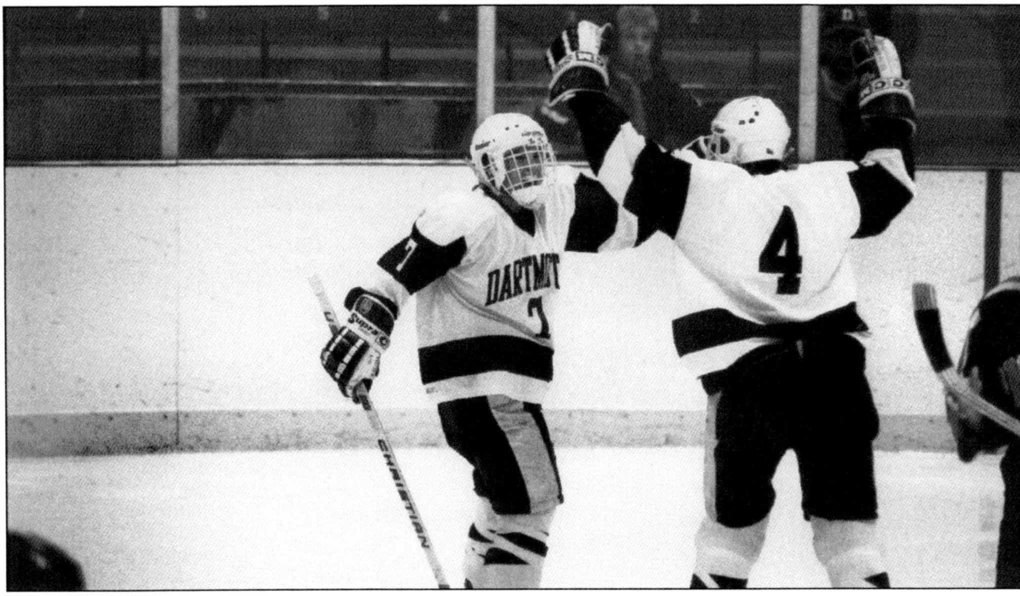

RACHEL ROCHAT '95. Growing up in New Jersey, Rachel Rochat (No. 4, celebrating a goal with Gretchen Ulion) was the only girl on a boys' team. The local media took notice, and she became a target, on and off the ice. She lettered twice in boys' hockey before quitting the team. Rochat resumed play at Dartmouth and collected 127 career points. In 1994–95, she was the captain and only senior on a young team that had a 16-8-4 record and won Dartmouth's third Ivy League title in five years.

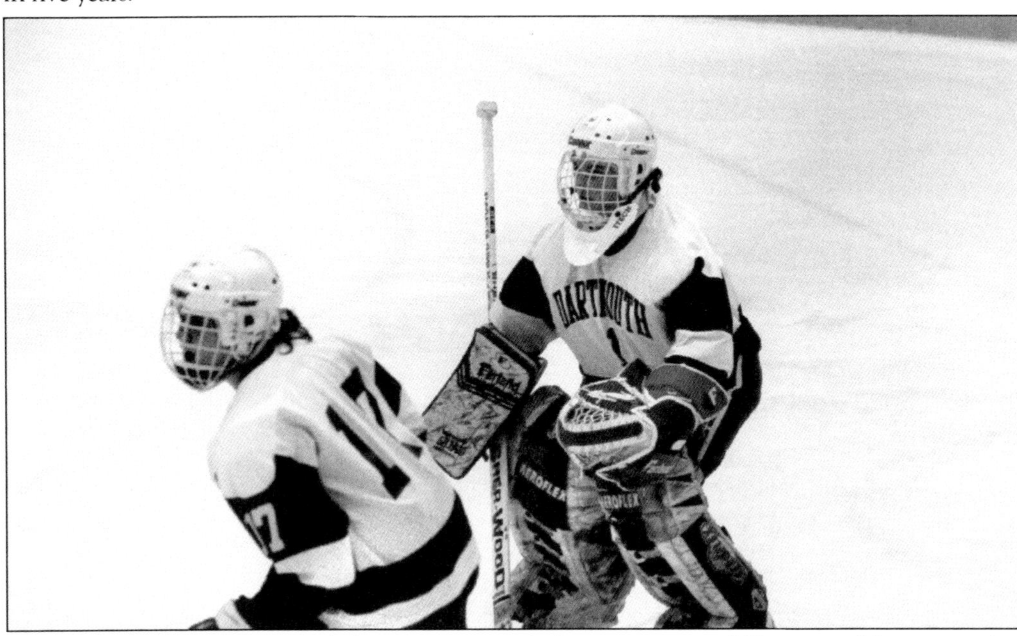

KIM COHEN '94. In 1994, defenseman Kim Cohen was named Dartmouth's outstanding female athlete. Cohen was selected twice to the All-Ivy League team in hockey and was also an All-Ivy second team choice as a goalie in lacrosse. In hockey, Cohen holds the Dartmouth assists by a defenseman in a season (36 in 1992–93) and a career (109). Cohen is shown here protecting goalie Sarah Lenczner '97.

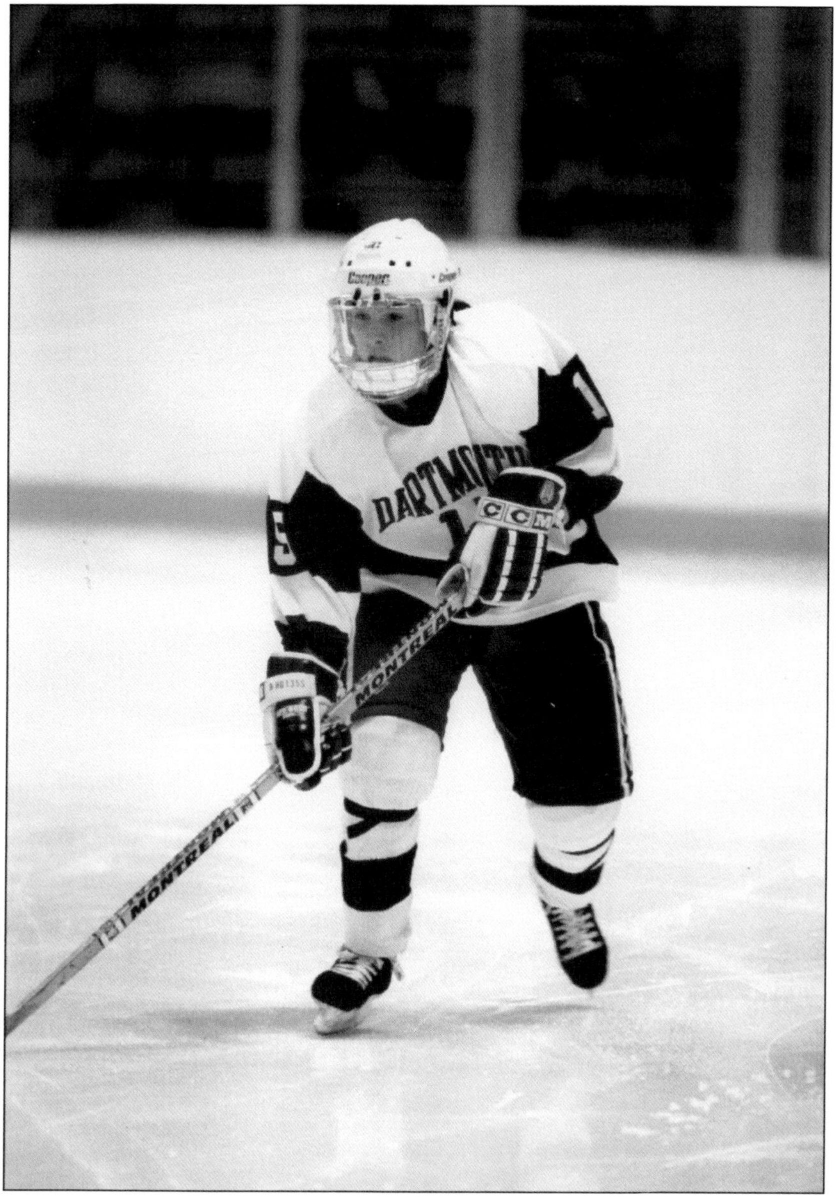

SARAH DEVENS '96. Sarah Devens was all-everything, perhaps Dartmouth's best-ever all-around female athlete, a standout in three sports (hockey, field hockey, lacrosse) who contemplated running the Boston Marathon in 1996. She would sneak in some skating at Thompson Arena during the summer, an outlet before field hockey began. She loved to play pranks, and one of her pet phrases was "Bring it on." It was a burden that "the Devil" from Essex, Massachusetts, hid from everyone—until the day in July 1995, as her senior year was about to begin, when Devens, alone at home, took her own life. She was co-captain-elect of Dartmouth's 1995–96 hockey team. In three seasons on the ice, Devens had already scored 108 points. She was the Ivy League and ECAC rookie of the year and All-Ivy in 1992–93. Twice, she was a unanimous All-Ivy selection in field hockey. She was a two-time All-American in lacrosse (though only second-team All-Ivy). "Sarah's death was a tragedy," said coach George Crowe. "She was a national level player in three sports."

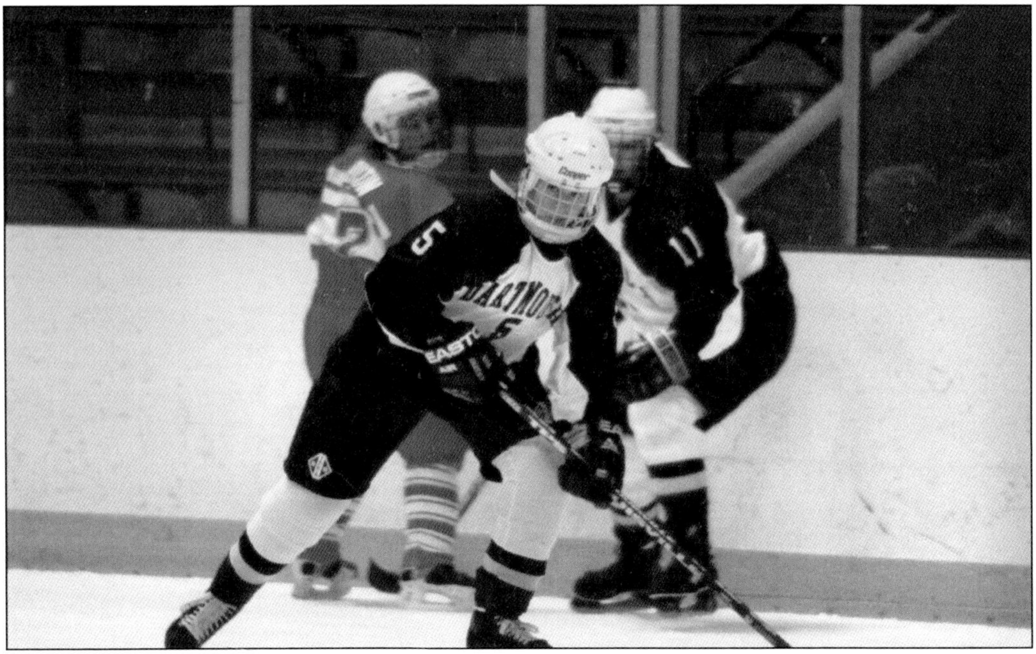

SARAH HOWALD '96. After Sarah Devens died, leadership of Dartmouth's team in 1995–96 belonged to Sarah Howald (5) and Michelle Erickson '96. They would lead the Green to their first 20-win season (20-9-3). Howald, the team's scoring leader and an All-Ivy selection, finished with 146 points, sixth on the all-time scoring list.

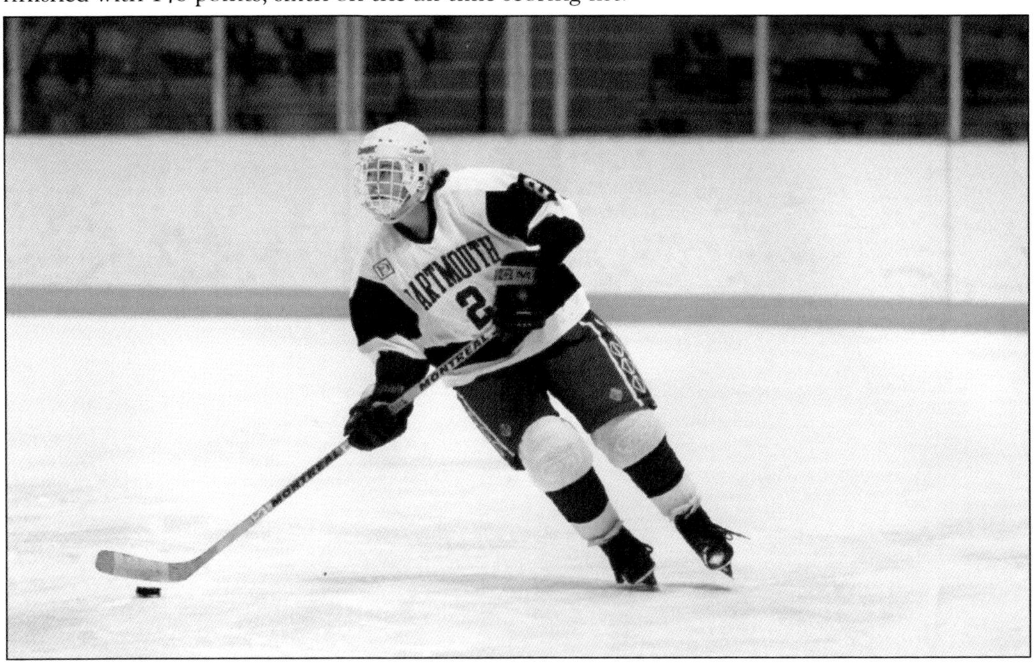

AMY COELHO '97. A defenseman, Amy Coelho was an All-Ivy choice as a junior and senior and was also named to the All-ECAC team in 1997. In 116 games, Coelho had 87 points (53 assists). After a knee injury ended her hopes for a place on the U.S. Olympic team in 1998, she made the U.S. national team (with Sarah Hood '98) in 1999.

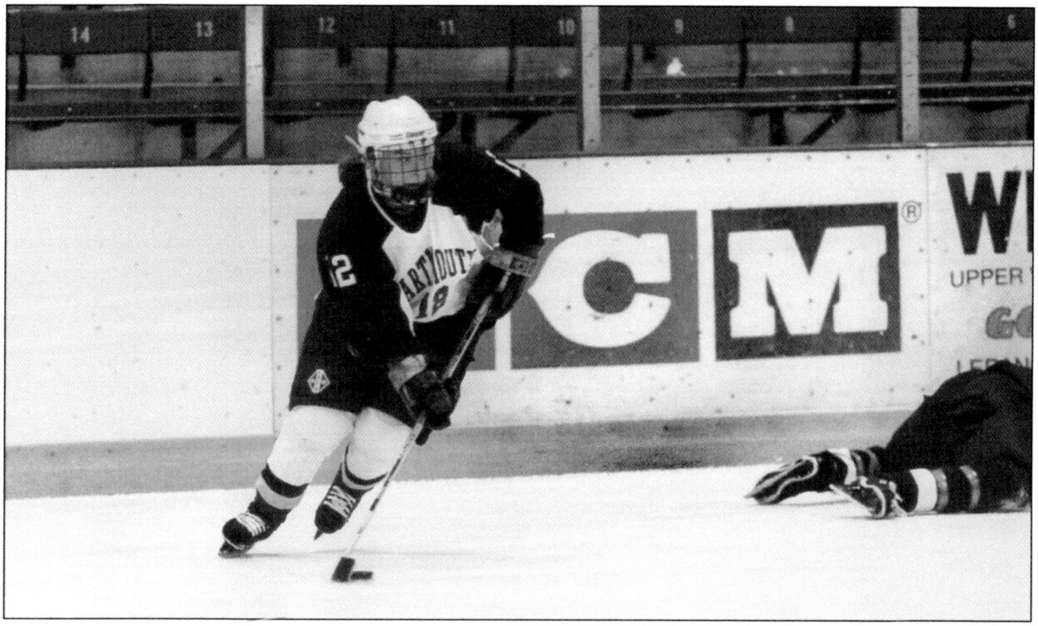

MICHELYNE PINARD '98. A forward, Michelyne Pinard was Dartmouth's third-leading scorer as the Green won its fourth Ivy League title in George Crowe's last season as the women's coach. Dartmouth had another 20-win season (20-9-1). She closed her career with 110 points (62 assists). Also a standout in soccer, she is now the women's soccer coach at Williams College.

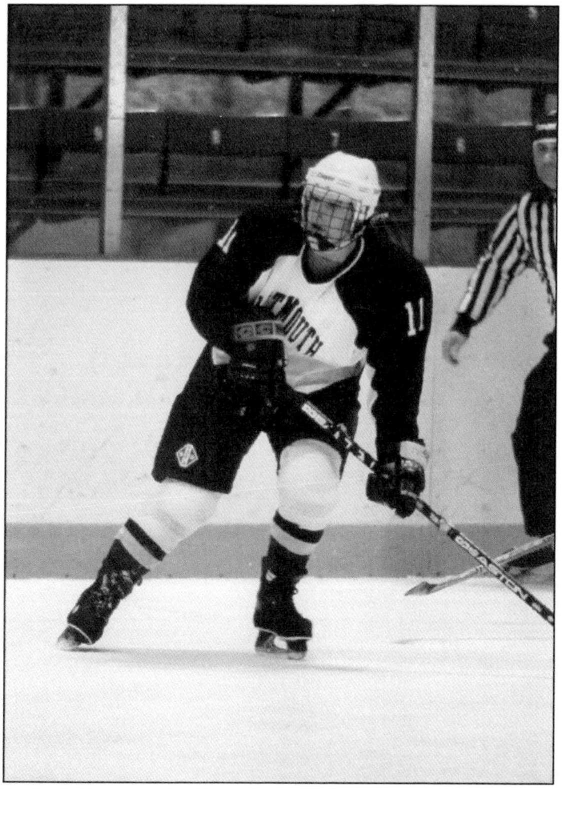

SARAH HOOD '98. Sarah Hood was named twice to the All-Ivy team (1997, 1998) and All-ECAC as a senior when she became Dartmouth's first All-American selection and a finalist for the inaugural Patty Kazmaier Award that recognizes the outstanding player in women's intercollegiate hockey. Hood ranks fifth all-time among Dartmouth scorers with 147 points (73 goals, 74 assists). She was a member of the U.S. national team in 1999.

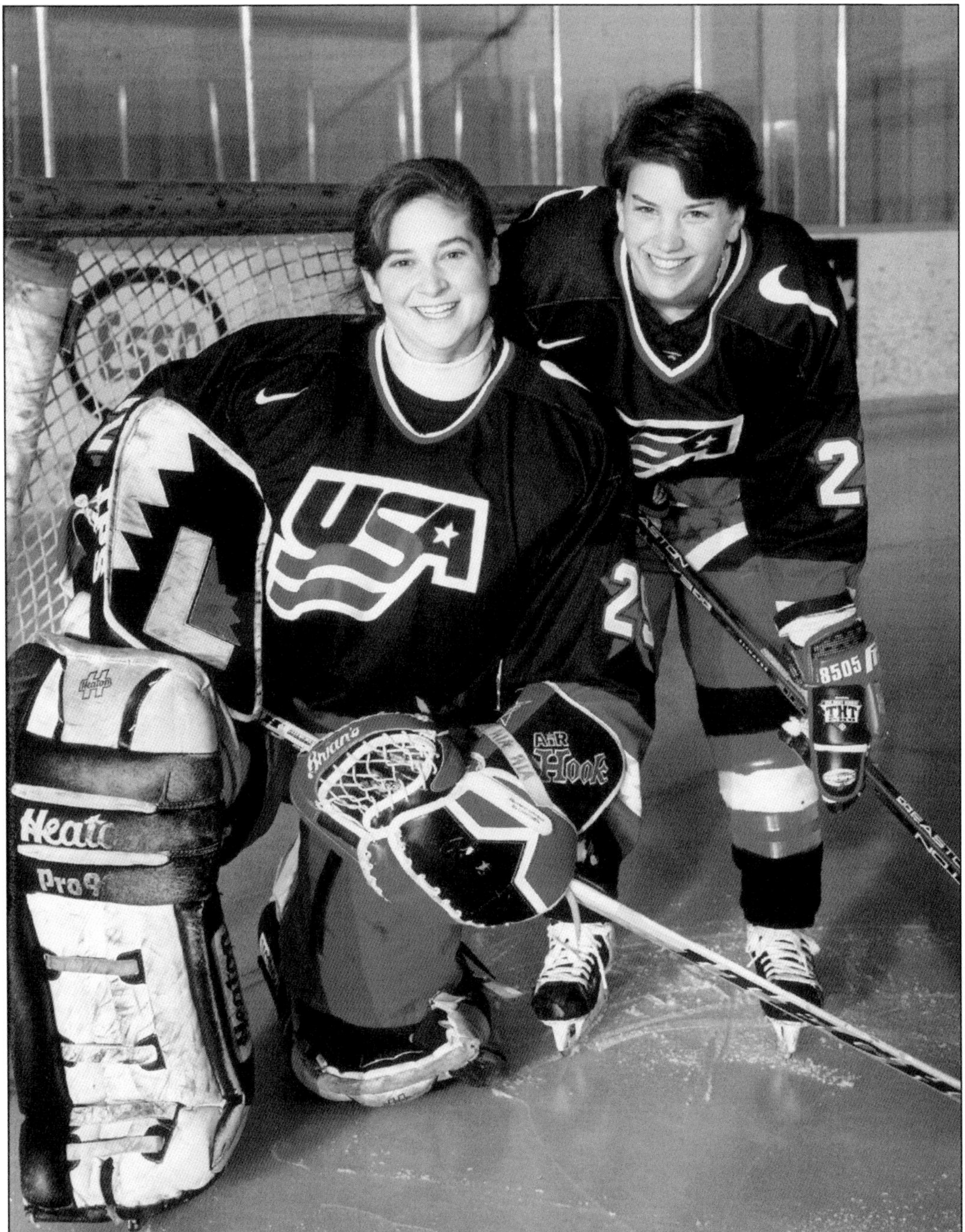

U.S. OLYMPIANS. In 1998 at Nagano, Japan, goaltender Sarah Tueting '98 and forward Gretchen Ulion '94 were members of the U.S. team that won the gold medal in the first Olympiad in which women's hockey was contested. In 2002, Tueting was also a member of the U.S. Olympic team that won the silver medal at Salt Lake City. Ulion's achievements at Dartmouth are found on page 91. Tueting played two seasons at Dartmouth (1994 to 1996) before pursuing, successfully, a place on the Olympic team. She had a 26-17-7 record and a 2.52 goals-against average and helped Dartmouth to the Ivy League title as a freshman in 1994–95.

SEVEN

Men, Years of Trying 1984–1997

For men's hockey at Dartmouth, this was a period of great expectations but only little success. On paper there was every element for triumph. On the ice, where games are won, there was only frustration. And this frustration ran deep. After the 1980 team went to the NCAA tournament, the men's team didn't have a winning season for the rest of the century. That's two decades of dashed hopes—and smashed dreams.

These years are proof that this game is not only physics but also chemistry. The physics were there: talented men, accomplished coaches, pent-up demand for victories. But they never came, or when they did they were too few to break the frustration. These were years of trying, to be sure, but mostly they were trying years.

Look, for example, at how long the drought lasted. The Green did not have a winning season through the final three years under George Crowe, all six seasons under Brian Mason, one under Ben Smith, six under Roger Demment, and the first three seasons under Bob Gaudet '81. Put it this way: the New York Rangers had a better two decades.

Which is not to say there wasn't something to watch, or remember. Steve Laurin '90 was a goalie of great mastery and left Hanover (having been drafted into the pro ranks) wondering what life might have been had the teams he had been on won more than two dozen games in four years. Dave Williams '90 was an All-American and played for several years with West Coast teams in the NHL. Scott Fraser '94 also skated into the NHL. They were the centerpieces of Dartmouth teams in the 1990s. Unfortunately they had few peers at Hanover.

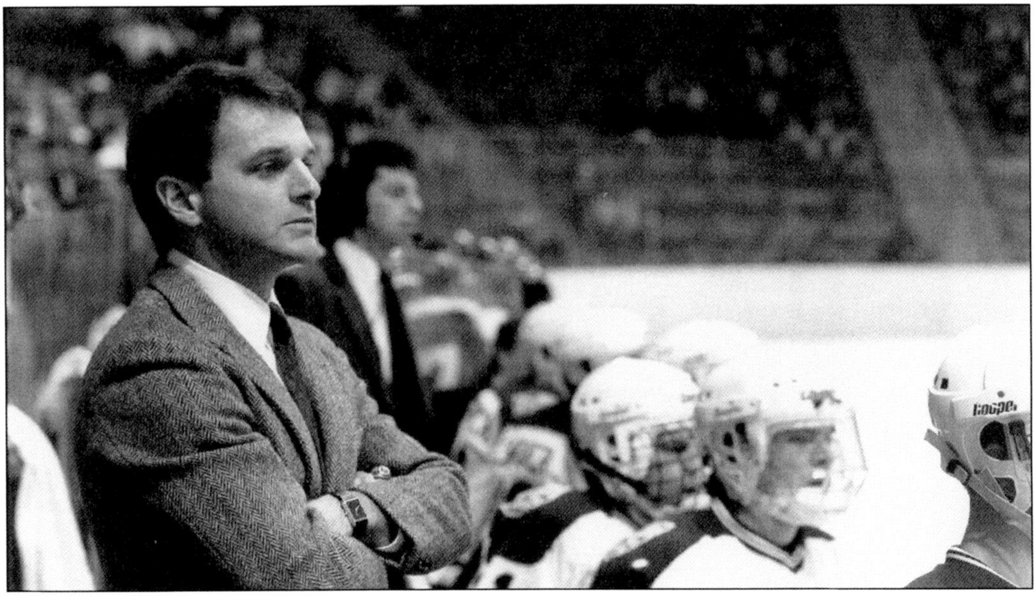

COACH BRIAN MASON. After coaching Rochester Tech to the NCAA Division II national championship in 1983, followed by a 29-6 record and third place in the nation in 1984, Brian Mason succeeded George Crowe as Dartmouth's coach. Mason had been a captain and two-time most valuable player at Clarkson. His credentials as a player and coach were not enough. A 10-15-1 record, in 1987–88, was Dartmouth's best season under Mason. He resigned in 1990 after six years and a record of 36-108-8.

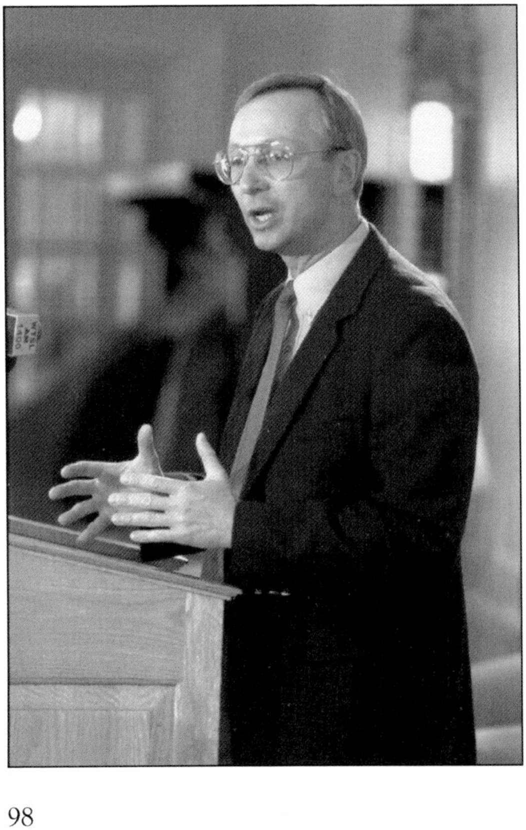

COACH JEFF KOSAK '71. Kosak was a steady wing (75 career points) at Dartmouth from 1968 to 1971. He coached Hanover High School to three state tournament appearances (one championship) from 1971 to 1974 and then assisted at Dartmouth for four years. He was the hockey coach at the Hotchkiss School from 1984 to 1999, except for 10 days in 1990 when he was hired—and then resigned "for personal and family reasons"—as Brian Mason's successor, Kosak coached Hotchkiss skaters to a record of 235-98-7. In 2004, the American Hockey Coaches Association honored Kosak for his achievements as a secondary school coach.

COACH BEN SMITH. After Jeff Kosak's 10-day tenure, Dartmouth turned to Ben Smith, a Harvard graduate and assistant coach, first at Yale and then at Boston University. Smith coached Dartmouth for one year, a 1-24-3 record in 1990–91. He returned to Boston and coached Northeastern for five years. Since 1996, Smith has been the head coach of the U.S. Olympic and the U.S. national women's teams.

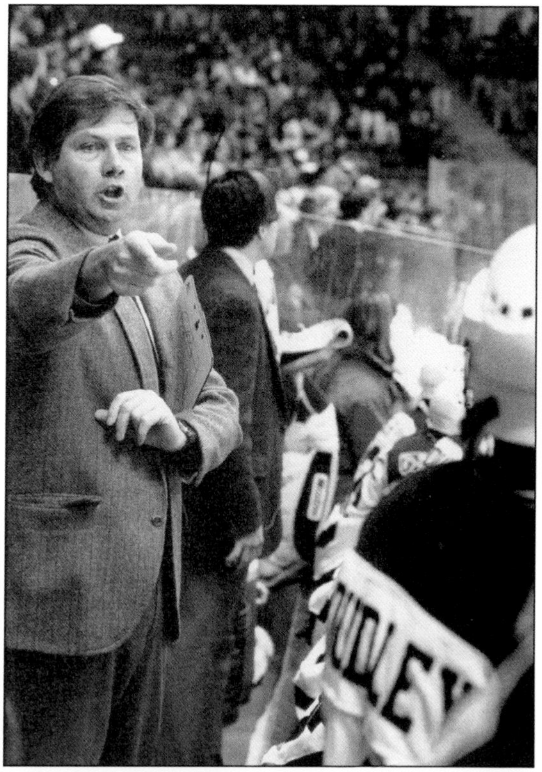

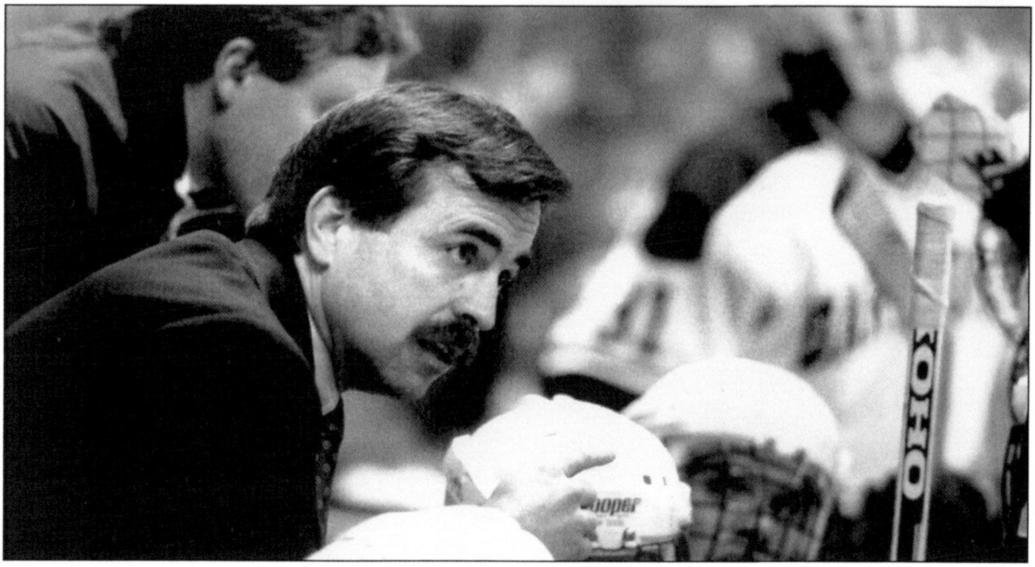

COACH ROGER DEMMENT. Roger Demment, Ben Smith's assistant in 1990–91, coached the Green from 1991 to 1997. Demment, a hockey captain at Yale, had been a player-coach in Europe and a prep school coach. Demment's six seasons produced a record of 45-111-10. Demment was named ECAC coach of the year in 1992–93 as the Green reached postseason play for the first time since 1980—an 11-16-0 record that included seven one-goal losses. Since 1997, Demment has been Dartmouth's director of physical education, intramurals, fitness, and recreation.

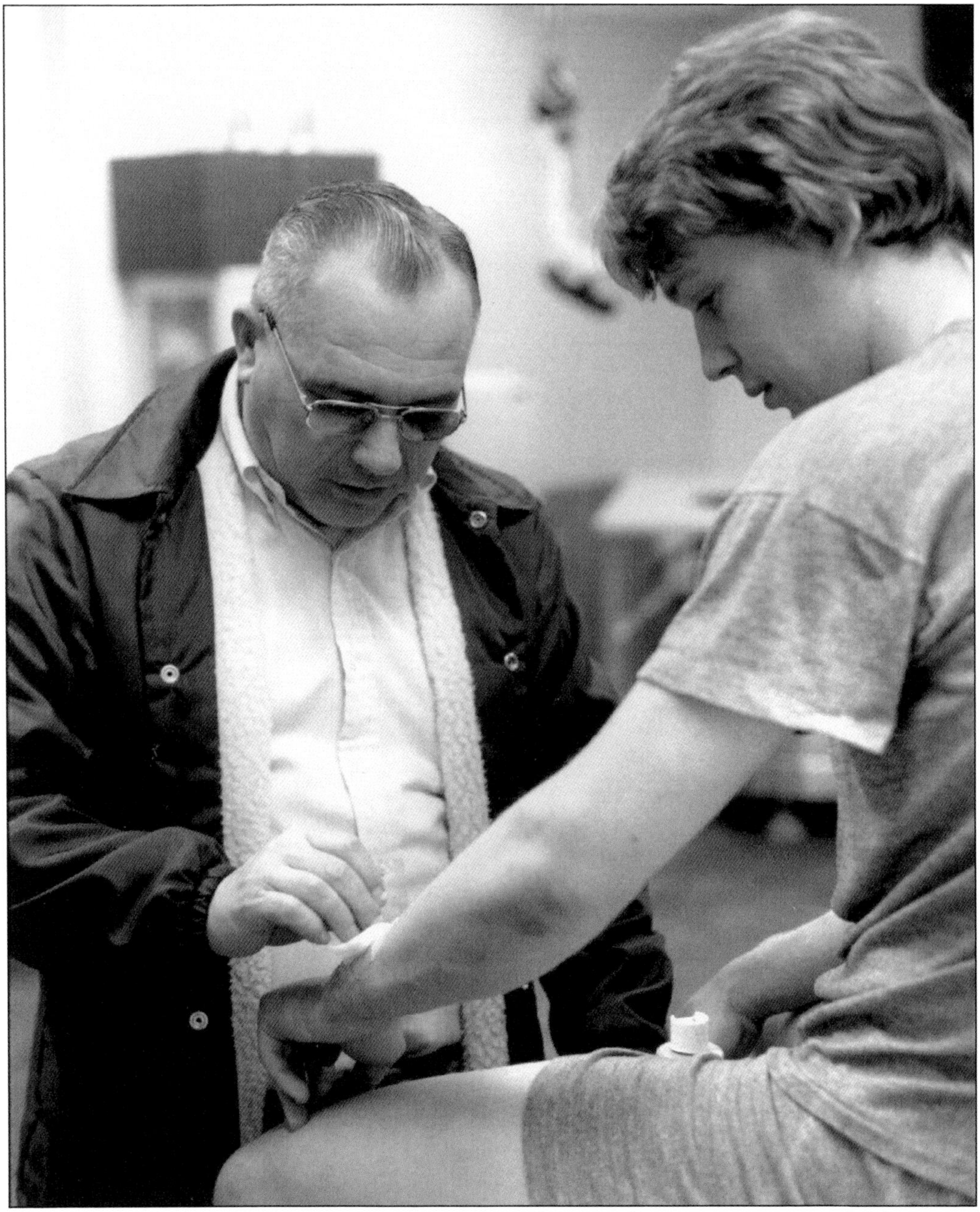

IRVING FOUNTAIN, TRAINER AND FRIEND. If Irv Fountain knew your name, it didn't matter. Irv's greeting to everyone was the same, "Hi, Chief." He became a trainer for Dartmouth teams, including football and lacrosse but primarily hockey, in 1957. He retired 37 years later. He served seven hockey coaches, from Eddie Jeremiah to Roger Demment, and Dartmouth's current coach, Bob Gaudet '81, when he was a player. He is shown above treating Gaudet's classmate, defenseman Chris McLaughlin. Fountain grew up in neighboring Lebanon, New Hampshire, and scored 13 touchdowns in six games for the Lebanon High football team. He did not have a college degree, but his words of encouragement and friendship while taping an ankle or shoulder were the type of healing medicine not taught in the classroom.

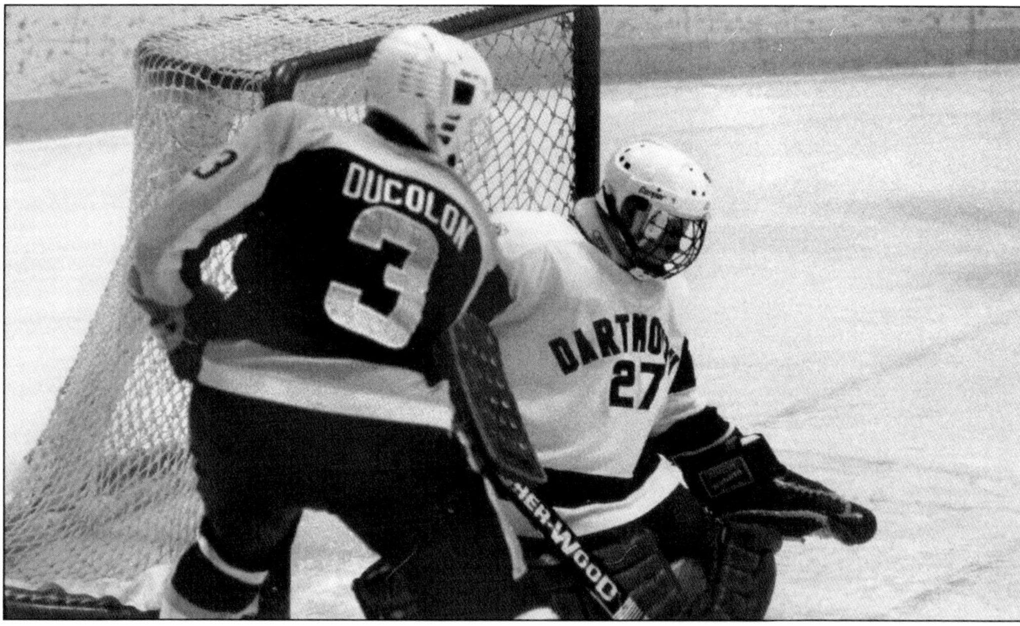

STEVE LAURIN '90. From 1986 to 1990, Steve Laurin was a mainstay in Dartmouth's goal. In 66 games, his 2,197 saves eclipsed the Dartmouth career record held by Bob Gaudet '81 (they now rank 1-2 behind Nick Boucher '03). He was drafted by the NHL's Hartford Whalers in 1987. Playing on teams that won only 24 games over four seasons, Laurin ranks sixth all-time in save percentage by a Dartmouth goalie (.885).

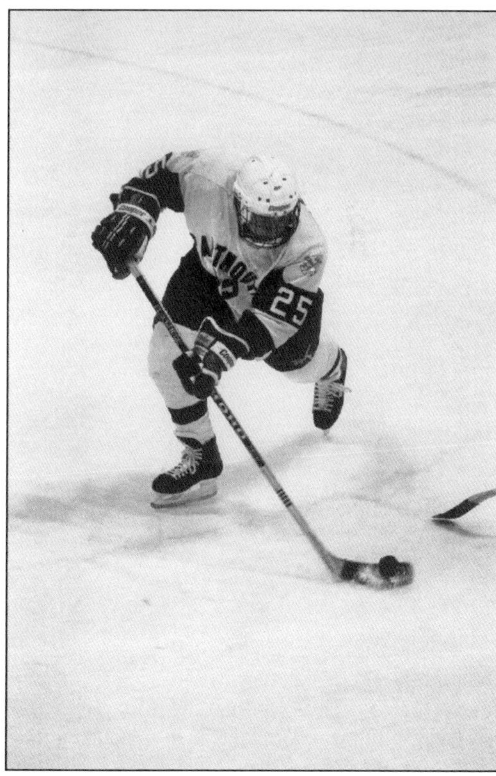

JAMIE HANLON '90. For two seasons, from 1988 to 1990, center Jamie Hanlon was Dartmouth's scoring leader. He was second to his classmate Dave Williams as a sophomore wing and finished with 88 career points (56 assists). Hanlon was one of several outstanding players recruited to Dartmouth by coach Brian Mason. Mason's dilemma was that he couldn't recruit enough of them.

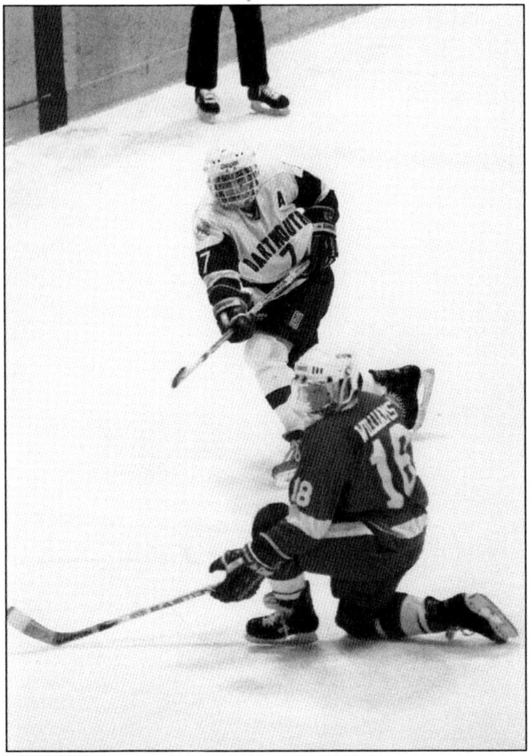

Dave Williams '90. Defenseman Dave Williams was Dartmouth's scoring leader as a freshman and sophomore. He had 73 career points. He was All-Ivy and All-ECAC as a junior and All-Ivy as a senior, when he was Dartmouth's captain. In 1989, Williams became Dartmouth's first All-American since Ross Brownridge '80. Drafted by the NHL's New Jersey Devils in 1985, he played in the NHL for several years in the early 1990s with the Anaheim Mighty Ducks and San Jose Sharks.

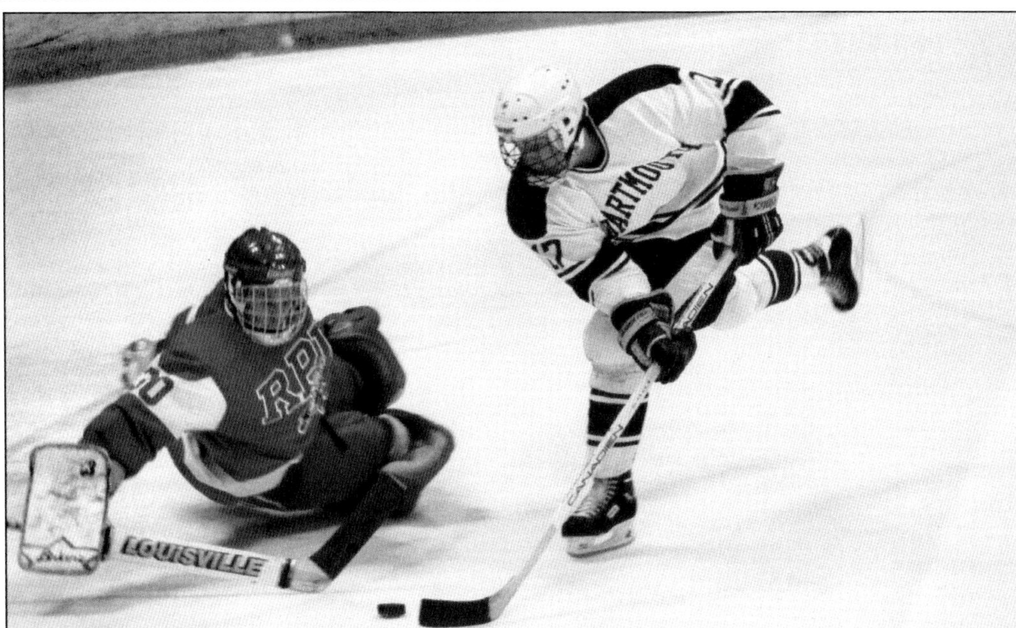

Scott Fraser '94. Scott Fraser became Dartmouth's second player to reach the National Hockey League during the 1990s, playing with the Montreal Canadiens, Calgary Flames, Edmonton Oilers, and New York Rangers. During four seasons at Dartmouth (1990 to 1994), Fraser scored 112 points (59 goals, 53 assists) and was the Green's scoring leader as a junior and senior.

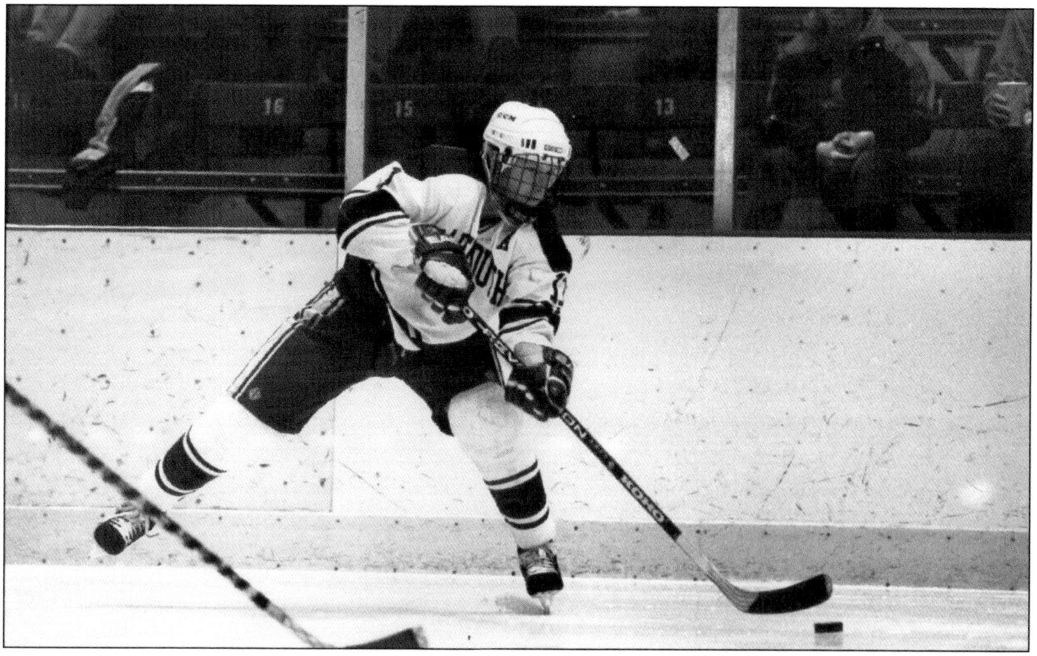

Dion DelMonte '95. A co-captain of Dartmouth hockey in 1994–95, when he was an All-Ivy League selection, center Dion DelMonte was the Green's scoring leader as a senior and had 108 career points (71 assists) from 1991 to 1995. DelMonte went on to play hockey in Europe for three years. He then played minor-league pro hockey in the United States.

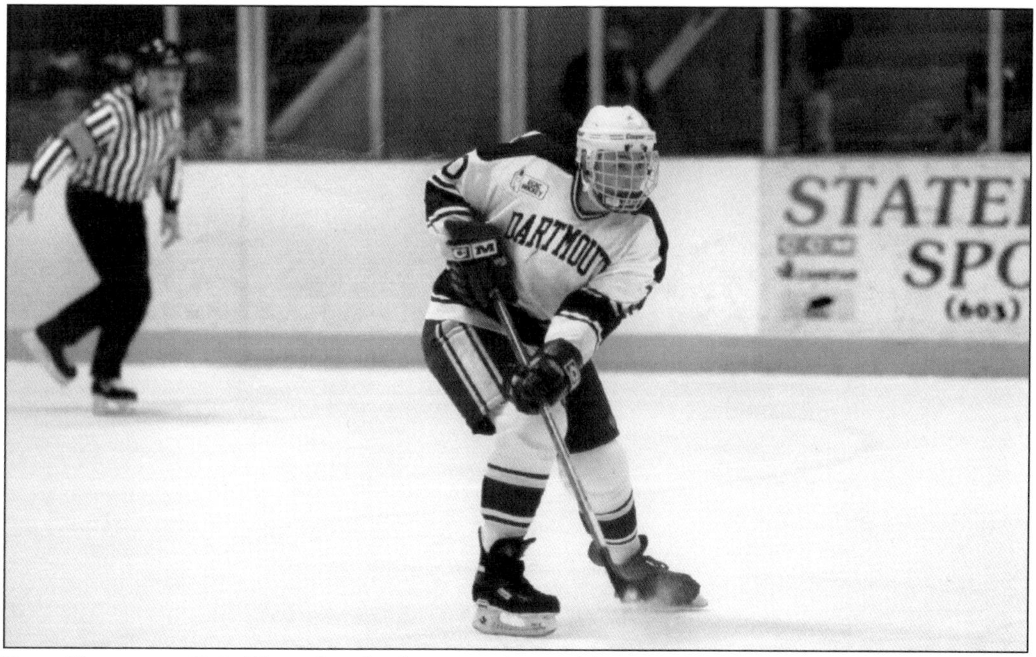

Bill Kelleher '96. Though a broken arm limited him to four games as a sophomore (he had been second in scoring as a freshman in 1992–93, behind Scott Fraser '94), forward Bill Kelleher closed his career at Dartmouth with 104 points (76 assists) and was the runner-up in scoring as a senior, this time to sophomore David Whitworth '98 (page 121).

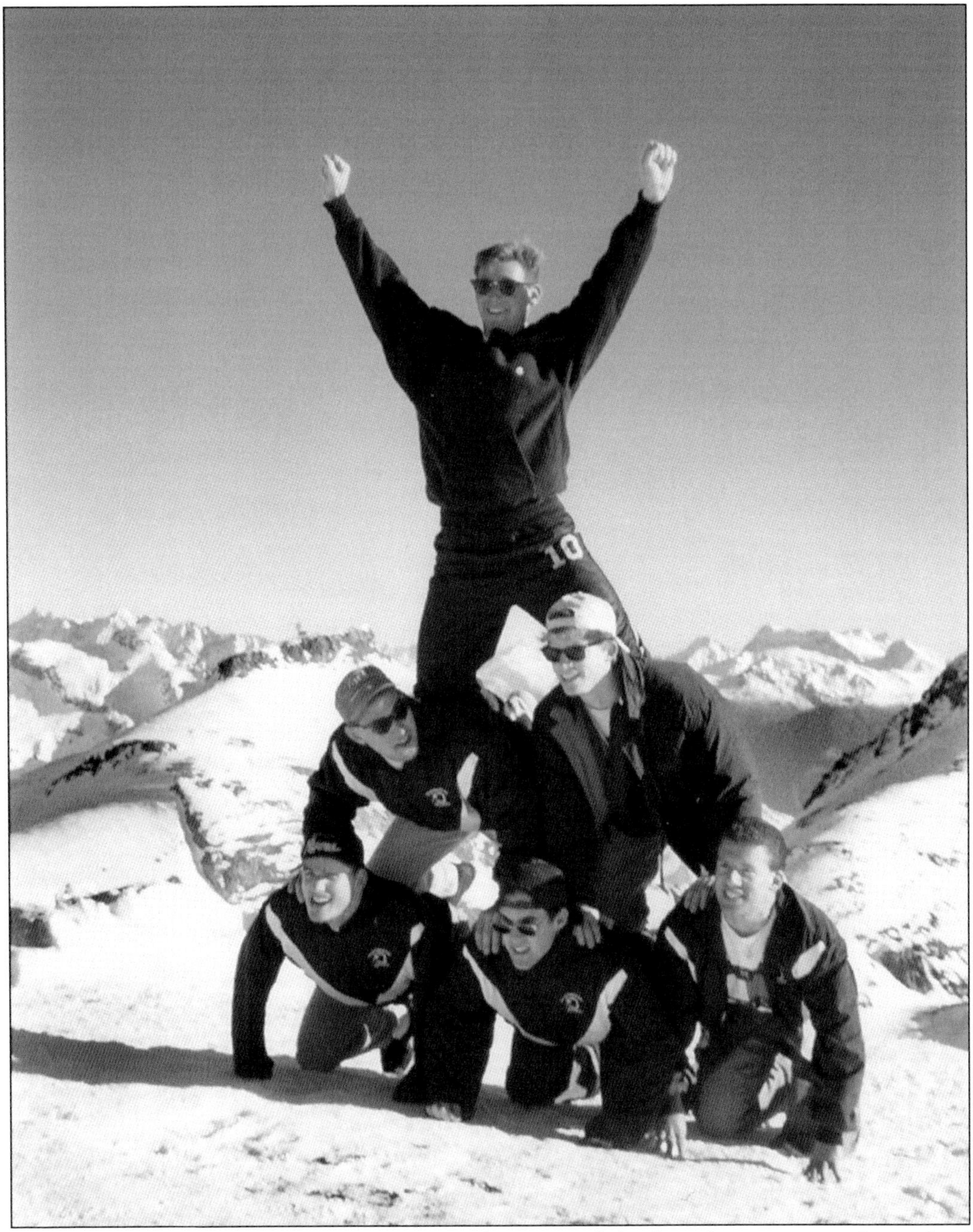

SWITZERLAND, 1994. In February 1948, several Dartmouth hockey players went to Switzerland for the Winter Olympics (page 46). Forty-six years later, in December 1994, Dartmouth's hockey team visited Switzerland to play a series of exhibition games during the 1994–95 season. (Dartmouth's hockey team made a similar trip to Sweden in 1986.) Dartmouth won all five games played against Swiss club teams, but the victories were not as memorable as the morning they rode to the top of 10,000-foot Plaine Mort in the Swiss Alps. The crowning moment for Bill Kelleher '96 was "being on top of the pyramid (of teammates) on top of the world." (Photograph by Kathy Slattery Phillips.)

EIGHT

Women, National Scene 1998–2005

In this period, Dartmouth's women established themselves among the premier hockey teams in the United States. They appeared in national tournaments, dotted All-Ivy and All-American squads (though not as often as they challenged for positions on national teams), and became known as perennial powerhouses. They had come of age and had established an age of glory of their own. It continues to this day.

One statistic bears witness to this feat. For 19 consecutive seasons (and counting), Dartmouth's women had winning seasons. Dartmouth's men share no such tradition. Few teams in the history of any sport do. But a winning tradition feeds on itself, and in this time Dartmouth's women are having a feast. They have yet to win a national championship, though the 2000–01 team was ranked tops in the nation for nearly five months. This much is beyond contention: they are consistently among the most accomplished, most skilled, and most feared hockey teams in the land.

Their record roars for itself. Judy Parish Oberting '91 built a 114-40-8 record in five seasons. In his first two seasons as the Green coach, Mark Hudak has built a 51-16-2 record. Oberting took Dartmouth to three NCAA tournament appearances, Hudak to two. Eight times in a decade's time, Dartmouth won 20 games or more. Four members of the class of 2006 entered their senior years with over 100 points. Cherie Piper '06 arrived at Dartmouth in 2002 with an Olympic gold medal already in hand. Others, almost too numerous to count—though Canadians Correne Bredin '02, Carly Haggard '03, Gillian Apps '06, and Katie Weatherston '06, as well as Tiffany Hagge '06, from Coon Rapids, Minnesota, come easily to mind—have taken frequent sabbaticals to represent their nations in global competition.

These Dartmouth women's teams were marked by equal measures of firepower and iron discipline. There were standouts, to be sure. Bredin was Dartmouth's second All-American; Carly Haggard '03, the third All-American, led Dartmouth in scoring for three years running; and Meagan Walton '05 finished her career with 108 points. But the reason Dartmouth's teams did so well was not merely on the power of individual performance. It was a matter of balance and an edgy excellence. They were ferocious on offense, nearly impenetrable on defense. All this not because they blasted past effete eastern teams. From 2003 to 2005, Dartmouth played Minnesota six times and Minnesota-Duluth twice. Then again, these Dartmouth women came from pioneer stock.

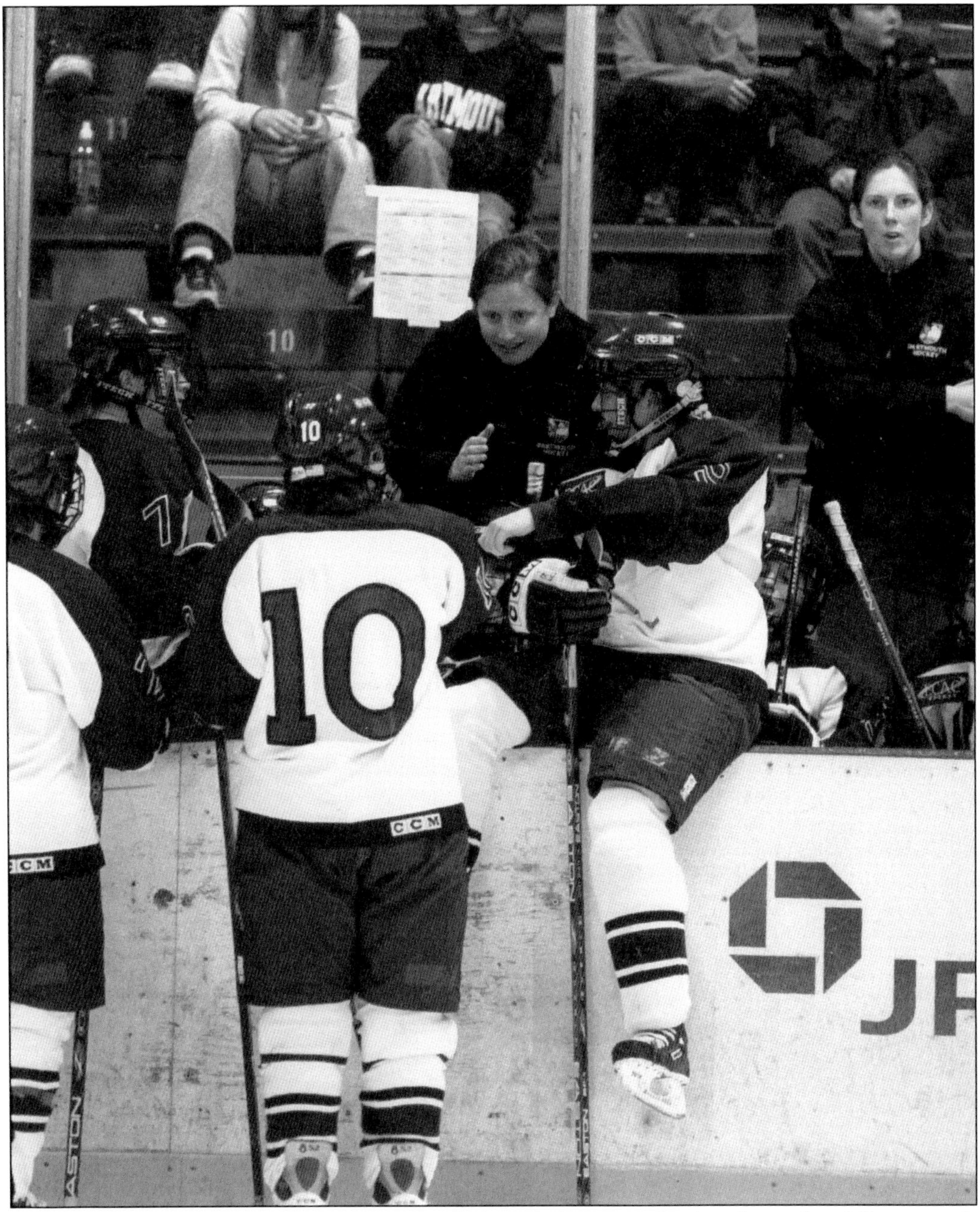

COACH JUDY PARISH OBERTING '91. Judy Parish became the head coach of Dartmouth women's hockey in 1998. During the next year, she married her Dartmouth classmate Kernan "Kip" Oberting. As a player at Dartmouth, she was a three-time All-Ivy League selection (page 88). Oberting succeeded George Crowe after five seasons as his assistant and associate head coach. During five seasons (1998 to 2003), she led Dartmouth to three national tournament appearances, a pair of Ivy League titles and two ECAC championships. When she left coaching in 2003 to be with her family, Oberting's teams had built a record of 114-40-8 and Dartmouth had solidified its place among the nation's best women's intercollegiate hockey programs.

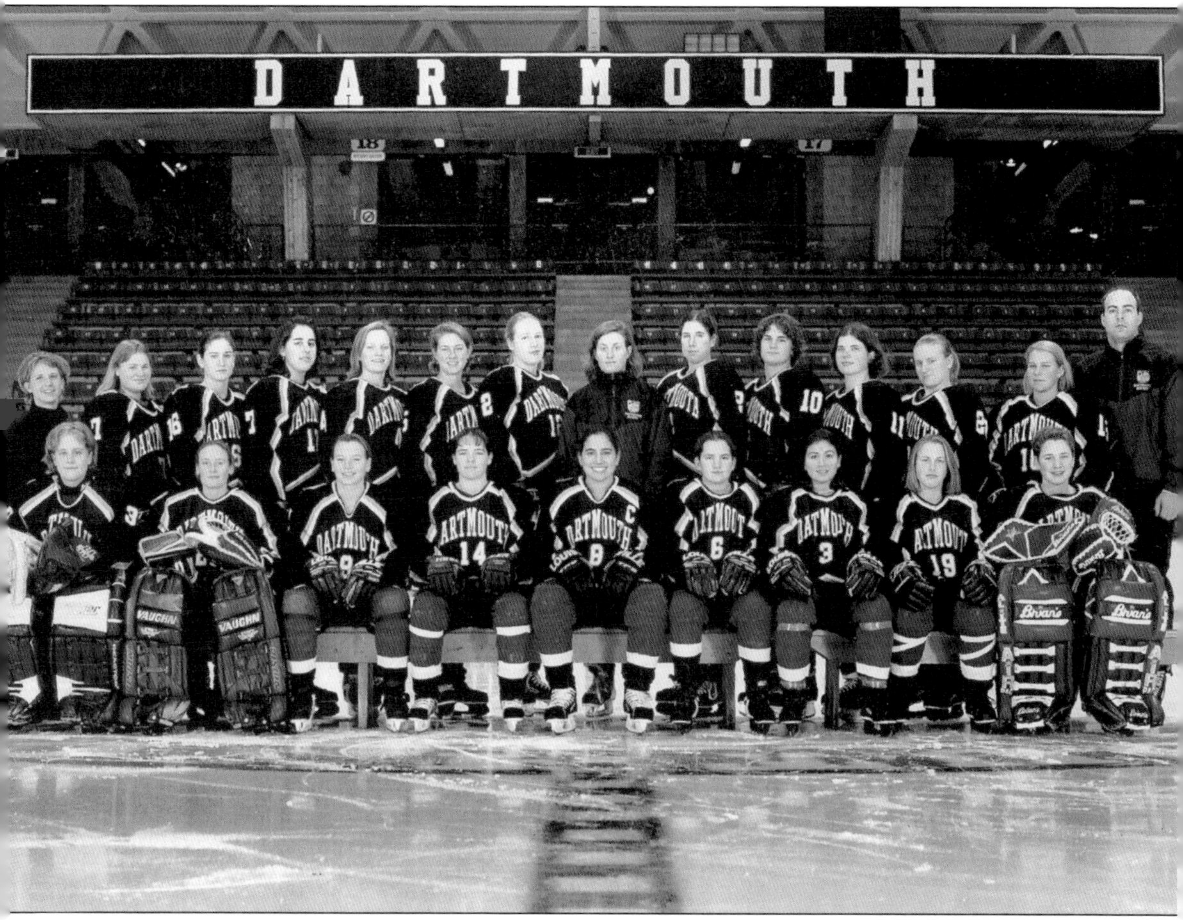

The 1999–2000 Team: Reaching the National Scene. Dartmouth capped a 21-12-0 record in 1999–2000 with a season-ending run that saw the Green take third place in the American Women's Hockey Coaches Alliance (AWCHA) championship in Boston. Led by two junior co-captains, forward Carrie Sekela '01 and forward Kristina Guarino '01, the quest for national honors began with a dramatic double-overtime win 1-0 over Providence to reach the ECAC Tournament at Brown University's Meehan Auditorium. After beating Harvard in overtime 3-2, the Green lost to Brown, the Ivy League champion, 6-3 for the ECAC title. The teams met again in the AWCHA semifinal match, and Brown won 4-2. The third-place game against Minnesota-Duluth belonged to Dartmouth 5-4 on the sixth game-winning goal of the season by freshman forward Carly Haggard (page 114). Dartmouth returned for the first women's NCAA tournament in 2001, but this team's performance earned coach Oberting recognition as the national and New England coach of the year.

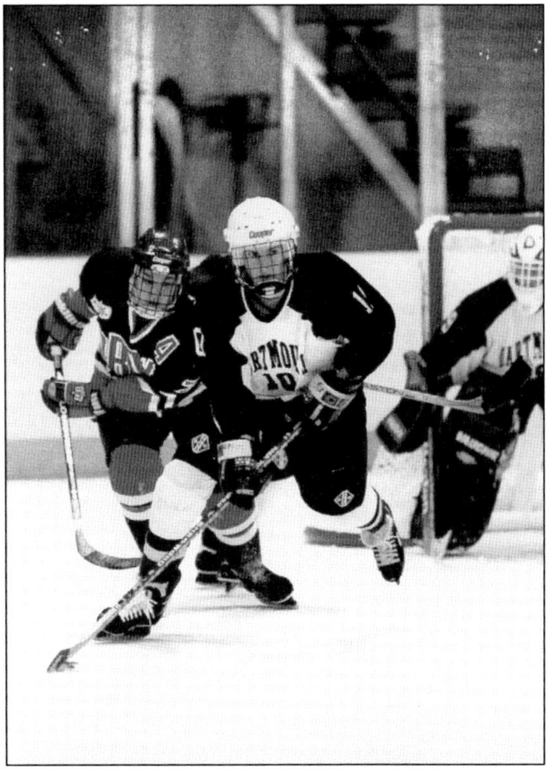

KATHLEEN O'KEEFE '99. One of Dartmouth's most versatile skaters, forward-defenseman Kathleen O'Keefe netted 103 points (67 assists) as she played in 121 of the Green's 122 games from 1995 to 1999 (she missed one game as a freshman). O'Keefe was a Dartmouth co-captain in 1998–99.

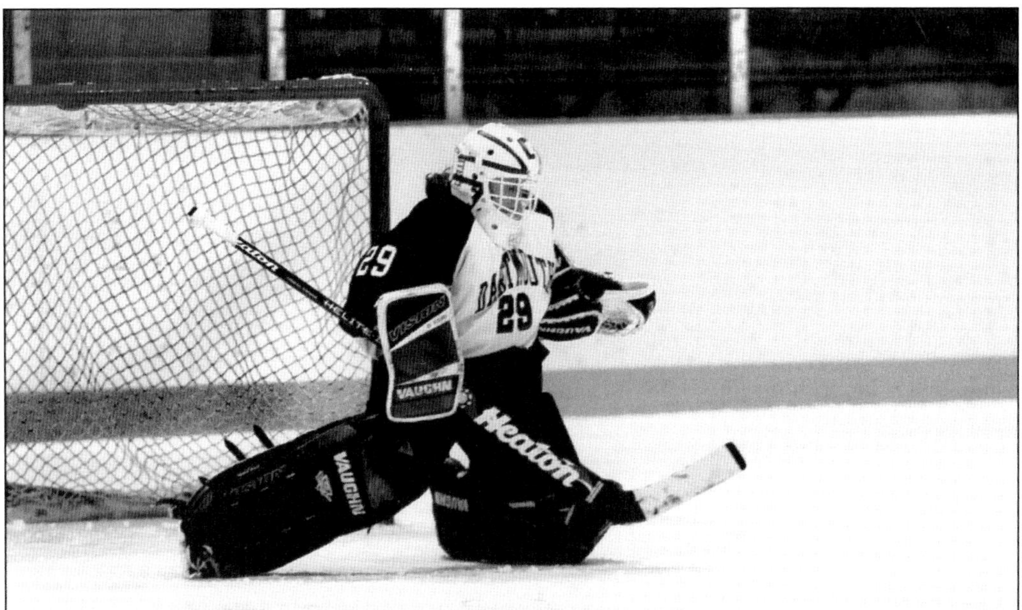

MEAGHAN CAHILL '01. Meaghan Cahill was the All-Ivy League goaltender in 2000–01, the season she set a Dartmouth record with 1.37 goals allowed per game. Cahill was Dartmouth's regular goalie as a freshman and sophomore. She and Amy Ferguson '03 became a goal-tending tandem from 1999 to 2001. Cahill set the Dartmouth record for saves in a season (749 in 1997–98). Ferguson holds the career record for wins (67).

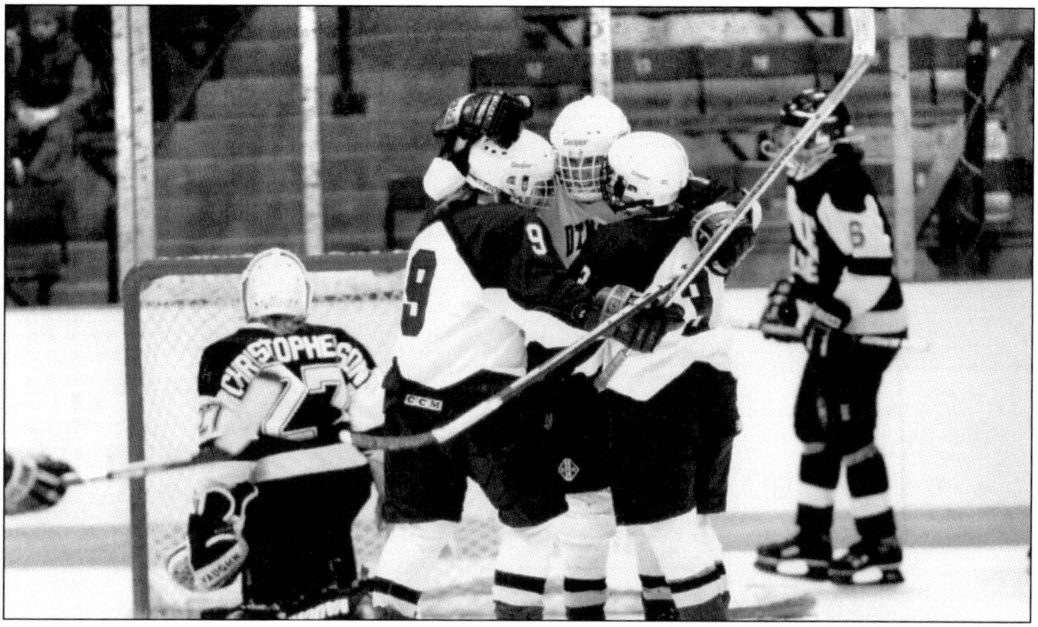

FOUR-YEAR LINEMATES. From 1997 to 2001, this photograph was duplicated many times—the line of Jennifer Wiehn (9), Lauren Trottier, and Kristina Guarino celebrating a goal. They were put together by coach Crowe as freshmen and stayed together for three more years with coach Oberting. When their careers were complete, the Wiehn-Trottier-Guarino line had accounted for 150 goals and shared in 83 victories.

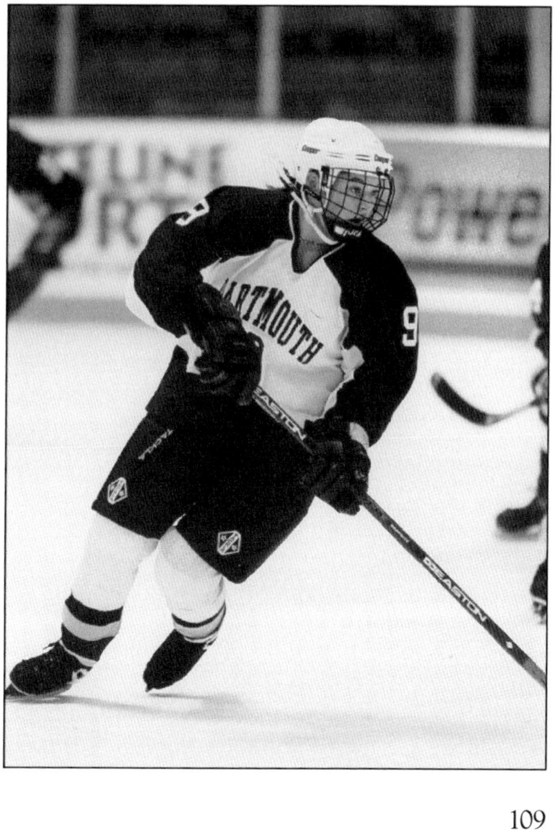

JEN WIEHN '01. Before Dartmouth, Jen Wiehn played three sports at Tolland High School in Connecticut: soccer, basketball, and track. She played hockey with the Connecticut Polar Bears, the midget all-star team that won the national championship in 1997. During four seasons at Dartmouth, Wiehn scored 126 points (62 goals, 64 assists), tops on the Wiehn-Trottier-Guarino line, as the Green won a pair of Ivy League titles. She was co-captain of the 2000–01 team.

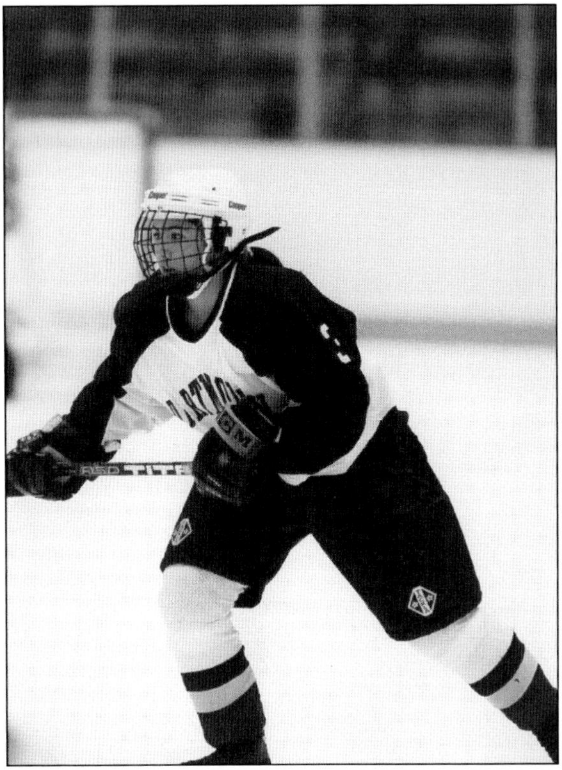

LAUREN TROTTIER '01. Lauren Trottier immediately established herself as a scoring threat. Her first goal came in the first period of her first game, a 2-1 win in the 1997–98 opener against Brown. During her career, Trottier also netted 14 power play goals. She finished with 57 goals and 60 assists (117 points).

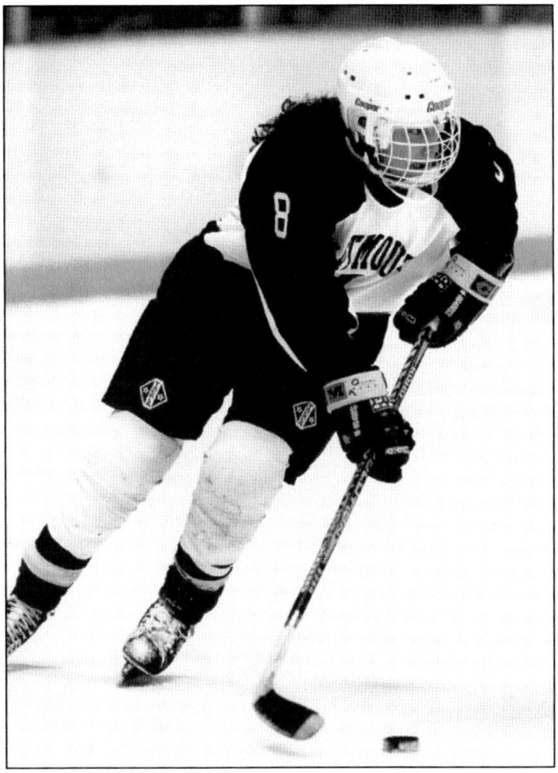

KRISTINA GUARINO '01. Guarino played on the first girls' hockey team at Hartford High School in Vermont and was a two-time co-captain at Dartmouth. While Jen Wiehn and Lauren Trottier scored more often than Guarino (she had 32 goals), no goal was more memorable than Guarino's game winner in the overtime win 3-2 against Harvard in the ECAC Tournament in 2000. Guarino returned to Dartmouth as an assistant hockey coach of the women's team from 2003 to 2005.

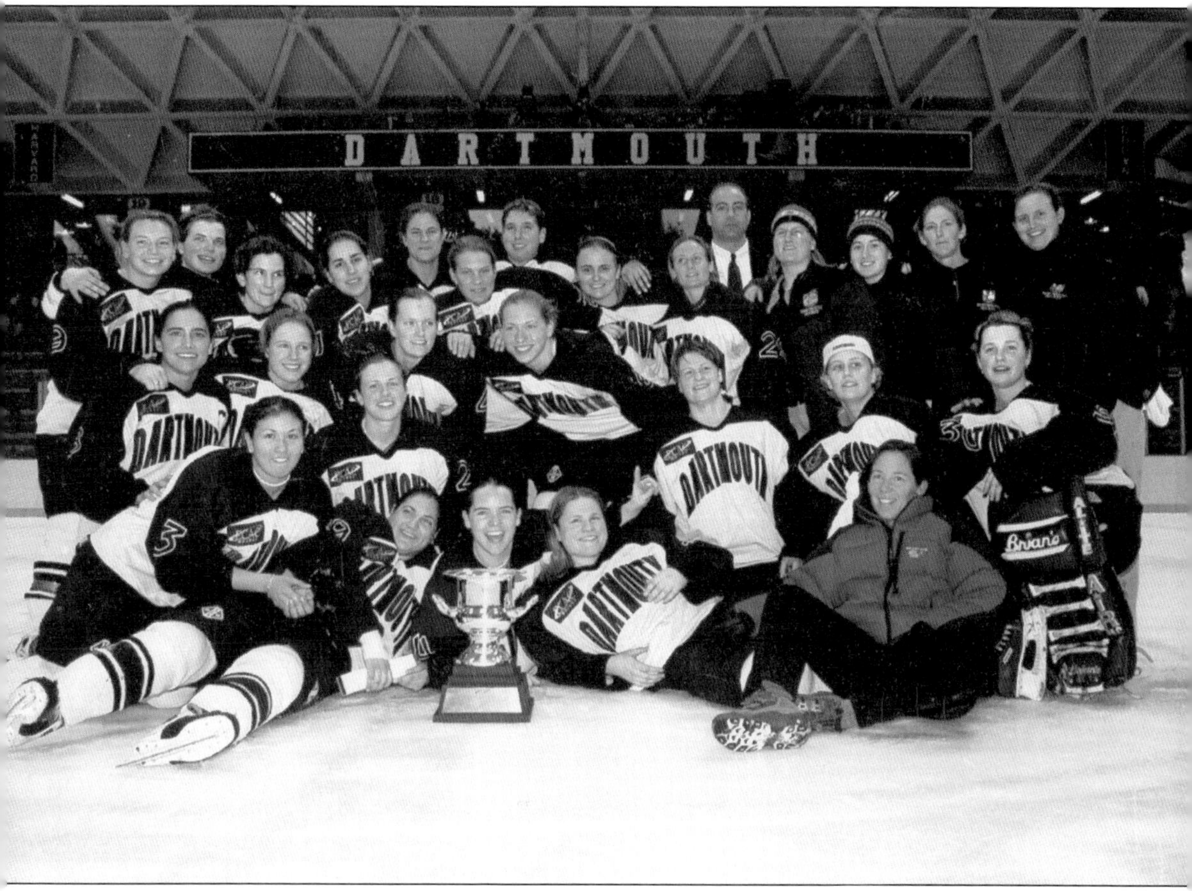

THE 2000–01 TEAM. The first NCAA women's hockey tournament was held in 2001, and Dartmouth capped a 26-5-1 campaign by taking fourth place in the inaugural Women's Frozen Four at Minneapolis. En route to the NCAA tourney, Dartmouth was the nation's top-ranked team for nearly five months, starting the season 19-1-1. The Green won the Ivy League title and then defeated Niagara, Brown, and Harvard to win (on the Thompson Arena ice) its first ECAC championship. Amy Ferguson '03 made 46 saves in the 3-1 win over Harvard, and Jen Wiehn was named most valuable player in the ECAC event. A week later in the NCAA competition, Dartmouth came up short; in the semifinal game, Dartmouth lost to St. Lawrence 3-1, a team the Green had beaten and tied during the regular season. Then, Harvard avenged its loss to Dartmouth in the ECAC title game, winning the third-place game 3-2. "It was disappointing," said coach Oberting, "but it doesn't take anything away from what this team accomplished."

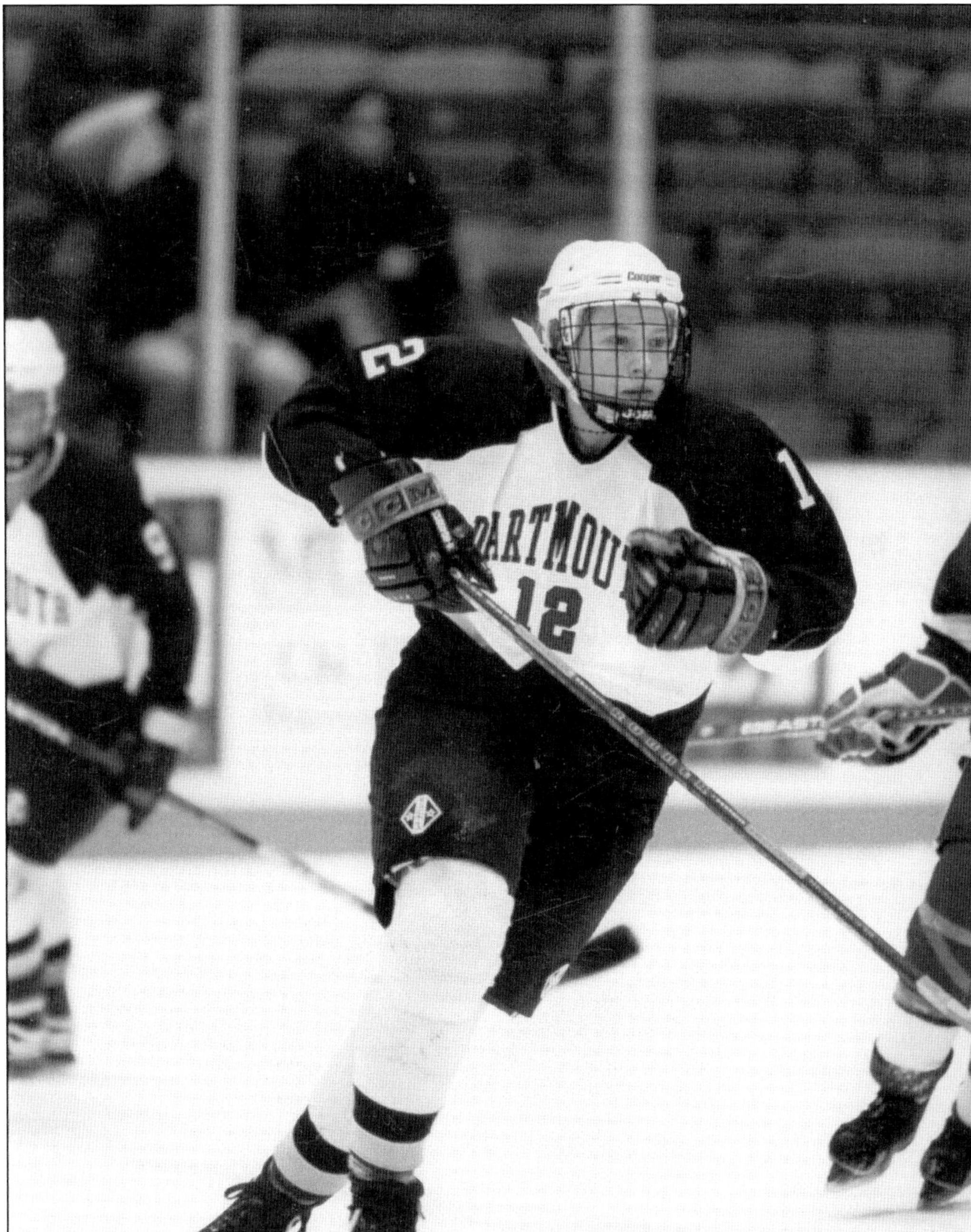

CORRENE BREDIN '02. In 2000–01, defenseman Correne Bredin became Dartmouth's second All-American player (joining Sarah Hood '98). She was also All-Ivy and All-ECAC that season. In 2001, Bredin was also a member of Canada's gold medal team in the women's world championships. She took the 2001–02 season off to compete with the Canadian national team and lasted until the final cut for the Canadian Olympic team that won the gold medal at Salt Lake City in 2002. Returning to Dartmouth for the 2002–03 season, Bredin was All-Ivy and a second-team All-American selection as the Green posted a 27-8-0 record in Judy Oberting's last season as coach. Dartmouth won another ECAC championship.

LIZ MACRI '01. Macri, a defenseman, joined classmate Jen Wiehn on the Connecticut Polar Bears national championship team in 1997. Also an outfielder on the Dartmouth softball team, Macri scored 80 points (47 assists). She arrived at Dartmouth in 1997 with classmates who were called the "Fab Freshmen." Four years later, they had become the keys on teams that built a record of 83-35-7.

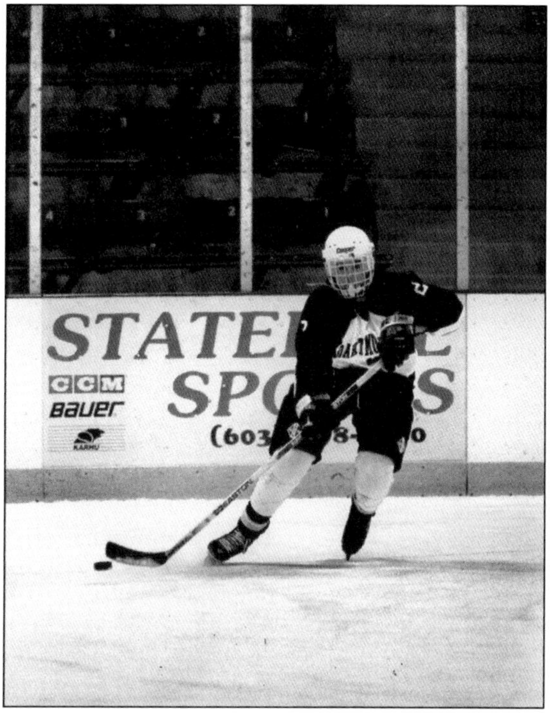

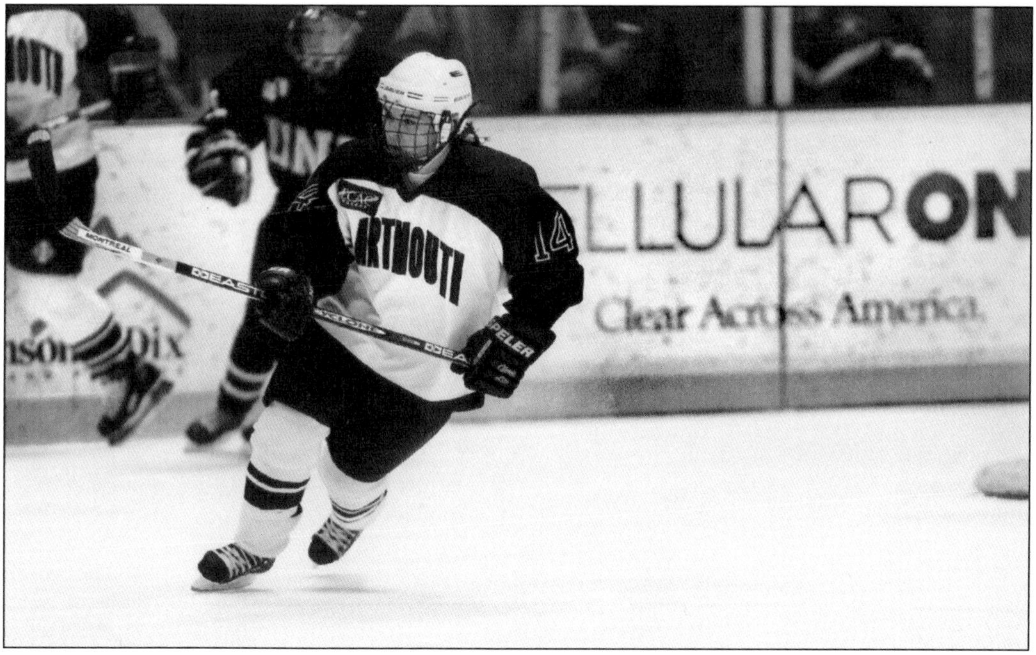

KRISTIN KING '02. King's high school in Ohio did not have a team, so she traveled to Michigan to play midget hockey. She also earned All-Ivy mention as a member of Dartmouth's softball team but made her mark on the ice. As a junior and senior, the versatile forward was named to the All-Ivy team and finished her career with 120 points, including 69 assists. Her two-sport career earned her the Archibald Prize as Dartmouth's outstanding student-athlete in 2002 and a place on the U.S. national team in 2003.

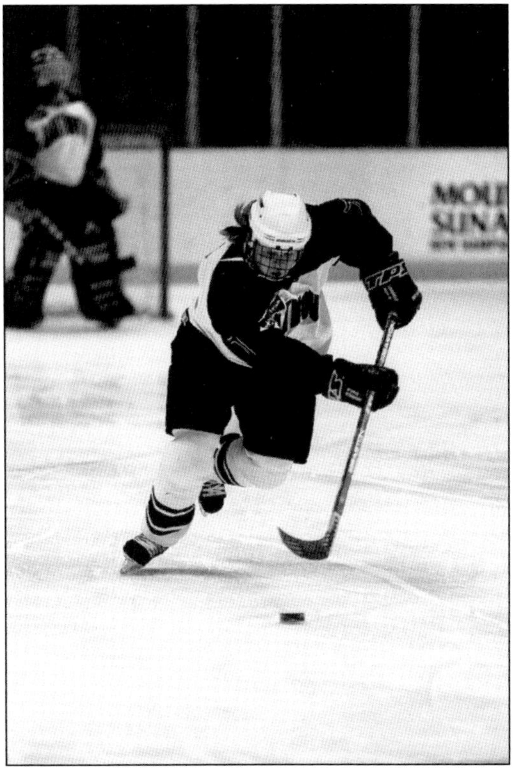

CARLY HAGGARD '03. Haggard was the Ivy League and ECAC rookie of the year as a freshman. She then led Dartmouth's scorers for the next three years. In 2001–02, Haggard was an All-American, All-Ivy, and the Ivy and ECAC player of the year. Twice she was a finalist for the Patty Kazmaier Award as the nation's outstanding player. In career points, Haggard ranks third behind Gretchen Ulion '94 and Judy Parish '91 with 204 (114 goals). For several years, Haggard was a member of the Canadian national team. She was also a four-year softball player at Dartmouth.

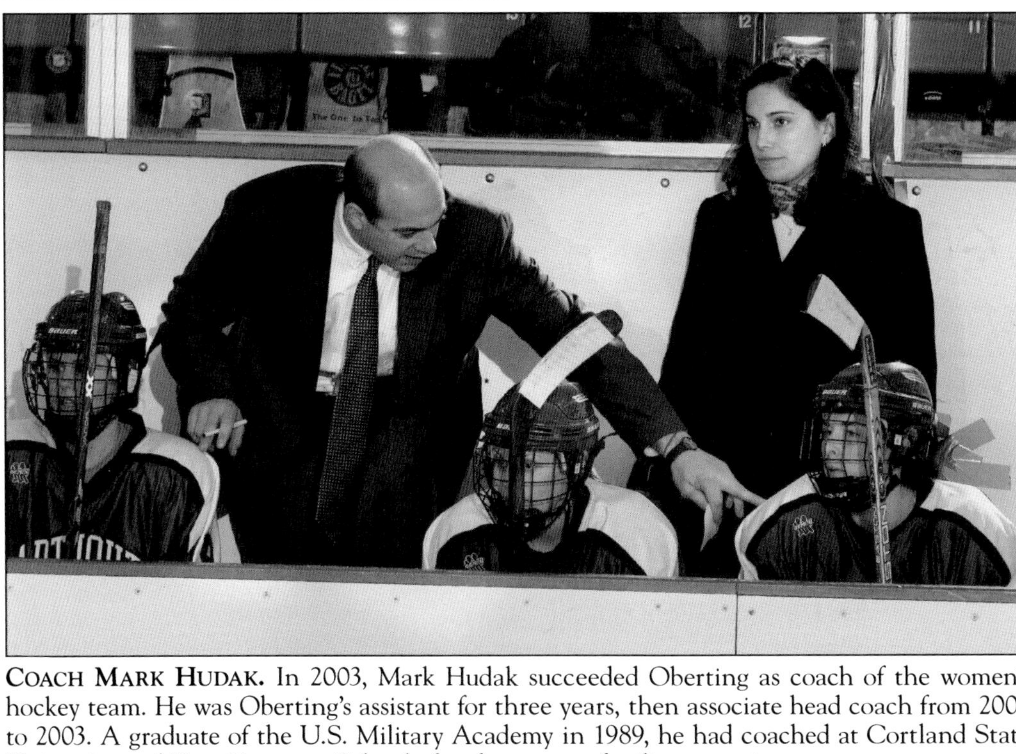

COACH MARK HUDAK. In 2003, Mark Hudak succeeded Oberting as coach of the women's hockey team. He was Oberting's assistant for three years, then associate head coach from 2001 to 2003. A graduate of the U.S. Military Academy in 1989, he had coached at Cortland State University and New Hampton School after four years of military service.

MEAGAN WALTON '05. After missing much of the 2002–03 season due to injury, forward Meagan Walton was Dartmouth's co-captain as a junior and senior. "Mother Meagan" was voted the team's most valuable player in 2004–05. Her 40 points were a personal high as the Green finished 27-8-0. Walton had 108 career points.

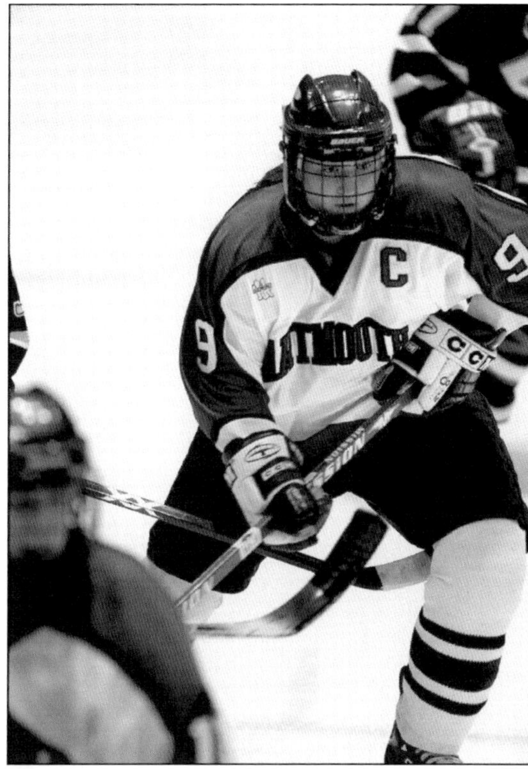

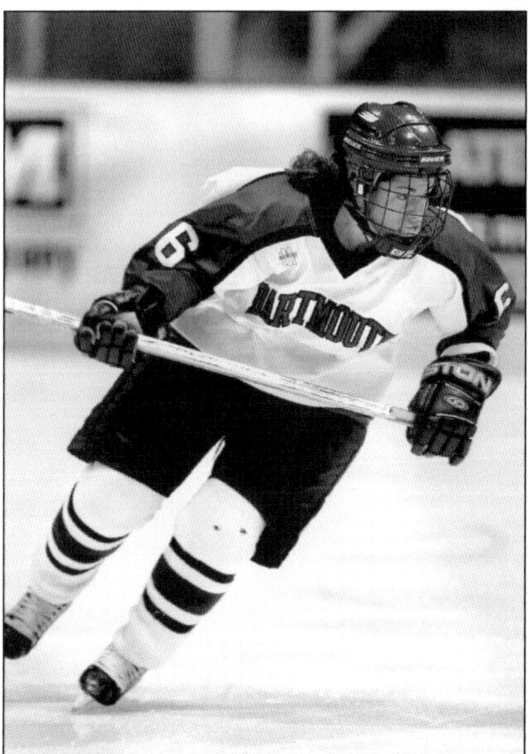

KATIE WEATHERSTON '06. Weatherston is one of four members of the class of 2006—with Gillian Apps, Tiffany Hagge, and Cherie Piper—who carry forward the story of Dartmouth women's hockey. With 148 points through three seasons, including 90 goals, Weatherston already ranks fifth all-time among Green scoring leaders. She was a second team All-American in 2005. Her three goals paced Dartmouth to a 5-1 win over the University of Minnesota that came into the game with a 27-game unbeaten streak as the nation's top-ranked team.

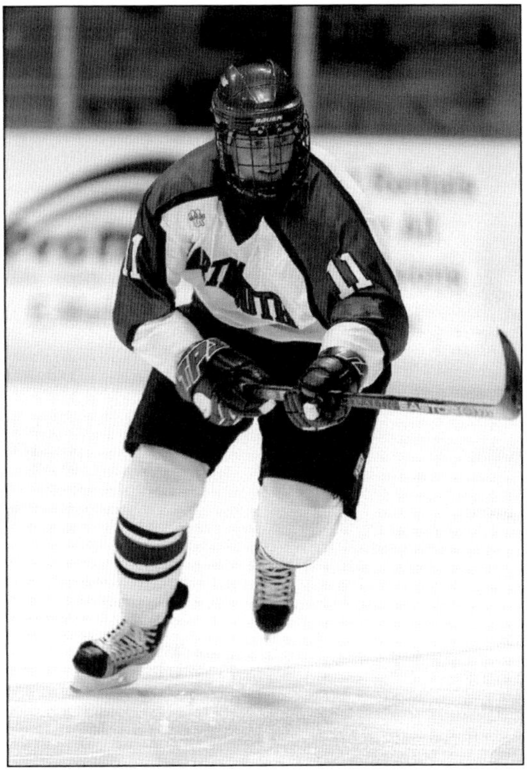

GILLIAN APPS '06. A forward and granddaughter of hockey hall of famer Syl Apps, Gillian Apps became one of five Dartmouth players to reach 100 career points during the 2004–05 season. She had 112 points through three seasons. She missed several games over her first three seasons while competing with the Canadian national team.

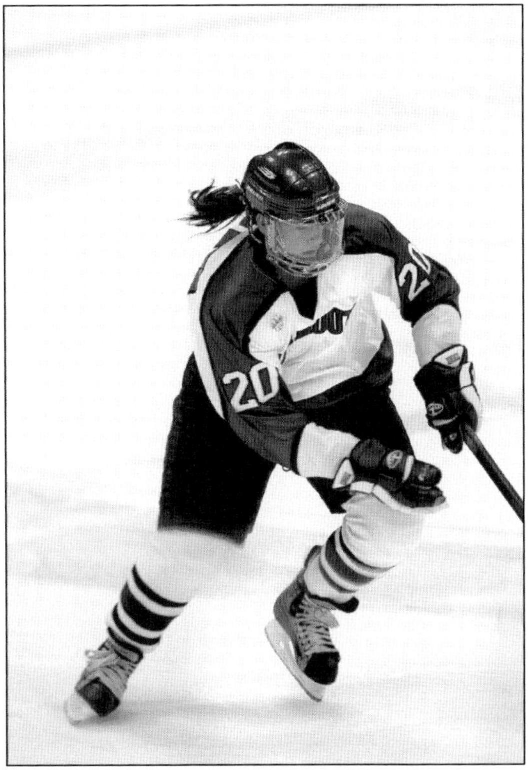

TIFFANY HAGGE '06. With 53 points, including 38 goals, in 2004–05, forward Tiffany Hagge had 122 career points through three seasons at Dartmouth. She was part of a prolific line with classmates Gillian Apps and Cherie Piper. During the 2004–05 season, Hagge also competed with the U.S. team in the Four Nations Cup tourney that included the United States, Canada, Finland, and Sweden.

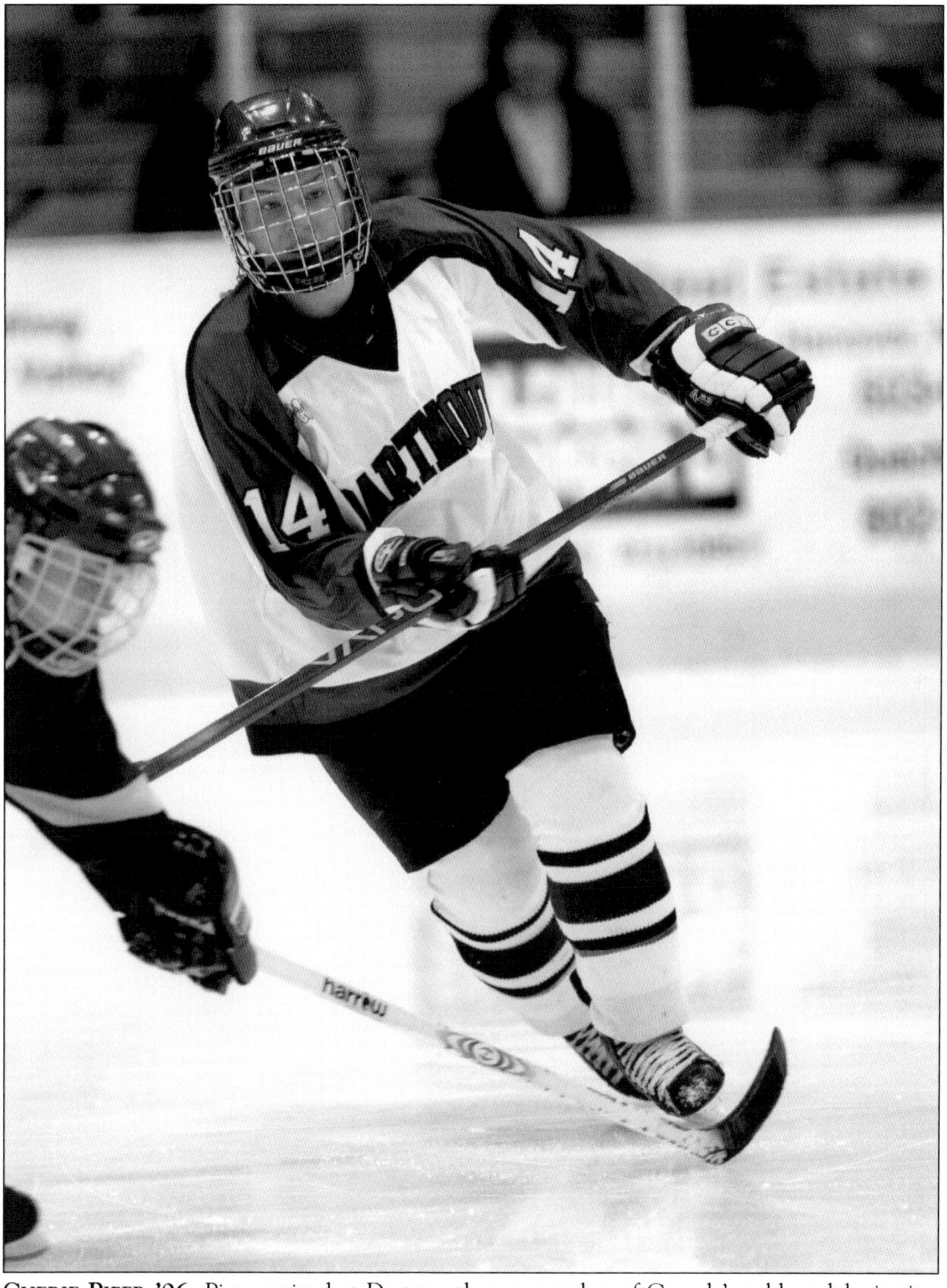

CHERIE PIPER '06. Piper arrived at Dartmouth as a member of Canada's gold medal-winning Olympic hockey team at Salt Lake City in 2002. Piper scored 138 points (60 goals, 78 assists) over her first three seasons, even though she missed part of the 2003–04 season, including the NCAA tournament, to compete with the Canadian national team. She was Dartmouth's scoring leader in 2004–05 with 60 points.

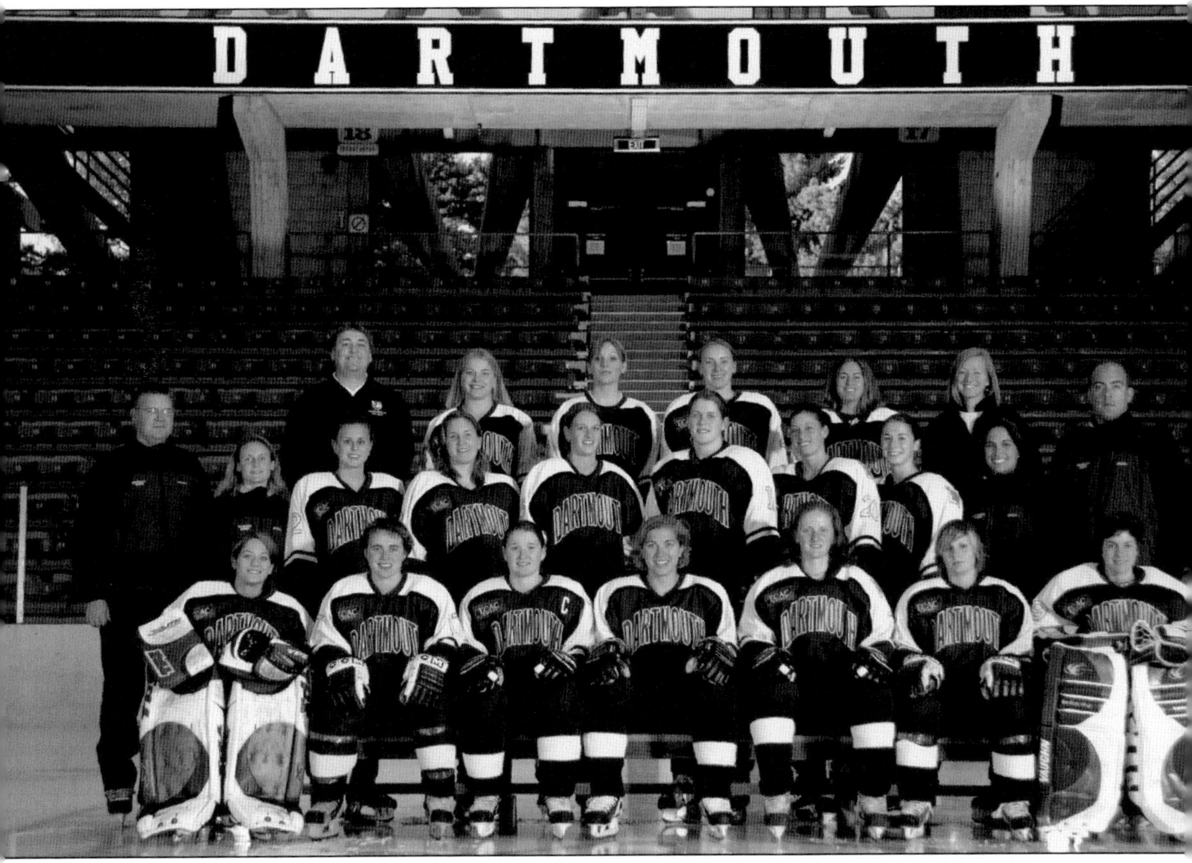

The Dartmouth Women's Team, 2004–05. Continuing the remarkable achievements of Dartmouth women's teams in recent years, the 2004–05 team posted a 27-8-0 record that matched the 2002–03 team for most victories in a season. Led by its co-captains, defenseman Alana BreMiller '05 and forward Meagan Walton '06, it marked the eighth time in 10 seasons, and the sixth straight year, that Dartmouth won 20 or more games. The Green fell to Harvard in the ECAC tourney championship game but made a fourth trip to the NCAA tournament. After beating Wisconsin 4-3 in the quarterfinal game at Thompson Arena (Katie Weatherston '06 scored the game-winning goal), the Green finished behind Minnesota, Harvard, and St. Lawrence in the Frozen Four at Durham, New Hampshire. Since 1986, under coaches Crowe, Oberting, and Hudak, Dartmouth has produced 19 straight winning seasons and has established itself among the nation's outstanding women's intercollegiate hockey teams.

NINE

Men, Restoring Tradition 1997–2005

For Dartmouth's men's hockey teams, the first years of the new millennium have been nothing short of a restoration. A restoration of competitiveness, spirit, and the natural order, in which hockey has a place in the very first tier of sports at Dartmouth and in the life of the college.

The ascendancy of men's hockey at Dartmouth is congruent with the ascendancy of Bob Gaudet '81. As a goalie, Gaudet left tracks on the Hanover ice. As a coach, he is leaving an impression even deeper—not only on the Hanover ice but also on all of Hanover itself. For the first time since the 1940s, Dartmouth has had five consecutive winning seasons (so far). The future seems even brighter. Men's hockey is back, where it ought to be.

It is back as one of the great powerhouses of the East, perhaps of the nation. It is back as a force on campus. There are many reasons, but one of them surely was that the team was full of hot tickets. Several of them have been drafted by NHL teams. (Three were drafted on one afternoon. One arrived at Hanover as a freshman with a draft letter in hand.) Several of them had played together at the prep level, had tasted success, and wanted more. (Two were related; they were brothers.) Several of them excelled in other endeavors, some in other sports, and some in the classroom. They knew that the winning spirit could be contagious. Whatever the reason, they played like a team, and as a team they played well.

These were, it seemed, the best of times—or, with so much potential, soon would be. There was a sense, on the ice as well as in the stands, that these young men could do anything: come from behind, preserve a lead, prevail in a nail-biting cascade of sudden-death tiebreakers in holiday tournament play. There was, for the first time in decades, a sense that all things were possible, and that some of them actually would come true.

Like their counterparts on the women's team, they were having fun and having success. Also like the women's team, they had yet to have their breakthrough. No national championships, yet. No appearances in the final round of the Frozen Four, yet. But there was no reason to worry, yet. They would get there. It was merely a matter of time.

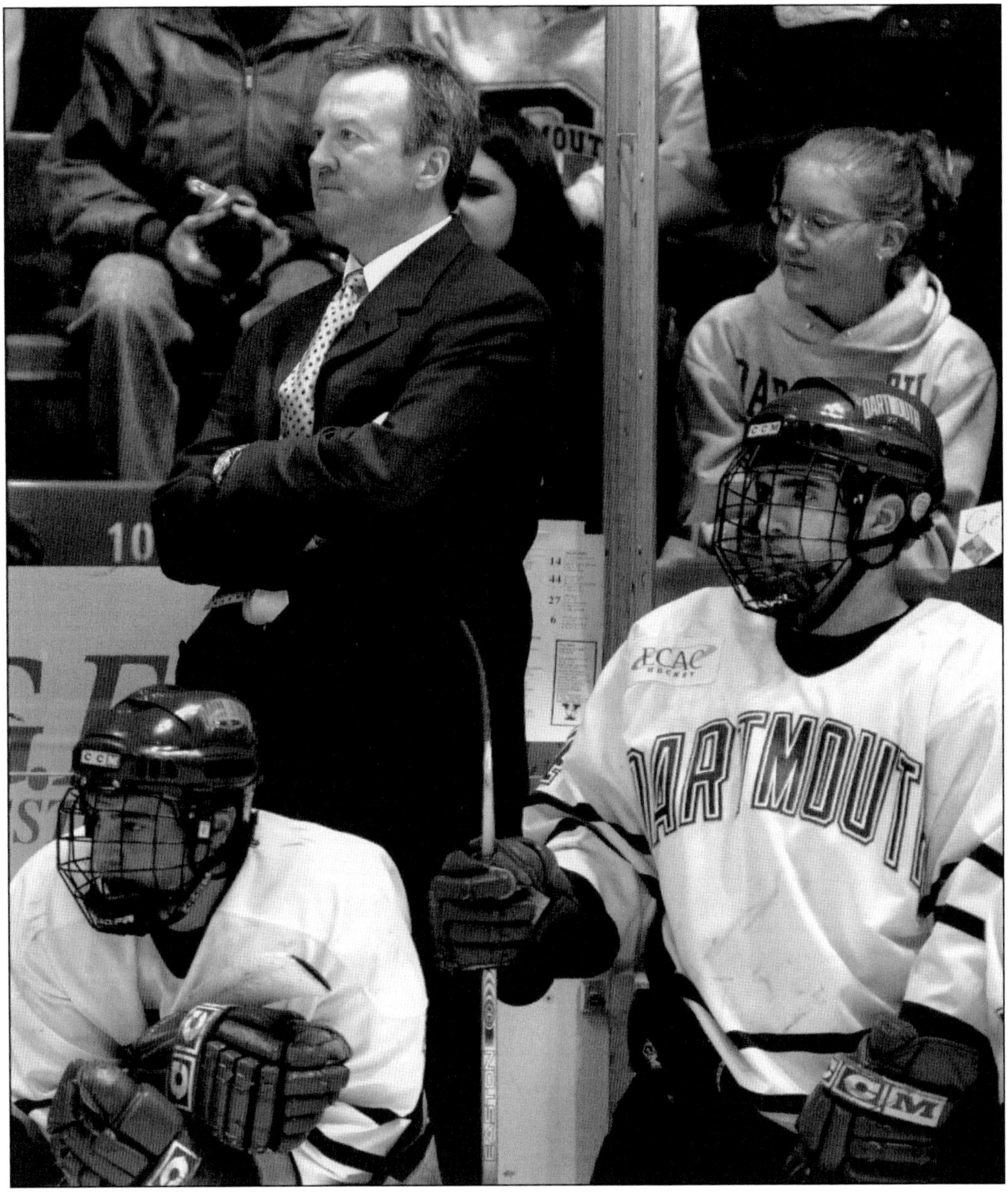

Coach Bob Gaudet '81. He described himself as "a cocky goalie" on Dartmouth's NCAA tourney teams in 1979 and 1980, and his friends called him "Gumby." Hockey had always been Bob Gaudet's life. Aspirations to play professional hockey were cut short by a knee injury, and Gaudet turned to coaching. From 1983 to 1988, he assisted George Crowe and Brian Mason at Dartmouth. In 1988, he was named head coach at Brown University. His first game was against Dartmouth, and the struggling Bruins won 5-4. They lost their next 25 games. From 1990 to 1997, Gaudet led the Bruins to the ECAC playoffs. When he answered Dartmouth's call in 1997, it took Gaudet three seasons to make Dartmouth an ECAC playoff team and four to launch a string of winning seasons that reached five in 2004–05, unmatched by Dartmouth teams since the 1940s. In 17 seasons as a head coach, Gaudet has a career record of 207-253-63, including 114-111-32 at Dartmouth.

DAVID WHITWORTH '98. From 1996 to 1998, forward David Whitworth was Dartmouth's leading scorer. As a sophomore and a junior, he won the Phelan Award as the Green's most valuable skater and was named to the All-Ivy League team. His 117 career points, including 74 assists, came in 113 games.

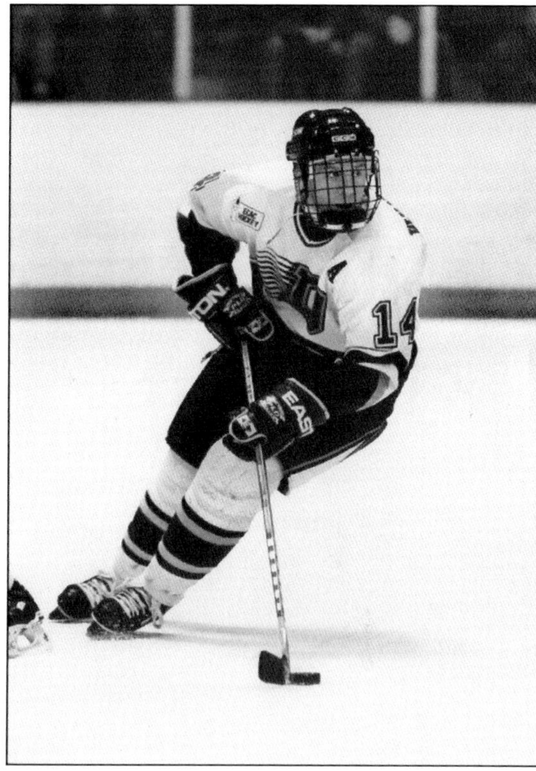

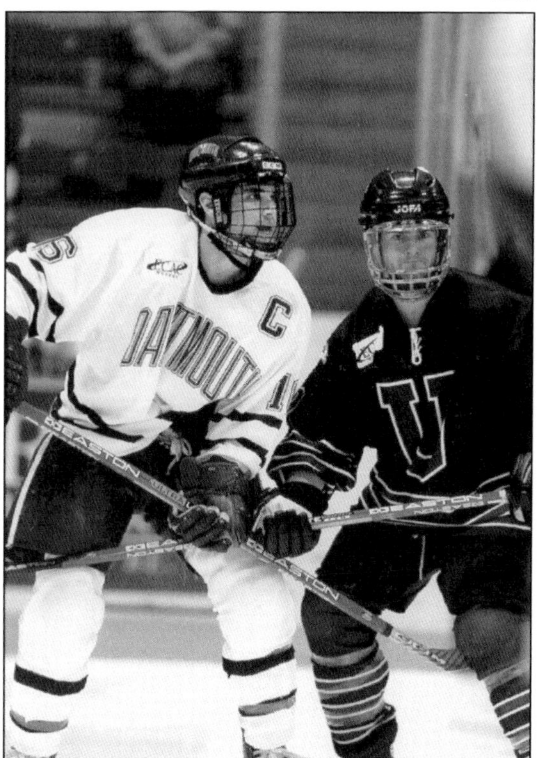

MIKE MATURO '02. As a junior and senior, Mike Maturo was a Dartmouth co-captain. In both seasons he was the Green's leading scorer and was named to the All-Ivy team. Maturo was Dartmouth's most valuable player as a junior in 2000–01. His 110 career points (49 goals, 61 assists) came as he played in all of the Green's 125 games and helped Dartmouth to three ECAC tourney appearances.

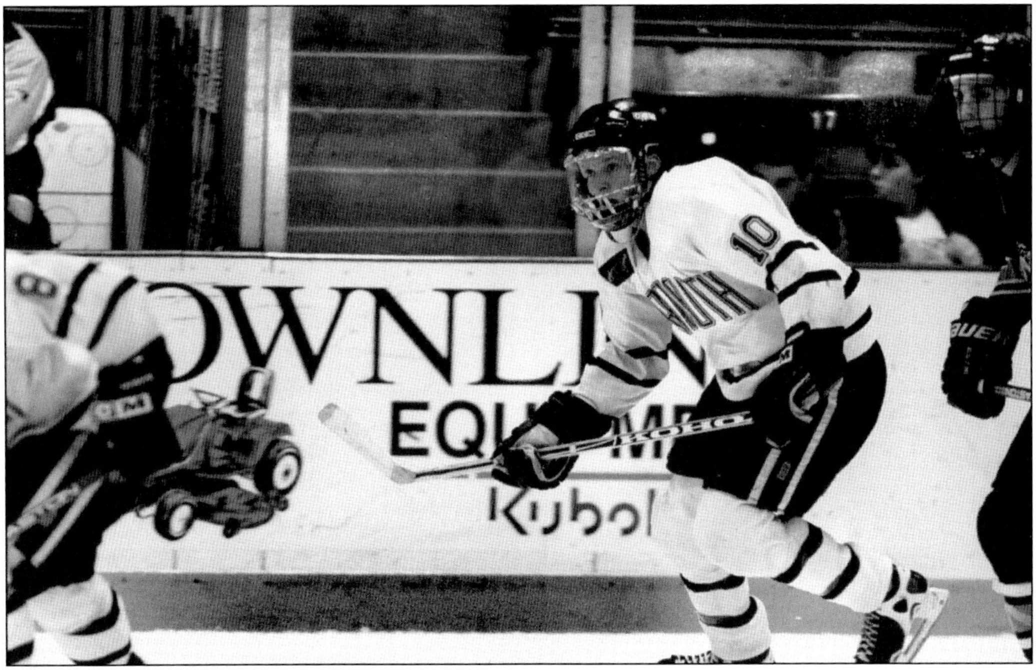

MIKE BYRNE '01. Like his brother Trevor '03 (below), Mike Byrne played at Deerfield Academy before arriving at Dartmouth. Byrne was a tri-captain of the 2000–01 team. He scored 39 points in 108 games though hampered by occasional injuries.

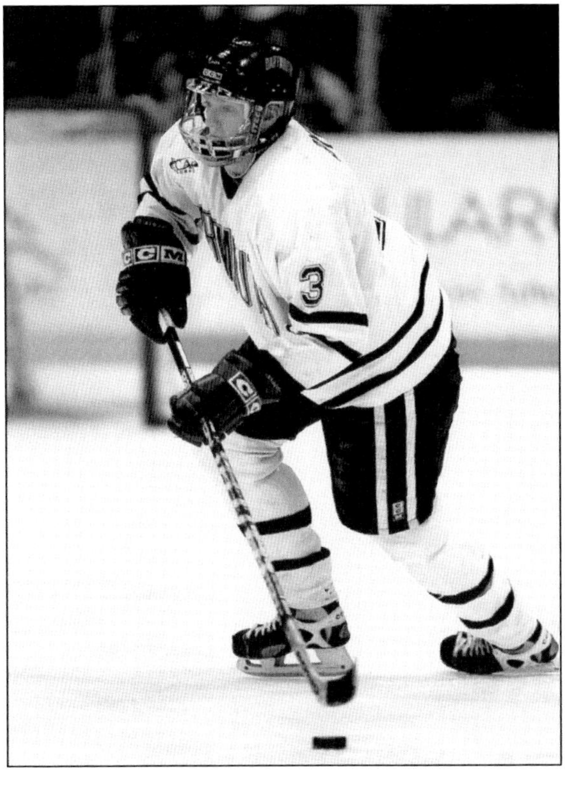

TREVOR BYRNE '03. When Trevor Byrne was Dartmouth's co-captain for the 2002–03 season, he joined his brother Mike as the first brothers to lead Dartmouth hockey teams since Jack Riley '44 and Bill Riley '46 in the late 1940s. Named to the All-Ivy team as a defenseman during his sophomore and junior seasons, Byrne played in every game (130) over four seasons. He was drafted by the St. Louis Blues in the fifth round of the NHL draft in 1999.

PETE SUMMERFELT '03. Playing in 129 games from 1999 to 2003, defenseman Pete Summerfelt had 18 multi-point games for the Green. His goal decided a 5-4 win, in double-overtime, against Colgate in the ECAC playoffs in 2002. Summerfelt had 80 career points, including 64 assists.

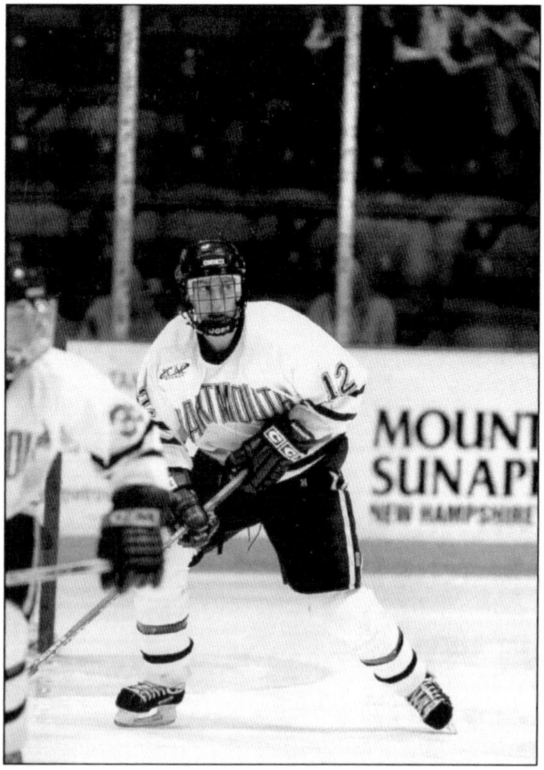

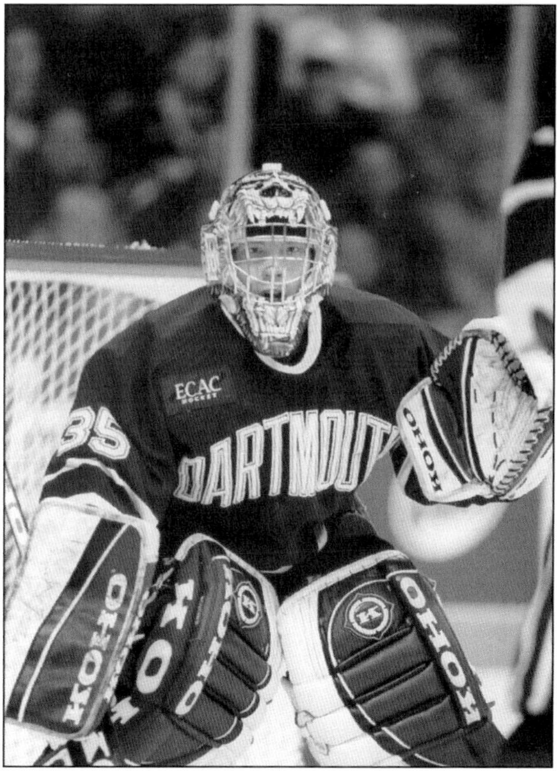

NICK BOUCHER '03. Early in the 2002–03 season, goalie Nick Boucher broke Dartmouth's record for career saves, 2,197, held by Steve Laurin '90. Boucher finished with 2,803 saves in 105 games. He set the single-season record for saves with 867 in 33 games in 2000–01. His career save percentage record of .907 was broken on 2004–05 by Dan Yacey '05 (.917). Boucher's 50 wins in the Dartmouth nets are 10 more than the runner-up, Bob Gaudet '81, his coach.

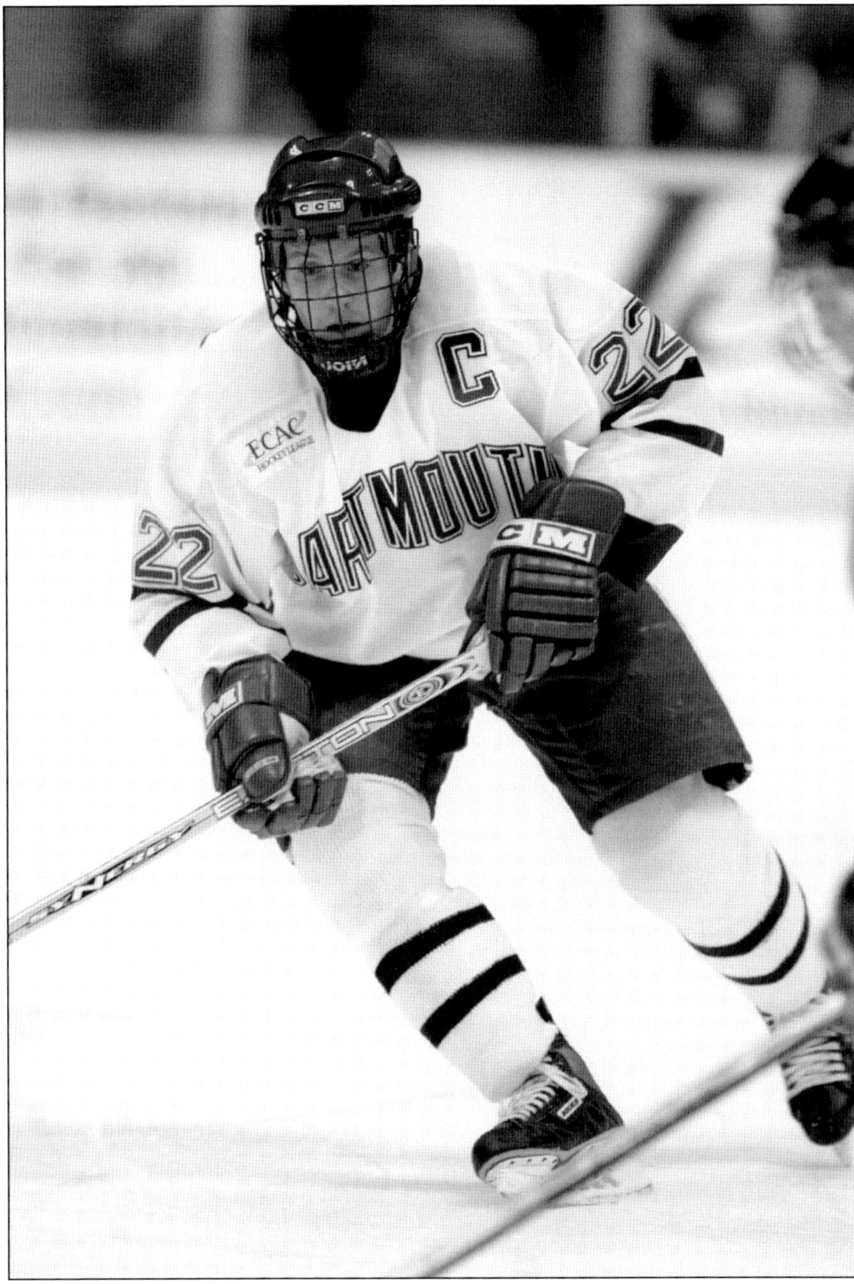

LEE STEMPNIAK '05. From 2001 to 2005, wing Lee Stempniak was Dartmouth's "go to" performer in a lineup that produced a pair of 20-win seasons. As a junior and senior, Stempniak became Dartmouth's first two-time, first team All-American selection since Bill Riley '46. The team captain in 2004–05, Stempniak's name dots the Dartmouth record book. He played in all of Dartmouth's 135 games from 2001 to 2005. His 151 career points are fourth-best all-time. He ranks third all-time with 88 assists and ninth with 63 goals. He was named All-Ivy League and All-ECAC twice and was the Green's most valuable player as a sophomore and junior. Stempniak was picked by the St. Louis Blues in the fifth round of the 2003 NHL draft.

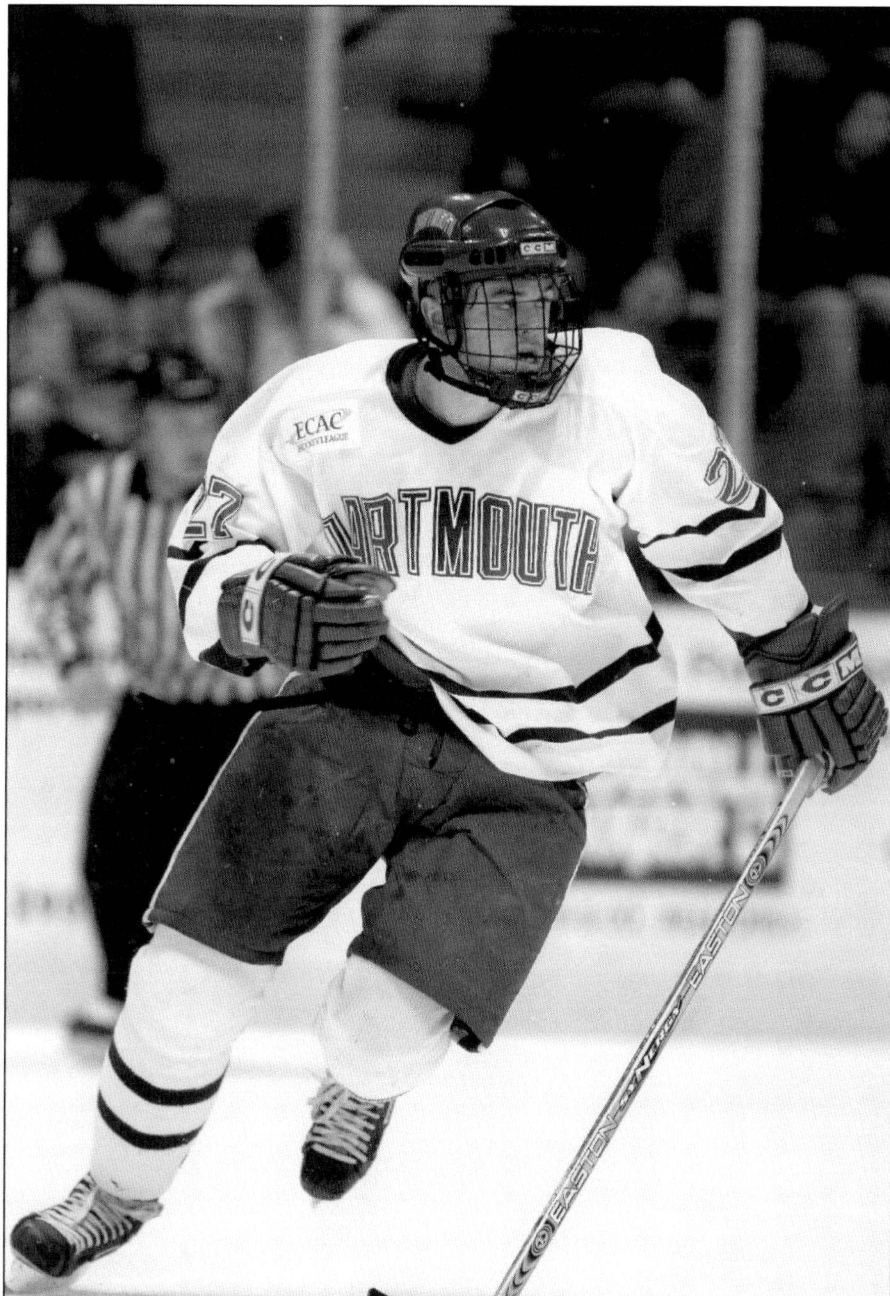

HUGH JESSIMAN '06. The highest Dartmouth player ever taken in the NHL draft (he was the 12th pick in the first round in 2003), forward Hugh Jessiman is probably Dartmouth's tallest player in history—he's six feet six inches. After scoring 80 points in his first two seasons and being named the Ivy League and ECAC rookie of the year in 2002–03, Jessiman turned down a contract from the New York Rangers to play at Dartmouth in 2004–05. His season was cut short when he broke his foot in the Green's fifth game, against Princeton, and didn't return until the ECAC playoffs four months later.

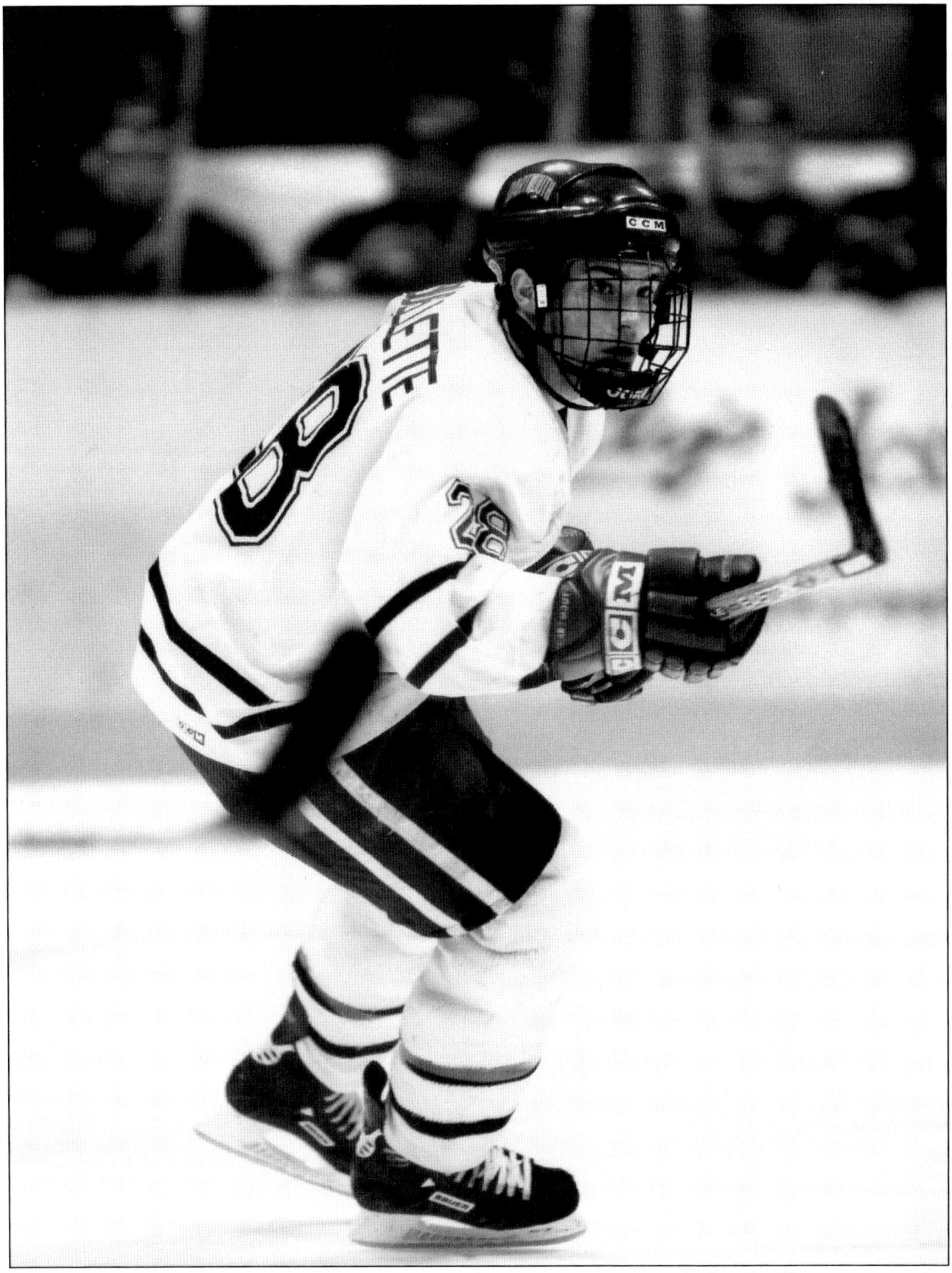

Mike Ouellette '06. With rare exceptions from 2002 to 2004, Mike Ouellette centered a line with Lee Stempniak '05 and Hugh Jessiman '06. Over two seasons, the line accounted for 106 goals and 227 points. Ouellette was second to Stempniak in scoring in 2004–05 (he had 41 points to Stempniak's 43) and was named Dartmouth's most valuable player. Through three seasons, Ouellette had 101 career points, including 56 assists.

GRANT LEWIS '07. After a freshman season in 2003–04 that saw him named to the All-Ivy, All-ECAC, and All-New England teams, defenseman Grant Lewis was picked by the Atlanta Thrashers in the second round of the 2004 NHL draft. Lewis was Dartmouth's fourth-leading scorer as a freshman with 25 points. He added 22, including 17 assists in 2004–05.

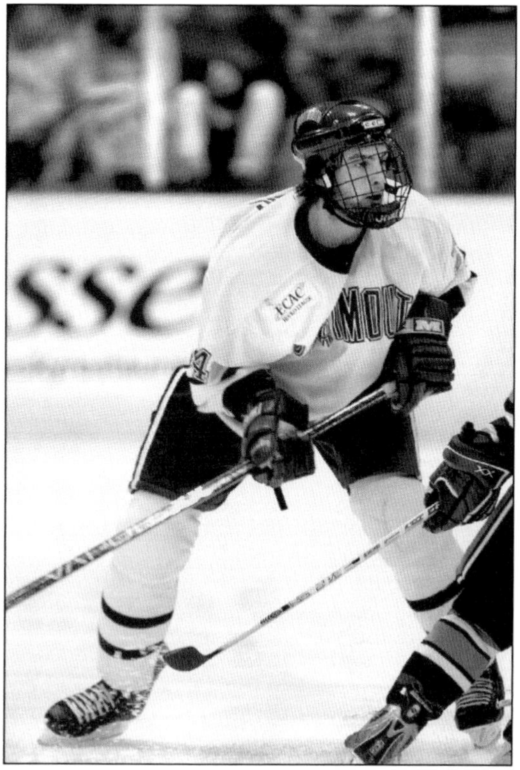

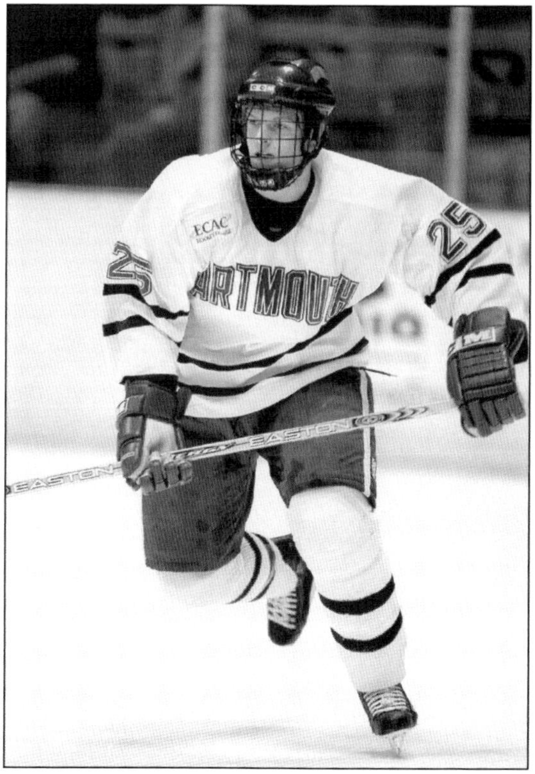

NICK JOHNSON '08. When Hugh Jessiman went down with a foot injury early in the 2004–05 season, freshman wing Nick Johnson moved into a line with Lee Stempniak '05 and Mike Ouellette '06 and became Dartmouth's third-leading scorer with 35 points (18 goals). He was named the Ivy League rookie of the year. Drafted by the NHL's Pittsburgh Penguins in 2004, Johnson followed his father, Kevin '77, and uncle, Dana '73, as standout performers in Dartmouth hockey.

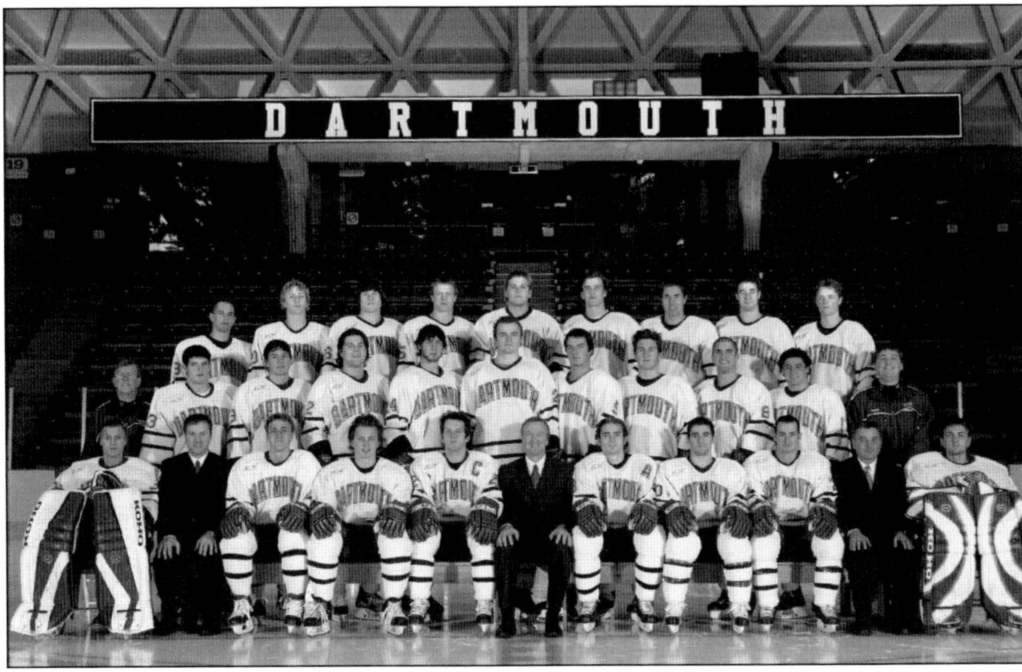

THE DARTMOUTH MEN'S TEAM, 2004–05. While the Dartmouth women's hockey team reached the NCAA tournament in 2004–05, the men missed by a whisker. Dartmouth's regular season ended with a 17-10-2 record, including nine wins in the last 11 games. In the ECAC playoffs, Dartmouth beat Yale but then lost two of three games at Vermont, all decided by one goal. In a ranking process that hinged on a number of one-goal games, Colgate edged past Dartmouth for the last berth in the 16-team field. Dartmouth finished 20-13-2. It was the Green's second 20-win season in three years and sixth straight winning campaign. Measuring Dartmouth's competitive position in Eastern collegiate hockey during the season: a scoreless tie with Maine at Thompson Arena and a 9-8 victory over New Hampshire that saw the Green rally from a 7-3 deficit at the Verizon Center in Manchester, New Hampshire. "It's been a fun year," said coach Bob Gaudet, reflecting on a team that included only five seniors. After nearly a decade of success, the Big Green plays to packed houses in Thompson Arena (as it did during the 1970s).

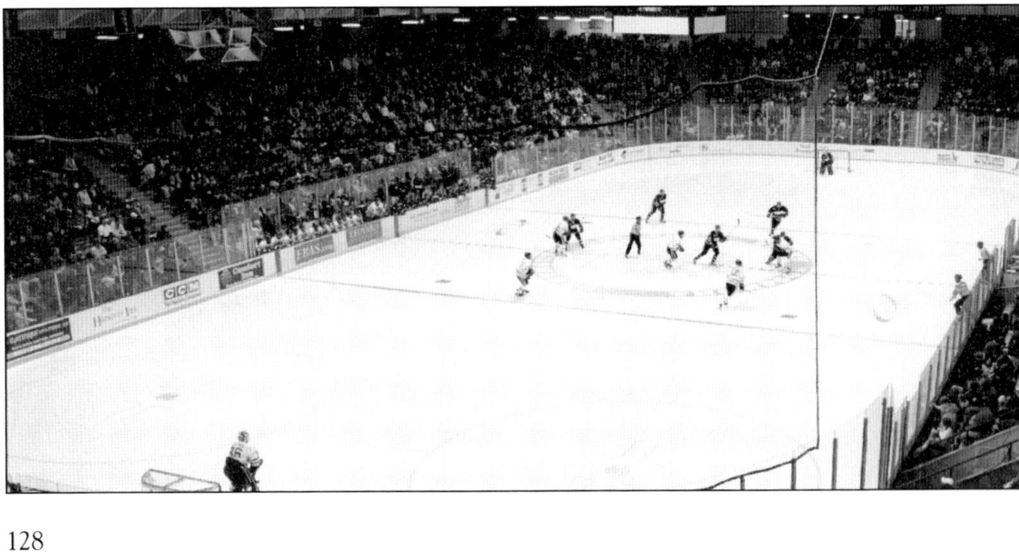